SHREDDED

WHAT READERS ARE SAYING ABOUT
SHREDDED

...this book really blew me away! So many nice little Christian novels out there, but so few that really attempt to be life-changing....It makes such a difference!... I was so taken away with the story. All the emotion, the drama, the romance and tenderness, the action, adventure. I couldn't wait to see what happened but I didn't want it to end either. I really can't say enough good things about it and how much I enjoyed it. WOW!... I was nervous with anticipation and crying and so caught up in it all. I had to put the book down to give myself an emotional break. :) ... I rarely cry over books, but I think that other than Karen Kingsbury, [Rae is] the only other author that has made me cry while reading a book. -Sue

Shredded was compelling, convicting, and compassionate at once...a deeply disturbing reality packaged with grace, humor, and a sweet love story. I couldn't put it down. –Joy

I love it!!!...[Rae's] best book yet I think! Can't put it down. –Mary

I couldn't put the book down... a compelling story of suspense and romance. -Jeanie

...incredible. –Michael

I think this is [Rae's] best book yet. It is so relative to today's church and how we treat people. It is a wonderful mix of relationships, interwoven with suspense and love. It is a must read for anyone who thinks their past defines them and gives them no hope, whether they are a victim of human trafficking, child abuse, or just bad decision making, because Jesus can wipe the slate clean. - Wanda

This is an intense book! Very well written, great character development....I don't know someone that couldn't identify with one or more characters in it, the heart, the heartbreak, the discomfort with someone they don't know/understand, the living in fear. I LOVE Candy's character....She is so raw and real....I literally cried. I cannot say enough about this book. I literally couldn't put it down. It was SO GOOD. –Amy

...hands down my favorite author. –Tiffany

Warning!! You won't want to put it down once you get started!! ...there's no stopping. Awesome, awesome book!!!! -Sue

SHREDDED

YOUR PAST DOES NOT DEFINE YOU

Kimberly Rae

Library of Congress Cataloging-in-Publication Data
Rae, Kimberly
Shredded/Kimberly Rae - First edition.
Pages 376
Summary: "Jean has kept a secret for fifteen years. Only she knows that she has remained at Brookside Baptist to protect the children, and only she knows why. When a new pastor and his brother arrive at the church, a chance encounter with the town prostitute starts a chain reaction that will change Jean's life, and the rest of the church, forever."
-Provided by publisher.
Library of Congress Control Number: 2015910211
ISBN-13: 978-1514701515
ISBN-10: 1514701510
[1. Childhood Sexual Abuse-Fiction. 2. Abuse within the church-Fiction. 3. Romantic Suspense-Fiction. 4. Freedom from Fear-Fiction. 5. Overcoming-Fiction. 6. Restoration-Fiction. 7. Human Trafficking-Fiction. 8. Power of Gospel-Fiction.] I. Title. II. Title: Your Past Does Not Define You.

DEDICATION

*to the friend
who asked me
not to tell*

*and all others
with unhealed wounds
and untold secrets*

CHARACTERS IN SHREDDED

Jean Louise Jameson - Children's Director at Brookside Baptist Church

Stewart Henderson - New pastor at Brookside Baptist Church

Brenda Henderson - Stewart Henderson's young wife

Grant Henderson - Stewart Henderson's brother

Candy - Oakview's older town prostitute

Champagne - Oakview's younger town prostitute

Jamaica - Coffee shop owner and source of town news

Gladys Simmons - Oldest member at Brookside Baptist Church

Florence Simmons - Gladys Simmons' sister and Jean Jameson's former teacher

Rod Carson - Head deacon at Brookside Baptist Church

Alice Carson - Rod Carson's wife

Susan Meeks - Church pianist

Ian Craig - Oakview's sheriff

Once, long ago,
a woman of scandal and shame
cried on Jesus' feet
and wiped them with her hair.

If such a thing were to happen
in a modern context
on a larger scale,
who would respond like
the judgmental religious leader,
who would respond like Jesus,
and what would happen
to the woman
who was forgiven much?

*No one
would
believe
her.*

Jean

Grace Jameson's daughter did not intend to eavesdrop. It was five o'clock on Sunday afternoon. Ten-year-old Jean Louise Jameson always found her mother at exactly five o'clock.

"Routine leads to a feeling of security," Jean heard her mother say. She must be counseling another worried parent. Probably one of the ones who moved away, since the conversation was over the phone rather than in their living room, where Jean usually heard that phrase about security.

Mrs. Jameson had rules about not interrupting phone conversations, so Jean sat crossed-legged on the carpeted floor just outside the open kitchen doorway and wondered what new routine she could start. Already, her day was meticulously ordered. She brushed her teeth from right to left, top to bottom, every time. Ate her waffles with exactly one dip into the syrup per bite. Dressed in the exact same order each day: slip first, then top, skirt, socks, and shoes last. Her mother said she would need a training bra soon. Jean did not want to think about needing such a thing

"Well," her mother said into the phone, "expressing past hurts leads to freedom from them."

Jean curled into a ball where she sat, arguing within herself. Expressing it out loud was impossible. Everyone loved him. Almost worshipped him. Even Mother.

No one would believe her.

"Let me take my tea into the living room and you can tell me more."

Jean heard the click of her mother's Sunday heels on the kitchen tile and tried to skitter away before being seen, but she was not fast enough.

"Oh, Jean, honey, could you help me?" Grace Jameson pulled a set of keys from her purse on the living room coffee table, set there in readiness for the evening service at six. She handed the keys to Jean and then used her free hand to cover the mouthpiece on the phone. "This is a really important call," she whispered to Jean. "Could you go over to the church and unlock the doors? I might be running a bit late if this lady needs to talk long."

No, no, no, Jean said inside her head, but the words did not come out and even her body seemed frozen in place. Her mother noticed after a few seconds and waved her hand toward the door.

"Get going," she said with a smile.

Jean ran, through the front door and out into the cool evening air. She was alone. It was not good to be alone right now. Not at five o'clock.

Her chest heaving, panic flooding through her thin arms, she looked wildly for a place to run and hide. But if she hid until church time, people would be waiting at the locked doors, and her mother would get upset. Grace Jameson never yelled, but her sad look was something Jean always tried to avoid.

She would have to go. She could run, unlock the doors as fast as she could, then run back. Brookside Baptist was close, just across the creek, so she would only be alone for three or four minutes total.

The teeth of the church key bit into her palm as she ran, while the other keys dangled from the key ring and clanged against each other in discord. Jean jumped over the creek and sprinted to the church. Her hands shook so much, it took three tries to get the main front doors unlocked. Down the sloping hill beside the church, she had to slow her steps or risk a painful tumble, but at the bottom she was able to run again, around the corner of the church basement to the back door.

Just as she reached the door, an idea came so swift and clear Jean thought it must be from an angel. Inside the church, if she could bear being there and being alone, she could express it, and Mother said she would be free.

Jean unlocked and opened the door, then fought terror when the door swung shut behind her and left her in darkness. The basement was really a hallway lined with rooms, but all the windows were inside the rooms and all their doors were shut.

Except one. Jean ran toward the light coming through the open doorway of the pastor's office. She sat at the small secretary's desk inside and tried to stop shaking.

Talk, she told herself. Express it. She could speak out loud there. No one would hear.

But what if someone did? What if someone was out in the hallway, listening? Or outside the window?

What if *he* heard her?

Jean whirled and shut the office door, locking herself inside. Back at the desk, she saw two piles of church bulletins. The church secretary always saved the leftover ones in case visitors came to the evening service. It would not be stealing to use one. An usher always gave her one anyway.

A pen lay beside the stacks of bulletins. Jean picked up the pen, then chose a bulletin and began to look through it. Below the birthday announcements on the inside fold, she found some white space. How long would it take? People came to church early sometimes. She might have to stop around five-thirty and come back later at night if she wasn't finished. Her mother always kept her keys in the side pocket of her purse. It would not be hard to borrow them, or to sneak out of the house once her mother put her earplugs in and drifted off to sleep.

"Expressing hurts leads to freedom from them," Jean said out loud. She stared at the bulletin for long moments, then uncapped the pen and forced herself to write, sentence after sentence, putting into words things she spent all day, every day, trying to forget.

Sunday Evening, June 29
Fifteen Years Later

Jean

Jean collected the church bulletins people had left on pews or in hymnal racks, turned out the lights, locked the front doors, and carried the bulletins downstairs.

Arms forward, as if swimming through the thick darkness, she felt her way down the hallway, bulletins clutched in one outstretched hand and a light jacket in the other.

Fourth room on the left. Her hands had long ago learned to count the doorways along the wall. Her key opened the door and from there it was six steps forward and two to the right.

The desk was where it should be, and a moment of blind searching brought her hands to the small lamp set just to the left of the desktop paper shredder.

She draped her jacket over the lamp before switching it on. Even at that, she winced at the faded light which spread across half the desk.

Jean stood still, fighting the feeling someone was watching, knowing she was there. Knowing why.

Pulling the desk chair backward out of the circle of light, she sat and placed the bulletins in a neat pile on her lap. Her hands stretched into the light and set the first bulletin onto the desk alone next to the paper shredder, separate from the pile.

For a moment that small movement took on meaning. One bulletin out of all of them had been chosen and plucked away from the others. Placed separate, alone and helpless, at the mercy of someone's choice. Someone's hands.

Her own hands trembled. Jean reached for the ink pen always left next to the lamp and began to write. Fast, hard strokes shaped words along the margins, under announcements, between paragraphs listing nursery schedules and coming events. Black letters formed dark words, fragments, sentences, until every portion of white space succumbed to pressure and ink.

Once filled, she set the burdened sheet of paper aside and reached for another. It, too, she methodically filled, then another, until the stack reached five high.

She stared at the papers, at the words, then quickly lifted the stack and fed each bulletin into the paper shredder positioned half-inside the light. The small machine vibrated on the desk, chewing with loud, harsh sounds like a child who refused to learn manners, before releasing the shreds over a trash can adjacent to the desk.

Jean wrote on five more papers, and one by one, held them up to the shredder's mouth and watched them destroyed. The chopping sound paused after the fifth paper, but left a silence that seemed to breathe, as if the machine waited, impatient and greedy for more.

After an hour, possibly two, all the bulletins lay silent and powerless in the trash. Long, thin, shredded secrets.

Another Sunday night was over, but the routine had given no security. The words she wrote offered no freedom.

Jean knew next Sunday would be the same. And the next. Forever.

Her mother had been wrong, about so many things.

Jean's hands, with no bulletins left to hold, opened palm up to capture and cocoon her face as she dropped her head and sobbed.

"You aren't actually worried he'll get mugged in this sleepy little town, are you?"

Grant

"Recalculating."

Grant Henderson grinned when his brother Stewart's rarely seen exasperation came to the surface. "If that thing says 'recalculating' one more time," Stewart said, "I'm going to throw it out the window."

"Recalculating."

He reached for it and Grant pulled it away just in time, laughing. "We've got to be close. Just drive around a few blocks and we'll likely come across it. How hard can a church in a small town be to find?"

"Hard," Stewart said half an hour later. Oakview, North Carolina, hosted a quaint downtown lined with old wooden storefronts, historic signs, a few cobblestone alleyways, and multiple large, brick churches topped with traditional white steeples. They had passed a Presbyterian, Methodist, and Episcopal church, but no Creekside Baptist. "It's getting dark, which will make it even harder to find the place, and the deacon's meeting I'm supposed to attend starts at eight." He pulled the steering wheel toward the left down a cobblestone lane they'd crossed twice already. "Is she still asleep?"

Grant looked over his shoulder at the passenger curled between mounds of blankets and pillows piled high across the backseat. "Yes, though I don't know how. You need new shock absorbers on this car."

"I'm glad." Stewart adjusted the rearview mirror. "Today was tough on her, leaving her hometown for the first time."

"We left our hometown today, too."

"Yeah, but we're not girls."

"No kidding. You just figured that out?"

Stewart punched a fist in his direction which Grant easily dodged. "Keep your eyes on the road, Jimmy," Grant said, enjoying the smile that broke through at the childhood nickname. "We all want you to get to your first church in one piece."

"Well, let's do it without Miss Recalculating driving me crazy." Stewart shut the GPS down and dropped the device into the consul between them.

Dusk merged into darkness and a quiet settled over the brothers. Grant was surprised when Stewart glanced at him and asked, "Why did you really come with us?"

Grant turned his gaze out the side window and thought about the day he'd decided. Six months, his father had requested. Stewart knew that part. Should he tell him the rest? Should he admit that an old-fashioned town in the deep South was about forty-nine states from where he wanted to be? He clenched his hands on the thighs of his jeans.

"Are we there yet?"

Grant turned to see Brenda sit up and fought back a smile. Stewart's young wife was not one of those people who looked great when first waking up. Her curly hair fuzzed out all around her head and her eyes were squinty. She yawned.

"Hey, beautiful." Stewart looked at his wife through the rearview mirror and Grant shrugged. Love must do serious altering on the eyesight. "We aren't there yet, but will be soon."

"Yeah, right. We'd be there already if your hubby would stop to ask somebody where the church is."

"You mean we're lost?" Brenda immediately started biting a thumbnail, her lips colorless without her usual lipstick on. "Oh, Stewart, you should have called. You don't want to be late for your first meeting."

"I tried, three times. No answer." He tossed the GPS over to Grant. "And I would have asked for directions, except you may notice there is nobody around to ask."

"Okay, I'll give you that. Oakview seems like one of those towns where the streets roll up at night. But we could find some gas station or something." He turned the GPS back on. "If nothing else, we could get a cup of coffee to keep you awake while—"

"There's a couple of people." Stewart made a sharp turn and Grant's shoulder bumped the side door. "I'll ask them."

A little squeak of protest erupted from the backseat, but Grant did not look up to see why. He continued punching in letters to find a gas station, in case these pedestrians were as lost as they were.

"Don't worry," Stewart said, unbuckling his seat belt and opening the car door. "It's just two women." He pulled his wallet from his back pocket and tossed it on the seat with a smile at his wife. "There, now even if they do try to mug me, they won't get anything."

He shut the door and Grant heard the squeak again. He looked back at Brenda's horrified face. "What's the matter? You aren't actually worried he'll get mugged in this sleepy little town, are you?"

"What is he thinking?" Her face pinched up. Her hair still waved in several unnatural directions. "Can't he tell?"

"Tell what?" Grant finished supplying information to the GPS, then looked in the direction Brenda was staring. Stewart had approached two women standing under the only streetlamp on that stretch of road. His eyes took in the spiked heels, miniskirts, revealing tops, and excessive makeup. The women looked as out of place in the town as a neon sign strapped to an Amish buggy. No wonder Brenda had that look on her face. "Brenda…"

She squeaked one more time. "My husband, the new pastor in this town, is out on the street talking to prostitutes."

Saturday Evening, July 5

Rod

"He's late." Rod Carson had been watching the clock. He'd arrived first, ten minutes early, committed to setting a good example, something for which this new pastor obviously had little regard. "That's not a good sign. It shows disrespect for us and our office."

"Maybe something happened," John Standard, one of the other deacons, offered. "Maybe they had car trouble."

"He could have called." Rod pulled back the sleeve of his tweed suit jacket and set his watch. "I'll give him ten more minutes."

"If he did call, it would ring in the church office and no one would hear it."

Rod glared in the man's direction. "You do realize this will be the seventh pastor we've invited here in the last four years." Murmurs rose from the men assembled at the table, but Rod continued on. "The others were too modern, too radical, disrespectful, or just not a good fit for our church." He stood and eyed each man present. "Brookside needs strong leadership, someone to take charge and not waver, a person who can handle power and authority."

Me. Rod wanted to pound his fist on the table and shake the apathy out of these men. By now they should all recognize his rightful place as leader. How many times had he listed the qualifications, and they had merely nodded and gone back to their list of potential candidates? How many new pastors, fresh out of seminary, without any experience handling a flock, had come and gone?

It was ridiculous that he had been forced to take drastic measures. He'd chosen the last three pastors specifically for their youth and lack of experience, each time certain the deacon board would come to their senses and realize they didn't need to keep trying to find someone from the outside to lead their congregation. They needed him. He was the one who kept the church going through every pastor and interim pastor. He had presided over the deacon board for twenty years. They knew he could handle power and would not run from the problems in the church. He would not be yellow-bellied and try to facilitate when dissention arose. No, he would stamp it out, make sure everyone knew the chain of command and who was at the top of it.

That's what this church needed. It was dying because people these days had no sense of authority. They questioned everything, pushed their opinions, wanted change.

"We need to get our church back to the way things should be," he concluded. He heard no agreeing amens and frowned. Apathy. It disgusted him.

He checked his watch. Five more minutes and this new pastor would have a black mark against him before he even started.

"I didn't
ask to
hear your
sob story."

Candy looked from the bright red halter top to the green cutout blouse with a ring of gold at the neckline. "Which do you think will cause less of a stir?"

Her roommate laughed. "When have you ever not wanted to cause a stir?"

Candy set aside the red shirt and slipped on the green one. She tugged on her loosest pair of jeans and looked into the full length mirror. "They're tight."

"Of course they're tight. Customers need to see the merchandise."

With a sigh, Candy sat on one of the two twin beds in the small room. She looked over at the young woman adjusting her skirt to hang shorter. "You know, we've been roommates for, what, five years or something? And you've never told me your real name."

"You know my name. It's Champagne. Light, bubbly, and unforgettable. Like the color of my hair and the softness of my skin." Champagne picked up the discarded red shirt and looked it over. "I've always liked this top."

"You can have it."

"Really?" Champagne pulled it on, but paused as soon as her head was through. "What's going on with you? You never let me even touch your best clothes before. Are you sick or something?"

"Something," Candy said. She looked over herself in the mirror again and tried to get her jeans to stretch away from her body a little. It didn't work. She pulled her thick mane of bleached blond hair away from her face and stretched the skin where wrinkles fanned out from her eyelids. She was getting old. "I keep thinking about that man we talked to last night."

Champagne smirked. "You mean the preacher? The guy who turned all red in the face when I asked if he was looking for some fun?"

Candy smiled. "Yeah, him. It was nice to talk to a guy who didn't want a piece of me for a change. Did you notice he only looked at our eyes?"

Champagne stilled. "Yeah, I did. I don't think I've had a guy look into my eyes since middle school."

"How did you end up here, anyway?"

The girl's eyes hardened into a woman's. "My dad offered me to a trucker friend of his as a birthday present. Dad owed him money for drugs and I got him off the hook. It worked so well, he figured he could make some extra income on the side, so I'd go to school during the week and he'd sell me on the weekends." Champagne yanked off the red top and threw it. "This doesn't fit right after all."

Candy caught the top. "That preacher man said something I can't get out of my head. My grandmother used to say the same thing."

Champagne flopped back onto her bed with a moan. "A preacher and your grandmother. I'm dying of anticipation. What did they say?"

Candy flung a pillow at her. "It's not like your life's so full of excitement, you know."

"I know." Champagne's voice lowered. This time there was no sarcasm in it. "I hate my life. If I wasn't so scared of dying, I'd kill myself and be done with it."

Candy took a few deep breaths. Hadn't she thought the same, many times?

"So…" Champagne lifted her head. "What did they say that you can't forget?"

Ducking her head and purposefully focusing on zipping up her heeled boots, Candy spoke softly. "He said God works in mysterious ways. That sometimes what seems like a random coincidence is really God at work."

"Hah! So you think that guy getting lost and coming to ask us for directions is something God did? All you had to do was take a look at the woman in the backseat of his car to know that's a no-go. She about had steam coming out her ears." She chuckled. "I bet he got an earful when he got home."

"But what if it was?" Candy asked. "My grandmother took me in when my mom got arrested. My dad had disappeared a long time ago. She loved me and tried to put me on the right path, but I was too wild by then. Didn't want rules and quiet nights. I wanted independence and excitement." She looked around the nearly bare room, decorated only by a few pieces of clothing hanging on nails pounded into the wall. "I didn't know it would end up here."

The pillow hit Candy from behind. "Shut up. I didn't ask to hear your sob story."

Candy turned to see Champagne flop over and curl up on the bed, her back to her. She stopped talking, but after a minute or two heard a muffled, "If your grandma was so great, why didn't she come find you?"

A quick grab for a tissue gave Candy time to blot her makeup before any moisture could damage the perfect line of green eyeliner she'd just applied. "She tried. For over a year, she put ads in the paper looking for me. I was hiding out but still nearby; I got the paper every week just to read them. Every time, the ad said she loved me and wanted me to come home. After a few weeks, I'd have given anything to go back, but at first I was too ashamed, then I was too broke. Then..."

"Then we got stuck here, with him."

Champagne pointed toward the only photo in the room. It hung loose on the wall, crooked, a handsome man in the center with his arms draped around two young, fun-loving girls with side ponytails. The girls smiled at him.

Candy pushed the tissue against her eyes again. "I did get one letter from her. A sheriff who arrested me once contacted Grandma and she said she would come get me. I actually started to hope."

"I heard about when you got arrested." Champagne sat up. "Why didn't you go with her?"

Candy gestured toward the photo. "Slash came and bailed me out. By the time Grandmother got to the jail, we were across the state border at another truck stop." Giving up trying to stop the rebellious tears, Candy went to the sink in the room's tiny adjoining bathroom and washed off her makeup. It was probably better not wearing any today anyway. They might have issues with stuff like that. She pulled her hair up and the mirror showed a long scar just below her hairline, strategically placed where clients would never see. Her reminder of how Slash got his name, a permanent warning to never try to leave him again.

She made her way back into the room and picked through several tops piled at the edge of her bed, wishing she owned a long, baggy shirt. "The message she left was that she had prayed for me every single day since I ran away, and she would never stop until the day she died."

"So she's out there somewhere, still praying for you?"

"No." Candy grabbed her purse and emptied it on the bed. She picked through the items, putting several back into her purse, leaving the rest on the bed.

"What do you mean?"

"I used to call that sheriff when Slash was stoned and I could get away for a few minutes. He'd update me on Grandma if he could. He's a nice guy."

"And…"

Candy zipped the purse and stood. "I hadn't called him in months but on a whim I called yesterday. My grandmother died four days ago."

Champagne sat silent until Candy opened the door. "Where are you going?"

"I should have been there. If nothing else to show up at her funeral. Whether God sent that preacher or not, he's the first man to treat me like a person for as long as I can remember. He invited us to come to his church, and I'm going."

Her friend stood, mouth open. "You're going to church?"

"Just once. To pay what I owe him, and pay back a little of what I owe Grandma." She stepped into the stairway and made sure no one was in sight before turning back to say, "Maybe from there I can say thanks for not giving up on me, and God'll get her the message."

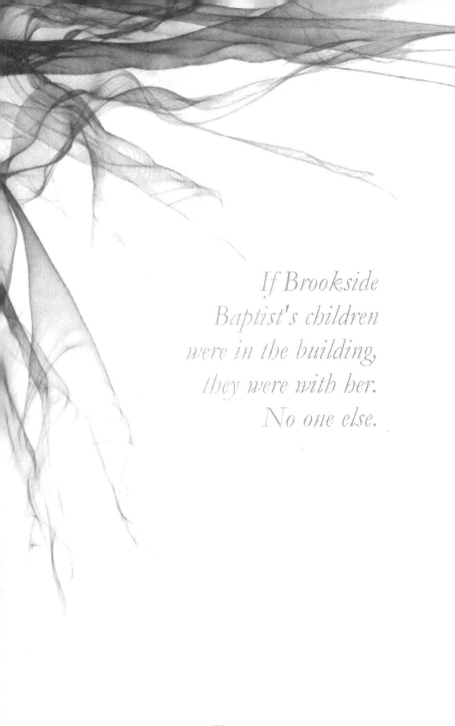

If Brookside
Baptist's children
were in the building,
they were with her.
No one else.

Jean

Jean Louise Jameson blew her nose, threw away the tissue, then doused a generous amount of sanitizer on her hands for the third time that morning. It wasn't a serious cold and would likely be gone by Monday. She'd only had two or three colds in all her twenty-five years. Nevertheless, she didn't want to risk any of the children catching it.

She turned to the small group of boys and girls. "This is a special Sunday. We have a new pastor, and I want you to be able to hear him preach today, so instead of children's church, we will go upstairs to the auditorium for the service. You may sit with your parents, or you may sit with me."

She gave them time to whine and object as they climbed the stairs, feeling guilty for requiring them to sit through a service rather than enjoy their usual snack, story, and craft. The children ranged from toddler to pre-teen, but Jean did not mind. She took her position seriously. If Brookside Baptist's children were in the building, they were with her. No one else.

Florence Simmons, in a dress that looked nearly as old as she was, approached and greeted Jean as soon as they entered the sanctuary. "Are you sure you don't want me and Gladys to take the kids today? You looked a little peaked, child."

"Thank you, but I'm keeping them here today so they can hear the new pastor."

Jean was thankful for the excuse. If she'd admitted she was sick and not up to teaching, surely someone would take advantage of the situation and force her to change her policy. A quick look at Gladys Simmons, imagining her with ten small children, nearly had her grimacing.

"Look, Miss Blue Jeans." Four-year-old Thomas pointed back at Gladys. "That lady looks like I do when my mom makes me eat asparagus."

That did warrant a grimace, especially when Gladys' "Harrumph" could be heard three rows up. "Florence," Jean heard her say, "you can teach those little whippersnappers anytime you want, but don't you go offering me to do it with you."

Gladys Simmons gave her sister the glare that used to scare Jean as a little girl. It did not seem to faze Florence much anymore. "Don't worry, Sister. I knew she would say no. She always does."

"Then why keep asking?"

The music started and Jean did not hear Florence's answer. She stifled a sense of pride when the few children who remained at her side refrained from wiggling through the singing and announcements. During Susan Meek's offertory, Jean noticed several of the younger ones start to fidget and pulled out small coloring pads and twistable crayons. She passed one pad and two crayons to each child, then sat back to enjoy the rare treat of getting to listen to a sermon.

She assessed the new pastor as he approached the podium. Stewart Henderson was of average height and somewhat lanky, not unlike herself. He had sandy blond hair, parted to the side, and his wire-rim glasses and nearly pointed chin gave him a scholarly appearance. He looked honest, and a little nervous.

He welcomed everyone and took out his notes, but instead of reading them, kept glancing toward the left side of the auditorium. Jean followed his gaze and gasped. Halfway back, sitting as if she'd done it her whole life, sat Candy. Jean recognized her by sight. Everyone in the church would, except maybe the new pastor and his family. She'd been in the papers a couple of years ago that time she got arrested for selling drugs.

What was a prostitute doing in their church?

Jean looked forward again and saw the pastor swallow. He gazed up at the ceiling, or maybe toward heaven for help, and swallowed again. He cleared his throat and glanced over at his wife, who sat in front of Jean, then bowed his head right there and started praying.

No one could hear the prayer, for his lips moved but he did not speak aloud. Jean glanced back again. Candy wasn't wearing much makeup, if any, which was surprising. Her outfit was far from demure, but not as declarative as it could have been. Jean wondered if the pastor knew who she was, if that's what he was praying about.

People all around the sanctuary began to whisper. Some subtly pointed in Candy's direction. Others were not subtle at all. Candy could have come to church years ago if she'd wanted to. Why was she at their church today?

Pastor Henderson lifted his face and the room stilled. He picked up his notes, folded them, and stuffed them into the inside pocket of his suit jacket. Jean stopped watching for a moment to pick up a crayon one of the children had dropped. She returned it to the child before focusing on the pastor again. He now had a worn Bible in his hands and was flipping through to find a passage.

No introduction. No joke or illustration. He just started reading.

Within a minute, every person in the church, except Candy likely, knew which story he had chosen. Several gasped. Jean felt her eyes widen. He was reading about the woman caught in adultery.

"They said to Him, 'Teacher, this woman was caught in adultery, in the very act. Now Moses, in the law, commanded us that such should be stoned. But what do You say?'" The pastor looked up and said, "In that time, the law clearly stated that anyone who committed adultery, or other such sins, must be stoned."

Jean bit her lip, wondering what Candy would think of his topic. She did not have long to wonder, for Candy's hand shot up, as if she were a child in school.

Pastor Henderson had opened his mouth to continue when he looked her way. He cleared his throat. "Um…yes? You have a question?"

Again, as if they were in school, Candy stood to her feet. "My name is Candy. You remember me, Preacher? We met last night."

Sunday Morning, July 6

Susan

Susan Meeks clamped her lips shut and covered her mouth to keep shocked sounds coming from it, glad she no longer sat at the piano where everyone could see her. She looked around and realized she could have put her red hair into pigtails and jumped up and down on the piano bench and no one would have noticed. All eyes were on Candy. Comments and questions flew around the room, as if Candy had taken a stick and busted open a verbal hornet's nest.

She watched Candy roll her eyes at the commotion, unlike Pastor Stewart, who stood still as a statue and was about as pale as one, too. "He was lost and asked for directions. Don't get your panties in a bunch," Candy announced, which if anything only made the buzzing worse.

The Pastor closed his eyes and seemed to be praying. Susan didn't blame him. What a way to start his first Sunday there. He kept his head down until Candy said, "So do I get to ask my question?"

He looked at her, took a deep breath, and said, "Go ahead."

"Where was the man?"

His eyebrows rose. "What man?"

"The man who was guilty, too." Candy crossed her arms. "The guys who brought this lady to Jesus said she was caught in adultery, in the very act. Well, you can't be in the very act, if you know what I mean, without there being a guilty guy there, too. Why did they only bring the woman? Did they set her up so they could kill her? Where was the man?"

Again, the congregation was far from quiet. Susan noticed Gladys muttering while fanning herself at record speed. Jean looked a little stricken, but Susan never could tell what was going on with her. In the pew in front of Jean, the pastor's wife chewed her nails as if her life depended on it. The pastor's brother, Grant, looking handsome and broad-shouldered in his solid grey shirt with lighter grey tie, was the only person in the building who appeared calm.

Susan watched Grant gaze around the room. When he caught her staring at him, he smiled and she felt her whole face flush. She dropped her bulletin and bent down to retrieve it, thankful that by the time she sat up, the pastor was talking and Grant was once again facing front. She waved the bulletin in front of her face to cool the flame across her cheeks.

"The Bible doesn't say where the man was," Pastor Stewart answered slowly. He seemed to be waiting for the noise to die down, or perhaps he was trying to figure out what to say next. "But you bring up an interesting point. Later in the passage, it says clearly that the scribes and Pharisees brought this woman to Jesus to test Him. They didn't really care about justice. They—"

"They didn't care about her either." Candy's interruption once again had everyone looking her way, except Jean. She was busy tapping a child on the shoulder and motioning for him to turn around. Susan shook her head and smiled. Jean had chosen the wrong service to have the children attend.

"What was that?" Pastor asked. He removed his glasses and blinked several times. Susan felt sorry for him.

"The woman. They were using her to frame Jesus. They didn't care whether she lived or died; they just wanted whatever they were after. Men are jerks." She sat down, but then looked up at the pastor and said, "No offense, Preacher."

Even though he bit both his lips together, a smile crept through. "Thanks," he said. He glanced over at his wife, but then his gaze traveled toward the children in the row behind her.

"You know," he said, closing his Bible and loosening his tie. His voice relaxed and he actually grinned. "Jesus wasn't your typical preacher. He liked to tell stories. Everybody likes stories, right?"

Every child on Jean's row nodded, and Susan saw Jean smile. That was rare.

Pastor Stewart left the podium and walked down the altar steps to be on the same level with them. "So I'll take His example and tell you this story. As you know, religious men brought a woman to Jesus. She was a sinner." He looked at the children. "She had done bad things. Things that God didn't like."

The children nodded again and he continued. "They wanted her to be punished. They wanted to see if Jesus would condemn her, like she deserved."

Susan risked a glance across the pew and saw several other people do the same. Candy never noticed. She was on the edge of her seat, her eyes locked on the pastor.

"Jesus didn't give an answer right away. He didn't say the men were right and she deserved to be punished."

"What did He do?"

The question came from Candy, quieter this time, her voice so full it seemed to carry with it a lifetime of longing.

Pastor Henderson smiled directly at Candy. Susan did not care how the others might interpret that smile, but she could see it was as pure as a smile from Jesus Himself would have been. "He stooped down and wrote with His finger in the dirt."

"He ignored them?"

"He did. They kept after Him to respond."

Candy grinned. "I bet they did."

Pastor Stewart walked to stand in the middle aisle between the two front pews. His finger reached out and trailed circles around the edge of the pew to his left. Susan wondered if he was aware he was mimicking what Jesus must have looked like, doodling in the sand. After a time of silence, he spoke. "Finally, Jesus stood and said, 'He who is without sin among you, let him throw a stone at her first.'"

"Really?" Candy's arms uncrossed.

"Really."

"Then what happened?"

Susan wondered if the pastor's wife would have any fingernails left by the end of the service. She admired the pastor's courage as he let his gaze take in every person in the room. "Then all those who accused her, from the oldest to the youngest, thought about the fact that they, too, deserved to be punished.

That they, too, were unclean. They walked away and the woman was left alone."

Candy stood, as if she was the only person in the building, and asked, "What happened to her then? What did Jesus say to her?"

Susan had heard the story all her life, but it had never meant much until this moment. She watched their new pastor speak to Candy as if the accusers around her had left and she was the only one in the room. "Jesus said, 'Woman, where are your accusers? Has no one condemned you?'"

Candy looked around, then back at the pastor.

His smile became tender as he finished the story. "She said, 'No man, Lord.' And Jesus said, 'Neither do I condemn you. Go and sin no more.'"

Susan was having a hard time seeing through her tears. Candy walked to stand before the pastor. "Would He say that to me?"

Stewart Henderson nodded. Susan watched him send a rather pleading look toward his wife. When she shook her head and he looked rather lost, Susan knew what she should do. Rising, knowing Gladys and probably a few others would disapprove, Susan adjusted her skirt, picked up her Bible, and walked across the pew into the aisle. She ignored the stares as she approached the front of the auditorium where the pastor and Candy stood.

"Hello, Candy," she said. "Will you sit here on the front row with me for a few minutes? I can show you what the Bible says."

"Will you show me that story in the Bible? I want to read it for myself."

"Gladly." Susan motioned for Candy to sit on the right front pew and sat beside her. The church remained silent except for Candy's questions and Susan's quiet answers. She was conscious there was no invitational hymn, since she was not available to play the piano. Susan felt a moment's guilt, then let it go. What she was doing now was more important.

Pastor Stewart needed no invitational hymn. He did not even give an invitation; he kneeled right where he was and prayed. Susan glanced up later just as his brother joined him.

Susan remained sitting when Candy stood and walked back to stand in front of the podium. "I just asked Jesus to save me," Candy announced to the church. "Now, some of you might think that I'm high or something and this might not be for real. Well, maybe it's not. Maybe I'm just going on feelings here. So I'm going to give it one week to see if it's real. If it sticks, then next Sunday I'll be back. If not, you'll never see me again. Well, not here anyway."

She turned and asked Susan, "Can I take that Bible with me so I can read it this week?"

Susan handed her Bible over. She, and every other person in the building, watched Candy take it, turn, then walk from the church without looking back.

*Brookside
would be the
laughingstock
of the entire
community.*

40

Alice

Alice Carson washed her hands before leaving the restroom. Hopefully by the time she got back to the table, the ladies would have found another topic. All they had talked about the last half hour was that prostitute woman coming to church on Sunday. It would be all over town soon. Rod said Brookside would be the laughingstock of the entire community.

She neared the end of the hallway and heard the ladies laughing, feeling a pang to know they did not miss her company when she was gone. There was no good reason to keep attending these monthly get-togethers at the coffee shop. She didn't even like coffee.

But it was the only time she got out of the house other than going to church. Any other time, Rod said she was needed at home. He only let her go to these events so she could be a good influence on other deacons' wives. Alice knew when she got home, he would be waiting for her report. He would want to know what the women talked about, if they mentioned him, and particularly anything critical they said about the current pastor.

Alice dreaded that part. Ever since that first time, when they were young and she didn't know better, she had not asked why he wanted to know all of this. Why should he care what women talked about over coffee? It was too complicated for her to understand, he had said. When she mentioned she might be smarter than he thought, he had thrown his plate of food across the room where it shattered against the wall. Shards of broken plate had cut into her hands as she cleaned them up, while he told her it wasn't her place to ask questions.

"If she says, 'Rod says' once more, I think I'll scream."

Alice was nearing the end of the hallway when she heard the words. She took a step back around the corner and out of sight.

"I know," another voice added. "Doesn't she have a thought in her head that is her own?"

"I don't think so." Alice recognized Susan's voice, the church pianist. "He's got her convinced that submission means being a doormat. I feel so sorry for her. Sometimes when he talks to her, I get so boiling mad, I decide I'm never going to get married."

"Not like there are many options around here to pick from anyway," another lady added and they all laughed like good friends.

Alice had heard enough. She wouldn't dream of relating this conversation to Rod, but he could always tell when she held something back from him. She had to stop the women before they said more. She walked into their line of vision and the conversation halted.

"Oh, hi, Alice," Susan said. "I was just going to get a refill. You want anything?"

"No, thank you." Alice sat down without further comment and let the uncomfortable silence remain.

One woman to her left, Samantha Albright, cleared her throat, then said in Susan's direction, "So, speaking of options, there is one more in town. What do you think of the pastor's handsome brother?"

"You talking about that tall, broad-shouldered thing that came in for coffee a minute ago and said hello on his way out?"

Alice turned to see Jamaica approach, owner of the coffee shop and waitress on slow days. Alice liked the smooth, warm confidence of Jamaica's voice, though she would never say so.

"Now that was a fine specimen of manhood." Jamaica placed a fresh bowl of creamers on their table. "He may be a white boy, but I'm no racist. I wouldn't mind looking at him again."

Alice watched the ladies laugh but didn't join in. There hadn't been anything inappropriate in her comment, had there? She would have to ask Rod later.

On second thought, she wouldn't ask Rod. He didn't like hearing about Jamaica.

"I just have to tell you all." Jamaica pulled up a chair and scooted between two of the ladies. "Now that all the other customers have left, I can come tell you the latest, and girls, the latest has some pretty juicy possibilities."

Alice watched Susan pat Jamaica's arm with a laugh. Susan was so pretty. And smart. She was in college. Alice had never been to college; she'd married Rod when they were both eighteen.

Jamaica wiped a finger to catch the foam overflowing from her cup. "Just yesterday morning that new pastor of yours and his big-muscled brother came in for a couple pastries. Did you know he was a quarterback? Even played in college."

"The pastor?" Susan asked.

"Don't be ridiculous. Grant, the brother." Jamaica blew into her coffee. She looked at Susan's playful grin. "Oh, you're a funny girl, aren't you?"

Jamaica sat forward. "Anyway, I got to talking with them, and after a little small talk, the brother asks me, all casual like, about the woman who is always with the children. So I say, 'You interested?' and he says, 'I'm curious,' like he doesn't really care or nothing. So I tell him her name is Jean Louise but growing up the kids called her Blue Jeans because she wore these baggy blue jeans and she was all sad all the time and didn't ever really have friends or do anything fun. 'Why not?' he asks, and I say, 'How should I know? I only moved here five months ago.' And I lean down and look into those brown eyes all melty like dark chocolate and I say, 'Why you asking me instead of asking her?'"

Alice was trying not to listen. She did not want to bring this story home. Rod didn't like her talking about Jean either.

"'I tried,' he says," Jamaica continued. "'Sunday night I asked her name and where she's from and then I asked if I could hang out with the kids for awhile and give her the chance to go hear the sermon for a change. I'd heard she worked with the kids every single week and thought she might like a break. It's not like I haven't heard Stewart preach before.' It was funny, the way those two brothers joked together. I like them. If your church wasn't all white, I'd think about coming over."

"You should sometime," Susan offered. "You know we'd love to have you."

Jamaica looked directly at Alice. "Um…yeah."

"So what did he say next?" Samantha Albright asked, getting Jamaica's attention again. Alice clenched her hands. Why had she looked at her like that?

"Grant said she clamped up and he didn't know what he'd said that was so terrible. His brother said he should leave it be, but then Grant said that he hadn't done anything wrong. Just tried to have a friendly conversation. I was watching his eyes as he said it, and I'm thinking that boy is used to having girls falling all around his feet, not clamming up and walking away."

Jamaica stood and picked up her empty cup. "So I tell him a little bit but I don't know much about her. She never talks when she comes in here. But just as I'm walking away I hear him say, 'That girl is so tight, it would take a crowbar to get her to open up.' He sounded frustrated, like he really is interested. Then he says to his brother, 'What should I do?'"

"What did he say?" Now even Susan was leaning forward.

"Well, he doesn't say a thing. Just shrugs, like guys do." She grinned. "But I walk back over there and put my hand on his big shoulder, and I say, 'Boy, you need to be finding yourself a good crowbar.'"

Saturday Evening, July 12

Stewart

Stewart Henderson watched his wife chug down a glass of milk like it was a jug of ale. He hoped whatever the milk was for would get resolved soon; he didn't want her getting another ulcer.

"Mm, that looks good." Grant looked over Brenda's homemade lasagna with an appreciative eye. "I'm going to get spoiled eating your cooking."

"Only for six months in our little parsonage," she reminded him with a smile. "Then you're on your own."

"You know, this *is* a great little place for a newly married couple," Grant said between bites after Stewart prayed. It was a good thing Grant exercised regularly since he still ate like a football player. "But not for a newly married couple and their brother. You should have a place to yourselves."

"Listen to him." Stewart gestured toward Grant while he smiled at Brenda. She grinned back and winked. If Grant had not been there right then, he would have gone over, pulled her into his lap, and kissed her until she couldn't see straight. "One week with us and he's already begging to move out."

She extended her smile to include Grant. "But where would you stay?"

"I've considered renting a place, but that wouldn't be prudent for only six months." He stood and motioned for them to come with him to the kitchen window. From there, he pointed across the yard to the church building. "See that one room downstairs where the ground slopes down? I looked in through the window yesterday while it was still light out. It's being used as some kind of storage room, but it looks like the boxes and desks haven't been touched in years. If I could clean that out, how about letting me move my stuff over there?"

Brenda cupped her hands against the window and put her face between them to see better. "You want to live in a storage closet?"

"It's not a closet. It's a small room, decent sized, plenty for a guy like me." He chuckled. "It's not like I need space for my knick-knacks or anything."

"But there's plenty of room here." Stewart could hear the I-feel-guilty-but-wish-I-didn't in her voice. She used that tone a lot.

"It's not about the space," he reiterated. "It's about privacy. And I'm not doing this just for your sake. I'm used to privacy of my own, you know." He turned to Stewart. "What would the logistics be regarding electricity and water? Would we have to run the whole building, or—"

A knock startled all three of them and Brenda automatically started toward the door. "Who would be visiting at this time of night?"

Grant reached for the knob before she could. "Here, let me get it. In case it's a bad guy." He smiled at her and opened the door.

The church piano player stood there, casually dressed, her long red hair pulled back, the beaming smile on her face directed at Grant.

"Hi, uh…"

"Susan," she said. "Susan Meeks. I know it's a little weird to come by so late, but...um..." She noticed Brenda and seemed to suddenly remember the covered plate in her hands. "Oh, hi, Mrs. Henderson! Here." She handed over the plate. "A welcome-to-our-church batch of cookies."

Brenda thanked her and she shrugged self-consciously. "To be honest, I didn't make them. I bought them and put them on a plate."

"Do you want to come in?"

"Oh no." She took a step back but remained on the porch. "I don't want to take up your time. I just...I have some news. I mean, well, I was wondering if I could talk with your brother-in-law for a minute?"

Stewart had to fight a smile at her asking for permission as if Brenda was the man's mother or something. "Be my guest," Brenda offered, tossing a grin in Grant's direction before heading for the kitchen.

Stewart followed her and reached for one of the cookies, then a second.

"Um, I don't really know how to say this..." he heard the girl say.

Grant's voice was casual. "I'm all for you coming straight out and saying whatever's on your mind. Less mosquito bites if you do."

"Oh, how inconsiderate of me. I should have let you close the door."

"It was a joke."

The young woman must have come inside because the conversation came closer.

"We should leave them to talk alone," Brenda whispered, offering him her cookie after taking two bites out of it.

"They're standing in the only path out of the kitchen." He lifted her half a cookie to his mouth.

"You're right. In that case..." She took her cookie back and bit into it. "I hope she doesn't know we can hear them. She seemed nervous enough already."

"Been watching that scenario play out with my popular brother all my life." He sighed. "When it comes to the girls, us smaller, brainy guys get left behind."

She crossed her arms. "Excuse me? Who's the one married and who's not?"

He chuckled and pulled her into his arms, kissing her soundly.

"Okay, I'll come right out and say it, if you're sure you don't mind me being blunt," he heard Susan say as Brenda snuggled up against him.

"Nope."

He felt Brenda smile against his chest. "Get to the point already!" she whispered.

"Well, you know the coffee shop on main street?" Susan asked.

"Jamaica's place?"

"Yes, well, um, I just wanted you to know that she's, well..." He heard the woman take in a big breath, then words came spilling out. "She told us all about the conversation you had with your brother about Jean and how she thinks you're interested in her and something about a crowbar. I just figured you should know that anything you say in her place is likely to get repeated and I didn't want you to end up in an embarrassing position because of a random comment that didn't actually mean anything."

Stewart swiped another cookie while he waited for Grant's reply.

"Oh," Grant said.

"Unless it did mean something...of course..."

"Okay. Thanks for letting me know."

"You're welcome."

"I'll remember that."

"Good."

"Yeah."

"Well, I should go."

Brenda shifted her weight from one foot to the other. "If she's waiting for Grant to ask her out, we'll be here all night."

Stewart chuckled. "True." Grant always said he wanted to marry his best friend, and you could only discover a best friend by making friends, not dating strangers. He bit into another cookie, decided they weren't worth the sore feet he was getting standing there, and led the way back into view.

"Oh, Pastor Henderson, I hope you're happy with this house. I always liked it here." When Susan grinned at him, Stewart smiled back even before he heard what was funny. "I have to say last Sunday was the most interesting service I've attended in my whole life. You sure are starting out with a bang, sir. I have a feeling this Sunday won't be boring either."

Grant laughed beside her. "I have a feeling you're right."

Stewart noticed her smile got a little wobbly when she focused on Grant again. "Well, I really should go. If you ever want a tour of the church, or if I can help in any way, just let me know."

"Thanks." Grant started to shut the door, then swung it open again. "Susan?"

She turned. "Yes?"

"We got lost on our way here because we were told to come to Creekside Baptist Church instead of Brookside Baptist. Any idea how the names could have gotten mixed up?"

She tilted her head. "No. It's been that name since it was built. That's...odd."

"Yeah. Well, thanks. Goodnight." Grant waved and shut the door.

Brenda joined them from the kitchen. "How many mosquito bites did you get?" she asked with a laugh.

"I don't want to talk about it." He ruffled her hair as if she really were his sister. "Let's get those cookies to the living room. There's a game on tonight."

"Okay." Brenda grabbed the plate and returned. "Grant, who told you it was Creekside Baptist?"

Stewart had hoped she would not bring that up. Once she knew, she was going to need another glass of milk.

Grant was halfway across the room. He looked back at her and all joking had left his face. "The man who gets to be in charge when there's no pastor. Rod Carson."

"It's not
your job
on the line."

Brenda

Oh, Stewart, what have you done?

Her husband stood near the podium, face pale, eyes wide and round. They had been married only six months, but Brenda already knew that look. She had seen it during their first fight, the moment she started crying. She'd seen it when his mother insisted Grant accompany them for the summer to help Stewart's first ministry here in North Carolina. It had appeared again last weekend when he'd gotten lost and knew he would be late for his very first church meeting.

If you hadn't gotten lost, you never would have met Candy, and we wouldn't have half the church furious at us already.

Brenda kept checking from her position on the front pew through the introduction, and again as they stood to sing the opening hymn. The double doors at the back of the auditorium were open, but the space between them remained empty.

She sighed with relief. *I'm sorry, God, if it's wrong of me to wish she wouldn't come. I know I should want her to genuinely be a believer and want to follow You, but couldn't something this divisive wait until after we've settled here awhile? This is only our second Sunday here.*

"You okay?"

Brenda turned sharply to her right. "What?"

Grant looked at her with concern. "You aren't singing."

"Oh." Her face flushed. "I was—I was praying."

He had the gall to grin and said quietly, "Looks like it was a pretty anxious prayer. Are you nervous about Stewart's sermon, or the fact that more than half the town is here today for reasons other than the sermon?"

The space between her eyebrows pulled together. "Grin all you want. It's not your job that's on the line."

Grant's smile faded. "You think—"

Brenda did not have to ask why Grant stopped talking. She had heard it too, a huge gasp that pulled in all the air around her, leaving her with none.

The piano player's fingers stilled and the music faded into heavy silence. Brenda turned and noted with misery that she was the last person in the building to do so.

Candy had come.

Between the double doors, her arms full of—*oh, goodness*—a heaping pile of lingerie items, other shocking pieces of clothing, and even a few pairs of stiletto heels, stood a woman everyone in the auditorium seemed to know by sight. Candy, the reason the church was packed today, the reason the deacon board had already called one emergency meeting.

Grant must have noticed the dismay on her face. "She said she'd come," he reminded her, "to testify if her new faith 'stuck' or not, remember?"

"I remember," Brenda ground out.

This time, Grant's voice was a whisper barely heard above all the other whispers echoing through the sanctuary as Candy began making her way toward the front. "Her coming back is a good thing, Brenda."

"For her. I know." Tears sprang unexpectedly to her eyes. "But did she have to be so—so open—about everything? Doesn't she know what this might mean for Stewart's testimony in this town? What people might think?"

Grant's gaze scanned the crowd of church members and curious visitors, all gaping. His survey ended back at her. "Should it matter what people think?"

"Of course not," she murmured, hating the moisture that rushed to glaze her eyes again. It shouldn't matter, but it did. It always had.

Sunday Morning, July 13

Gladys

How dare she? The brazen hussy.

If looks could kill, Gladys Simmons was certain that woman would drop dead right there in the middle of the aisle. And, not to be vindictive, but wouldn't that ultimately be a blessing? She said she got saved last weekend. If that were true—*Which it likely was not. Who knew what devious motives were behind all of this?*—she'd go to heaven. God would know what to do with her.

Pastor Stewart Henderson, young and green as he was, most certainly did not.

A gasp arose from the crowd when a long cloth, covered in bright pink feathers, dropped from the woman's arms onto the walkway between pews.

"Oh heavens, what is she thinking, bringing all her tools of the trade here?" Gladys leaned toward her sister Florence as if whispering, adding just enough volume to make sure those around heard as well. "She is desecrating the Lord's house!"

"Gladys, please. She'll hear you." Her sister Florence, meek and mousy Florence, of course did whisper politely. What need was there to be polite? Jesus wasn't polite when He threw out the money changers.

"Humph. I hope she does hear me," Gladys announced, but then lowered her voice to get that suffering look off her sister's face. "That trumped-up female has no business in my church."

Florence frowned. "It isn't your church, Sister. It's God's."

"Well, God is likely as mortified as I am." Gladys breathed in until her ample chest jutted out and overlapped the hymnal she held, which didn't matter because of course she knew all the words to the song. *And it* is *my church,* she argued silently. *I was here the year it was built. My own hands helped paint these walls. No one but God Himself has been here longer. I have the right to protest this…this atrocity.* "Just look at her!"

Florence followed her gaze and looked. Gladys herself had not stopped looking, staring in horror really, since the town prostitute had appeared at the entrance to the auditorium, arms stuffed to overflowing with the most bizarre clothing, shoes, and accessories.

Single word exclamations followed her slow, theatric, spike-heeled journey toward the altar.

"Outrageous."

"Unbelievable."

"Shocking."

A child somewhere asked loudly, "Mommy, why is that lady carrying all that stuff? Is she giving it to the church?"

Gladys nearly choked on her indignation. As loud as the question was, as loud as her own words had been, the woman of the street dared ignore them all and kept her face forward toward the holy altar.

Candy—what a ridiculous name—took step by slinky step forward. A garment so tiny Gladys would never even wear it to bed slipped from Candy's pile, the leopard spots and red lace falling into a silken heap of obnoxious color.

Two rows ahead, a woman elbowed her staring husband, and Gladys added her own, "Tsk, tsk," in support. "Mark my words," she said in Florence's direction. "This woman is going to singlehandedly be the ruin of this church."

Sunday Morning, July 13

Stewart

"God, what do I do now?"

Stewart said it aloud, but no one noticed or heard. Everyone's eyes remained on the woman walking down the aisle. From his position near the podium, he noticed his wife's worried gaze, his brother's calm one, and that one rather ancient woman on the third row, left side, whose perpetual grimace now glowed a deep, livid red. Everyone else was open-mouthed in shock, tight-lipped with disapproval, or flat out staring in curiosity.

He wouldn't be surprised if a few of the many visitors were from the local paper, waiting like vultures for a juicy story.

From the look of things, they'd get one.

She'd said to call her Candy. Wouldn't tell him her real name. As she walked towards him, she never once looked up, but kept her gaze firmly set on the steps at his feet. The altar, they liked to call it. Where people could come to pray or get right with God, or sometimes find Him for the first time.

Stewart had spent hours preparing for today's sermon, but there had been no way to anticipate, much less prepare, for what was happening at that moment. Candy reached the first step, stopped, and took in a deep breath.

He held his.

She let out a sob and threw her heap of...things. They landed on the steps, on the floor around her. A few of them floated upward and settled over his feet.

Should he step back? Move forward? Talk to her?

He never knew what to do when a woman cried, and this woman was weeping. The whispers that had broken the silence when she flung the clothing through the air quieted again at the raw sounds coming from her throat, sounds of grief and despair. The people in the auditorium looked as astonished as he felt. Their gazes swiveled from her to him, to her, to him.

God, what do I do? Seminary didn't train me for this.

Candy's wails continued. Loud. Uninhibited. Like nothing he had ever heard in church before.

She wiped her eyes with the underside of a blue scarf covered in sequins and edged with gold tassels. As her cries faded, the silence in the church fogged thick with expectation. Like everyone else, he stared and waited.

Candy looked up at him, hers a middle-aged face that once must have known incredible beauty, for it was beautiful still, even with her eyes swollen and red. Her eyes broke contact with his, she looked down at the clothing in front her, and cried again.

"God!" she shouted.

As if struck by lightning, the congregation jolted. Stewart involuntarily took a step back, noticed he'd stepped on a purple lace bra, and quickly moved to stand in a safer place.

"I'm sorry! I'm so sorry!" The volume of the woman's voice was astounding, as if she wanted her words to reach heaven itself. "Last Sunday the preacher said that if we confess with our mouth, then we'll be saved. I don't want everyone to know all I've done. How many men I got drunk so I could take their money. How many husbands I pulled away from their wives. But if that's what it takes to be forgiven, to be accepted, I've got to do it."

Her voice had quieted some, and several people leaned forward. The angry, red lady sat down and fanned herself.

That must have been the traditional cue, for pockets of assembled men and women also sat. The others, likely all the visitors, looked around, then followed suit. Only he remained standing, looking down on this woman prostrated below his feet who began spilling out details, sordid events, and even names.

She mentioned one name and several people shrieked. Another and they groaned. One man toward the front wrote furiously in a notebook. At the next name, a different man rose and rushed from the building.

This was bad. There was a time and place for public confession, but Stewart was pretty sure this wasn't it. Yet how was he to stop her? Even he knew it wouldn't be wise to go down and pray with her, putting a comforting arm around her shoulder as he normally would.

"Take them, please!" She was yelling again. Her eyes were closed, her face turned up to heaven, garments clutched in her hands. In a swift flash of movement, her eyes opened and fixed on him. "Take my sins away!"

She flung the clothes at him. He stood frozen, only his eyes moving from the woman, to the congregation, to his wife. Everyone stopped watching Candy and was now watching him, the pastor with a zebra-striped nightgown covering his shoes.

What was he supposed to do?

She was breaking three of her fundamental rules.

Jean

Breathing hard from her run up the stairs, Jean stopped just before the two open doors that connected the church foyer to the auditorium. Her eyes took in information, but her mind was slow to process it. Samantha was right; she wouldn't have believed it.

Jean had been setting out snacks for children's church, her eight young charges full of wiggles and curious questions, when Samantha Albright barely knocked, then rushed inside without waiting for a response.

"You're never going to believe it," her mother's best friend said, panting.

Alarmed, Jean rounded the miniature table and approached. "Is something wrong?"

Samantha had almost laughed. "Well, something is definitely not right. Remember the prostitute who came to church last Sunday?" She did laugh then. "What a ridiculous question. Of course you do. It's all anyone in town has talked about all week."

She took in a heaving breath. "You should see upstairs. The auditorium is more stuffed than my granddaughter's teddy bears. The service started, and we all thought she wasn't coming, but then, smack in the middle of a song, she shows up. Jean, she brought a whole pile of stuff with her! She walked it down the aisle and some of it dropped on the floor behind her. You should have seen Gladys' face! I think she's halfway toward a real swoon."

Jean sent a pointed glance toward the eight pairs of eager ears behind them. In case that didn't work, she whispered, "The children."

"Oh, sorry," Samantha said. "But you know it's all their parents will talk about at lunch today anyway."

A sigh was Jean's only acknowledgment of that likely fact. She was inwardly scrambling for some way to get Samantha to go back upstairs and leave the details for later, and hopefully for someone other than her, when her stomach tightened at Samantha's next words.

"She started crying and wailing, like somebody had died. Honestly, it gave me chills. I mean, I know she doesn't know how things are supposed to work in church, but surely even she knows it's not appropriate to be yelling in God's house." She put a hand to her heart. "And now, would you believe it? She's up there listing names. Names! She's already mentioned two politicians and one restaurant owner. She said she had to confess to be forgiven, like we were all one big confession booth and pastor Stewart was some kind of priest."

Jean felt her fingers contract into a fist and stopped herself before she crushed the small paper cup in her hand. With precision, as if it were important, she finished setting out each cup of juice along with exactly three cookies each to the waiting children.

"Samantha, would you—would you stay here with the kids while they eat their snack?"

It was understandable that the response was a dropped jaw. For ten years, Jean had presided over children's church and its occupants like a mother tiger would her cubs.

After Samantha put her jaw back in place and agreed, Jean sped from the room. As she ran up the stairs to the foyer, uncertain why she felt such a sense of urgency, she wondered if she had made a wrong choice. She was breaking three of her fundamental rules:

1. Never leave the children unattended or in anyone else's care.
2. Never act impulsively.
3. Never, ever, give people a reason to stare.

Now here she was, about to endure the stares of at least a hundred people, many of them strangers and many not. She was not sure if the thought of strangers staring or the church people staring made her insides clench more, but if they got any tighter, she would not be able to breathe.

Why was she even considering this? Why should she care what this woman did or who talked about it?

Jean quoted the children's memory verse for the week six times in her head as she walked down the aisle, focusing her gaze on Candy to keep her mind off the heads all around that turned in her direction.

It was certain that no matter how much shock the church members had felt at Candy's entrance, her current actions would surpass it.

Sunday Morning, July 13

Grant

Stewart had always been the more cautious one. More careful. He thought through every decision beforehand, calculated the risk, and analyzed the possible ramifications and consequences before developing a conclusion.

It drove Grant crazy. Grant was a man—and had been a boy—of action, ready to go, experience, discover. His quick decisions sometimes turned out to be bad ones, as Stewart often reminded him, but to Grant, actually taking the first step was worth the risk that his first step might need to be rerouted.

All their lives, they had argued over whose way was better, giving their mother grey hairs, according to her. She wanted them to be like Jonathan and David. Close and loyal and self-sacrificing.

No, that needed clarification. She wanted him to be like Jonathan while older brother Stewart reigned like David. Grant was supposed to be loyal and help his brother achieve greatness.

Stewart never believed it when Grant said so, but when their mother brought up her idea that Grant come with Stewart to start his first pastorate, Stewart finally saw what he had been seeing for years. Stewart was her chosen one, the favorite.

Naturally, Grant had balked at the idea. That night he had followed his father into his study. "Why is it always what Stewart dreams and what Stewart wants? He graduated a year before I did and floundered around trying to decide what to do. I've known what I wanted to do since high school. Why not have him come and help me?"

His father, a pastor himself, had calmly placed his elbows on the armrests of his desk chair. He clasped his hands, brought two fingers together into a steeple, and tapped that steeple against his lips, a gesture that always meant deep contemplation. To Grant, there was little to contemplate. He waited more out of respect than patience.

Finally, his father spoke. "Has it ever occurred to you that Stewart might need help more than you do?"

A quick negating comment came to mind, but again, out of respect, Grant let his father's words sink in and be considered. This wasn't just swimming in the deep end as opposed to the shallow end. This concept was an entirely different body of water, like a river or a lake. He had never enjoyed either: too slimy, and you couldn't see what you were swimming with.

And now here he was, watching Stewart sink in the murky water of indecision. Stewart wanted so desperately to do the right thing, but if he did not know what that one right thing was, he did nothing.

Now was not the time to do nothing. A new believer, lots of old believers, and plenty of unbelievers were all waiting for him to act. Grant's father had been wise when he asked Grant to come. His brother did need the balance of someone like him. And as his father had said that night, the need likely went both ways. Grant was finally willing to not only concede that point, but learn what it meant.

For the moment, however, Stewart needed rescuing. His wife was in no position to help. Brenda's face was layered with anxiety. "It's okay," he said with a reassuring smile. Then he rose from the pew and left the auditorium.

Sunday Morning, July 13

Florence

What is happening? Why isn't the pastor doing anything? Where is the pastor's brother going? And...oh my...

Rare was the moment when Florence Simmons' inner dialogue slowed, but this had it stalled completely. Jean Louise Jameson was not downstairs with the children. That itself was enough fodder for the gossip mill to run at full speed for at least a week. They would be talking for a month about the added fact that the young woman, who most often was hiding away somewhere to avoid attention, now walked down the aisle in front of God and everyone, picking up the dropped feather boas and sheer scarves like a misdirected flower girl.

"Merciful heavens, what now?" Gladys fanned at double speed. Florence could have used a little extra air herself, but they only had one hand-held fan, and of course Gladys never asked if Florence wanted a turn.

Florence felt her face scrunch up as it always did when Gladys got angry. It was no wonder she had so many wrinkles; she'd been scrunching up her face since she was fourteen years old. She knew today was going to be a bad day. Gladys had been spitting mad all morning just at the thought of the prostitute coming back. Florence would have loved to stay home and enjoy some quiet for an hour or two, but one must not miss church if the church doors are open, even if they are open for a prostitute crying on the aisle steps and shouting names like some hoodlum.

When Jean appeared, Florence had been thinking how hungry she would be by the time lunch was ready, for it always took twice as long when Gladys was upset. She would talk nonstop and misplace bottles of spices or forget to chop vegetables, but then snap whenever Florence tried to help.

Florence sighed. After fifty years, she should be used to it by now. Shame on her that she wasn't. She must just not have enough of the fruits of the Spirit, as Gladys said. She needed to spend more time working on that.

But later. For now, her mind had gone from blank to overflowing with questions as Jean, in her long, loose, brown-asmud dress approached Candy, who was wearing a fuchsia dress that was neither long nor loose. At the same time, the pastor's brother came back into the auditorium through the door to the left of the podium, the one that went to the baptistery and down to the lower level Sunday school rooms and fellowship hall. He carried a large, black trash can that he must have gotten from the fellowship hall.

"That doesn't belong in here," Gladys announced, in that annoying way she had of pretending to whisper but somehow doing it loudly. "What is that young man doing?"

For once, Florence ignored her sister and feasted her mind on what she saw. Something in her spirit told her this was an important moment, more than just drama to chew and re-chew later like mental cud. Something significant was happening right before her eyes.

The pastor's brother stopped when he saw Jean kneel next to where Candy still spouted her list of sins. His hands lowered and the trash can rested on the floor. Jean looked over and saw him, then turned her attention back to Candy. She put an arm around Candy's shoulders and Candy stopped to listen. Florence would have hobbled her sixty-four-year-old, arthritic bones up to the front row if she thought she'd be able to hear what Jean was saying. What could a tiny girl in her twenties, who didn't have the nerve to even wear bright colors, have to say to a prostitute?

Grant Henderson, trash can still in hand, moved to stand by the pastor's side. It was easy to see the relief on the pastor's face at his presence. Gladys would likely rip him to shreds over lunch for not throwing Candy out or whatever else Gladys would have done, but Florence was not one to decide what someone else should do. It was understandable that he was flummoxed. Who wouldn't be?

After a few minutes, in which time the crowd grew restless, apparently bored now that no one was giving out names or sharing sins, Candy and Jean stood and turned toward the congregation.

"Preacher," Candy said, looking back once then facing the group again. "This girl here just told me that I had that Bible verse wrong. It doesn't say I have to tell you everything I've done. It says I have to confess that Jesus is Lord. So that's what I'm doing right now. I confess that Jesus Christ is Lord." She looked over at Jean, who had inched half her body behind Candy's. Florence shook her head. Poor girl. "Am I saved now?" she asked Jean.

Jean whispered something to Candy and Candy said, "Oh, she says I got saved as soon as I believed in Jesus and asked Him to forgive my sins. Well, I guess that happened last week then!" She looked back at the pastor, who was a little farther away, having removed himself from that black-and-white nightie that had landed on his feet. "Don't take this personally, Preacher, but this is getting kind of confusing. I need somebody to help me study the Bible so I can learn how this works. If I'm going to follow Jesus, I want to do it right."

Florence felt her throat choke up with emotion as the pastor's brother held out the trash can and Candy's grin spread as wide as her face. She picked up pieces of clothing and started tossing them toward the trash can. Some of the items went in, some didn't. Little Jean, now with no one to hide behind, picked up a pair of sparkly platform shoes and looked them over in amazement before throwing them in, wincing as each made a loud thump.

Then Gladys said, "Impossible," and Florence couldn't stop smiling. People from the front rows, then rows farther back, rose to their feet, walked down the aisle as Jean had done, and picked up Candy's things to help her throw them away. Florence recognized the pianist, the former choir director, other church members and even some of the visitors. Candy started crying again when several women lined up to pull her into a hug.

"I don't believe it," Gladys said. For once, Florence nodded in agreement. She could hardly believe it either, but not for all the bad reasons she knew Gladys would share later.

Something remarkable just happened in their church. Something very good.

He looked
amazing.
And dangerous.

Chapter Seven
Sunday Afternoon, July 13

Jean

"Hello there."

Jean screamed and dropped her paintbrush. She whirled around. "How did you get in here?"

Grant Henderson stood just outside the nursery. Jean had opened the top half of the nursery door, but left the bottom half closed. Grant had a helmet in his hands, which he propped up on the door's ledge that reached a few inches above his waist. He wore a black leather jacket and must have been wearing the helmet, for his hair was damp and flattened to his head, and the drying edges were beginning to curl.

He looked amazing. And dangerous.

Jean saw his gaze drop to just below her collarbone. She felt her skin break out in a cold sweat. "How did you get in here?" She tried to keep her voice from shaking.

He reached into his pocket and pulled out a key. She looked at it, then back at him. His eyes were on her chest again. There were only two keys to the church building. She had one. If he had the other, and had locked the doors when he entered, no one else would be able to get in. Jean felt the shaking begin deep inside and spread outward. She clutched her Styrofoam cup filled with yellow paint in both hands to keep from dropping it.

"Um, you've got—there's—" He pointed at her shirt. "You sort of painted yourself."

71

Jean looked down. "Oh, no!" A line of yellow paint ran down her shirt, touched her jeans in several places, and ended in a small splotch of yellow where the paintbrush had landed. "The carpet!"

"That's my fault. I should have warned you I was in the building." He tried to open the nursery door and had to reach over to unlock it from the inside before it swung open. "I didn't know anybody was here until I came downstairs and saw the light on."

She was down on her knees, wiping up as much paint as possible with baby wipes from the changing table nearby. "Oh, this is terrible. I was trying to make the nursery better, not worse."

"It's just a little paint." Grant knelt beside her and she edged as far away as she could while still wiping at the paint. "Here, let me help." He touched her hand and she jerked away.

Backing away from him, Jean stood and placed the cup of paint on the counter near the wall farthest from Grant.

"Is it me?"

She did not face him, pretending to look through drawers for more wipes. She knew they were in the cupboards, but it kept her hands busy. "Is what you?"

"Are you scared of me or something?"

Jean looked at her hands. They were shaking. "Why would you think that?"

"Jean Louise, you are a complicated person to figure out." She heard his voice fade slightly and turned to see that he now stood back on the other side of the nursery door again. "I'll stay over here so you don't have to worry." He shrugged. "But it would help a guy out if I knew what it was that bugs you about me. The other day when I offered to teach the kids—and I like kids, by the way—you practically ran away. Just now I think you would have run if there'd been any place to go. I'm not used to girls running away from me."

His grin was so self-effacing she smiled before she realized it.

"Well, now, a smile is much better than panic. It looks good on you."

Her smile dropped instantly. "I doubt it." She knelt and began blotting paint from the carpet again. She knew what he saw. Plain Blue Jean, skinny as a rail, sharp, straight features. Straight, boring, dishwater-blonde hair. Long limbs and a long neck. Even her eyes were some bland shade of grey.

"Hey, I think you should give up on that paint on the carpet. It's not going anywhere. The walls look really cool though."

She had broken her routine and come early the past few Sunday evenings to decorate the nursery walls with flowers, butterflies, and ladybugs. "The nursery looked so bare. I felt sorry for the babies."

"Do you think babies can see that far? Oh, I bet that's why you painted them so big." He chuckled. "You really love kids, don't you? Your face softens up just talking about them, and at church you're off in your own world until a kid comes around. Then you light up. Are you a teacher?"

Why was he standing around talking with her? "No. I wanted to be, but..."

He opened the door again. "I'm just going to sit, if you don't mind." He sat on the floor near the door and set his helmet beside him. "But what?"

She shrugged, then surprised herself by telling him, "To teach you don't get to only work with kids. You have to interact with parents."

"Ah, so all adults scare you. Not just me." He grinned as if she'd given him a present. For some reason that bothered her.

"What are you doing here, anyway?" she asked.

"I was checking into something, but it can wait till later."

Jean felt one eyebrow slide up. "Oh? I'm curious."

"So am I. But about you."

She attacked the paint splotch again. Something deep inside started hurting. "There's no need to lie to me."

"I'm not. I don't like liars and have never wanted to be one. I like openness." He leaned back against the wall, looking completely comfortable sitting on the floor in a nursery, with butterflies painted behind his head. "See, me, I'm an open book. I'll tell you anything you want to know. Go ahead, ask me something."

The wipe was mostly disintegrated in her hand, but Jean continued using it. "Okay, what do you want to be when you grow up?"

He laughed. "When I was a kid, I wanted to be a superhero fireman who could fly but also had a motorcycle." He grinned. "At least I got the motorcycle part. You should come for a ride with me sometime."

That cold sweat was back. "No thanks."

She tossed the threadbare wipe aside and grabbed another.

"You're supposed to ask me now what I seriously wanted to be when I grew up."

She looked across the room at him. "Why aren't you off having fun with some cheerleader or something?"

"You know I played ball?"

"I had lunch at Jamaica's the other day."

"Ah, did she tell you about me on her own?" He wiggled his eyebrows like a circus clown. "Or did you ask?"

Jean rolled her eyes. "So, what *did* you want to be when you grew up?"

He shifted to sit cross-legged and smiled again. It wasn't fair that he could be so comfortable while she was in knots. "I wanted to do something important, something that really helped people. My dad was a pastor, but I'm not one for studying. I wanted to have some kind of ministry that had something to do with sports. Maybe using sports as therapy for natural disaster victims, or a way for believers to connect with non-believers in a setting comfortable to them. I like doing, getting in the action, being around people."

"If you like being around people, why come to the church when you think it's empty?"

"Nice. I'm impressed." He stood, approached, and reached a hand down to help her up. She backed away. "Okay, so you don't like adults and you don't like being helped. You're a tough case."

"You're probably used to girls falling over just to get you to hold their hand to help them up." Where were these biting comments coming from? She didn't talk to people this way. She didn't talk to people at all if she could help it.

He was still chuckling as he picked up her pile of used wipes and found a place to dispose of them. "Maybe that's why I find you so interesting. You're not like most of the girls I've met." He cocked his head and looked at her. "Now that I think about it, you're not like any girl I've met."

"You can give thanks for that."

"What did you want to be when you grew up?"

Jean felt her face harden. "Anything away from here."

He considered her for a moment. "But you aren't."

"No." She tossed the paint cup into the trash. "I should go." She turned around, but stopped and put a hand to her temple. "But what about the carpet?"

"Ah, wait," Grant said. He put a finger to his lips as if they shared a secret, then tip-toed across the room. He lifted the changing table and carried it back toward her, setting it right over the paint spot. "Problem solved."

She let out a laugh, then coughed on the shock of it.

"Not used to laughing much, are you?" He gave her a pat on the back, until she reacted and he pulled his hand back. "Sorry."

He followed her from the nursery, his helmet under his arm like a football. "Here's the thing: I can't figure you out. You don't seem to like people, which doesn't make sense because you're nice and funny and have a rare, quick wit. You want to be away from here but you aren't away from here. You're always around kids, but you just watch over them and don't play with them."

Jean walked faster, but he kept up. Why wouldn't he go away? She unlocked and opened the entrance doors to the church. "It's almost time for the evening service. Anything else you want to say, Sherlock?"

He leaned on the doorframe, too close to be comfortable. "I think I'm going to mess up your world, Jean Louise."

Her face was getting warm. Why didn't he call her Blue Jean like everyone else did? "Yeah? How are you going to do that?"

His mouth didn't smile but for some reason Jean felt like his eyes did. "I'm going to become your friend."

Sunday Evening, July 13

Church was over and Grant was still puzzled. Why did it bother him so much that Jean Jameson was edgy around him? She had joked about it, but it really was true that most of the women he'd known were the kind who deliberately tried to get his attention. Jean was different.

He chuckled. That was an understatement. She seemed to want nothing more than to get away from him. Maybe that was it; he saw her as a challenge.

Well, whatever the reason, everybody could use another friend, and she didn't seem to have many friends over four feet tall, so he'd volunteer for the job.

He whistled as he walked the short distance from the church to Stewart's house, glad to start thinking of it that way now that they'd agreed he could move into that room in the church. Tonight he would change into what his mother called his "grubbies" and go start cleaning the room out. He had planned to start before church, but got distracted by a willowy blonde who was a living contradiction, who had worn nothing but black or brown since he'd met her, but who painted brightly colored flowers in the nursery because she didn't want babies to have to look at bare walls.

She was an enigma all right. Tomorrow he was going to think of some way to get that woman to really smile. For tonight, however, he should find something else to think about before he gave himself a headache.

Thirty minutes later he had changed into an old pair of jeans and a t-shirt, eaten the last of the cookies Susan brought over, and was back in the church building with several large trash bags in hand. He would probably have to get approval before actually throwing anything away. Even if it looked like trash to him, that one deacon seemed to feel threatened anytime a decision was made without his approval. Grant wondered if his father had ever had a church member like that, and what he did about it. He didn't know how he was supposed to help Stewart when he was as new at all this as Stewart was.

Grant was two steps from the bottom of the dark stairway when something made him stop. He listened. It sounded like...like what? A toy motorcycle. Setting the trash bags down at the bottom of the stairs, he made his way down the empty hallway, pulling a flashlight from the back pocket of his jeans and holding it out, ready to turn it on if need be.

Just as the strange little motor sound stopped, Grant saw a hint of light coming from near the end of the hallway. He had not memorized the building's layout yet, but he thought that was where the church offices were. One for Stewart, an adjoining little room with a desk for a currently non-existent church secretary, and one more side room with a desk that deacon Rod said was for him. Grant wondered if it had been intended for him, or he had staked a claim on it during a lull between pastors.

Grant found himself slowing his steps and making as little noise as possible. He was not sure why he didn't just call out a hello and see who was there. Maybe Jean calling him Sherlock earlier had stuck in his brain and he sensed a mystery. He swallowed a chuckle.

The strange sound erupted again and Grant jumped, nearly dropping his flashlight. He returned it to its place in his back pocket and sneaked a little closer. The sound would start and stop, then start and stop, as if someone was turning a machine on and off.

Finally, at the doorway, he edged around to peek inside. The light came from the pastor's office. The lamp on the desk was weak, shining only over a bunch of papers that all looked the same—church bulletins?—and two distinctly feminine hands that fed the papers into a small paper shredder.

So that's what the sound was. Grant almost flipped on an overhead light to help the person see better when the slim hands fed the last bulletin into the shredder. He might as well wait. He didn't want to scare whoever this was the way he had scared Jean earlier.

He leaned in and was about to whisper his presence when whoever was sitting at the desk started crying. The light turned off and the cries intensified.

Grant stood mute and still as if someone had shot him with a stun gun. What should he do now? It didn't feel right to intrude. What would he say? "Sorry, didn't mean to interrupt your shredding and crying. Are you okay?"

He was no counselor. Besides, he shouldn't be in the church building alone with a woman anyway. Candy showing up had caused enough of a stir. He didn't want to start more trouble for Stewart to deal with, or Brenda to worry about.

Brenda. Of course. Grant backed away toward the stairs. He would tell Brenda, and she could come help this person with whatever was bothering her. It must be bad; she was crying as if her heart ripped apart.

He took the stairs two at a time, careful to keep quiet, and let himself out of the building. At a jog, he rounded the brick structure, ran down the sloping hill along the side, and nearly collided with a man.

"Whoa, sorry." Grant sidestepped to avoid the person.

"What are you doing here?" The man's voice was familiar. For the first time, Grant noticed there were no outdoor lights around the back of the church. Only in the front.

"I'm headed home." Grant's voice lowered. "What are *you* doing here?"

"Checking over the grounds."

Grant pulled his flashlight out while the man spoke. He turned it on. Rod Carson squinted in the light. He pushed himself to a full standing position and started to walk up the hill.

"I thought you were checking the grounds," Grant called out.

"I'm done. Goodnight."

Grant pointed the beam back toward where Rod had stood. When he'd shined the light on him, Rod had been leaning against the wall. He definitely had not been checking the grounds. Not in this pitch dark.

A look at his surroundings and Grant felt a shiver run up his spine. Rod had stood near the window closest to the back wall of the church building. Was it the window of the room where the woman was? Had Rod seen the light and was worried someone was robbing his office or something?

Grant turned and ran the yards between the church and the house. He opened the door and searched until he found Stewart and Brenda reading in the living room.

"Brenda, I need you to come with me. You might want to come too, Stewart. Something really strange is going on around here."

He wanted to
lay a hard punch
into every one
of their mediocre
expressions.

Brenda

"I'm so curious about who was in the church last night. I wish she hadn't left before we got there." Brenda stirred creamer into her coffee and smiled at Jamaica when she passed by.

"Me, too." Stewart took a generous bite of a poppy seed muffin. "Jean is the only other person with a key. Do you think it was her?"

"Possibly. Though anyone could have stayed behind after the service and then left. You don't need a key to get out of the church, just to get in." Brenda lowered her voice to a whisper. "It's knowing that Rod was hanging around in the dark that gives me the creeps. What on earth was he doing?"

Stewart finished the last of his muffin. "Beats me. So far several things since we got here have been odd."

"That's putting it mildly." Brenda took a sip of Stewart's frappuccino, then lowered it and reached across to take her husband's hand. "Can we talk about it now?"

"About what?"

She sighed and pulled her hand back. "About you talking to prostitutes. About the conversation I started over a week ago and you asked if we could talk about it later."

Stewart wrapped both hands around where hers now cupped her coffee mug. "Brenda, I had no idea. I forgot all about it. Please remind me if something's still on your mind like that."

"Seriously? You forgot?"

His smile at her words was something between wry and sympathetic. "I'm a man, Brenda. I focus on one thing at a time. The other stuff sometimes gets lost."

"You got that right." Jamaica was suddenly at their table, patting Brenda's shoulder with a hand covered by a padded oven mitt. "Girl, when people say men have one track minds, they aren't just talking about *that*. Men can only handle one thing at a time, so you got to keep track for them. There's a reason God said men needed helpers. You know, He never said that about us women."

Brenda laughed. "I'll write that down when I get home."

Jamaica meandered to the next table and Stewart smiled at his wife. "Now, what is it you wanted to talk about?"

Her fears seemed almost silly to mention after so much time had passed. "It probably isn't that important."

She started to pull her hands from his, but he grasped them tighter. "No, don't do that. Don't pull away. I didn't forget on purpose. Tell me what bothered you."

Brenda looked down at his hands wrapped around hers. "Well, you just walked right up to two beautiful prostitutes wearing revealing clothes, and you didn't think that would bother me?"

"I wasn't looking at their clothes, if that's any help."

Brenda recalled the low tops, skimpy miniskirts, and fishnet tights. "How could you not?"

"Well, it was a matter of will to avoid it, I'll admit that." He tipped her chin up until she looked at him. "Brenda, I'm going to tell you something important." He looked around, his gaze stopping at Jamaica. "But let's go outside first."

"Be right back," he called and Jamaica waved. They left their drinks and he led her outside to a bench on the sidewalk. "I was in eighth grade when a classmate brought several Playboy magazines and hid them in his desk. That was my first experience with pornography."

Brenda shifted uncomfortably.

"I knew it was wrong, but it was hard to keep from looking. I am a guy, and we guys are wired visually."

"I know," Brenda said. "That's why when I see someone like Candy, it—"

"Wait." He took her hand again. "Can I finish?"

She bit a fingernail on the hand he wasn't holding and nodded.

"When I gave my life to the Lord, I knew I would have to learn to not only avoid temptation when I could, but how to deal with it when I couldn't avoid it. Opportunities to look at women immodestly clothed are everywhere, Brenda. On TV, billboards, magazines in the grocery store checkout lines, even sometimes women at church."

"This isn't making me feel any better."

He smiled. "I'm not done yet. It took practice and willpower, but I learned the best way to keep my eyes and my mind pure was to not take the second look."

"What do you mean?"

"Well, look at that stop sign over there." She did. "Now don't look at it again." She looked down at her hands. At the sidewalk. At a building across the street.

"Wow, that's hard. My brain keeps wanting to look at it simply because you said I shouldn't."

"Exactly. I can't avoid ever coming across something I shouldn't see the first time. But it's a conscious choice to look or not look the second or third time. If I do the harder thing, and don't look the second time, I'm not in danger of giving in. So when I walked up to those ladies that night, I noticed what they wore, and then I made myself look at their eyes and only their eyes from then on. I'll be honest with you, it's not always an easy thing to do. But it is right, and I want to be right—with God, and with you."

She reached up to palm the side of his face. "Thank you for telling me that. And thank you for choosing the harder path. I really respect you."

He grinned and his cheek filled her hand. "Well, you could make it an easier path if we went home and you put on that little black nightgown your aunt Sylvia gave you for our honeymoon."

Brenda's laugh filled the space between them. "Is that the kind of help God was talking about that you men need?"

He pulled her to her feet. "We probably need a few other things, too, but at the moment it's the only one I can think of. We men are into one thing at a time, remember?"

"Well, Mr. Henderson." She tugged him toward the door. "Let's get our coffee and go home so I can get you something to focus on."

Wednesday Evening, July 16

Rod

Rod made a point of looking at his watch. "Late again. Let's go ahead and get started."

One of the older deacons spoke up. "Why doesn't somebody go over to their house and remind him?"

"We shouldn't have to remind him!" Rod slammed his Bible onto the table. "He should be the first one here instead of me. He should set an example to the others. He should be showing us all that he is ready for the responsibilities of his position."

"Seems to me he's been doing a good job in the two weeks he's been here."

Rod's regard for John Standard plummeted. "And just what has he done that's good? Bring an indecent prostitute into our midst to influence our whole church toward evil? Let her take over the entire service as if she owns our church? And the display last Sunday! I for one was horrified to see our church used as a place for her to air her dirty laundry."

John actually chuckled. "Well, you've got to admit, we had a bigger crowd Sunday than we've had since before my knees started creaking."

A few other deacons joined in. Rod wanted to roar. He wanted to lay a hard punch into every one of their mediocre expressions. Didn't they understand what was happening here? "This is no laughing matter."

He took in a deep breath and forced his voice to remain calm. He had to make the men feel as if they were making the decision themselves. "Gentlemen, I am gravely concerned for our church. We need to take care of our own. Stewart Henderson should get to know us and learn what we need as a church body before he goes out and brings the world in. We aren't to love the world, or the things in the world."

Finally, he had their attention. Now was the time to hit hard. "I hate to say it, but the fact that the first person he invited to church was a woman of the night is very disconcerting to me. Did you notice how she defended him? She said he stopped to ask for directions, but who among us would approach a prostitute for any reason? Why didn't he just look at a map? Or ask someone more reputable?"

They were nodding. He had them. "I have to wonder if there is something inappropriate happening here, and think we should be on our guard. We are the protectors of this church body. We have to make sure nothing comes in that will harm or destroy what we have spent years building up and overseeing."

John indicated he wanted to speak. Rod nodded permission, but with some irritation. If this kept up, John was going to need to retire his deacon position soon and someone more willing to work as a team under a leader would be chosen.

"Rod, it seems we're missing the target here. The Bible says—"

John stopped and turned, as they all did, when the door swung open and Stewart Henderson appeared. He greeted everyone cheerfully, walking around the table and shaking hands with each man, calling them by name. "Wow, you are all early birds, aren't you? I'm ten minutes early and seem to be the last one here."

"Ten minutes early?" John looked at his watch. "The meeting started at five."

Stewart did not look at his watch. He looked directly at Rod. "Really? I was told to come at five-thirty. Perhaps the time changed and you forgot to tell me?"

Rod held his gaze. "The meeting is always at five o'clock, every third Wednesday. It always has been. You're late."

Stewart kept his eyes on Rod, his hand still clasping a deacon's mid-shake. "Like I was late to my welcome meeting because all my materials said the church's name was Creekside, not Brookside?"

The deacons shuffled and murmured. "Creekside?" John chuckled. "Son, whoever you're getting your information from must be getting on in years and forgetting things, or just losing his marbles."

"Or deliberately trying to make me look bad." Stewart's voice was soft and the room quieted. Rod noticed several men's eyes shifted from Stewart to him.

His own eyes narrowed. "Are you accusing me?"

Stewart's gaze did not falter, but his voice got even quieter. "Let's go discuss this in private, Rod, as the Bible says we should."

"We'll discuss it here. Now." Rod wasn't going to fall for that. He was facing this man in front of them all. Let them all see the difference between him and this boy they'd called to be their pastor. "You have a few things to answer for."

Wednesday Evening, July 16

Florence

A mischievous smile crept across Florence's face, pulling her cheeks upward to places they hadn't been in years. She had escaped Gladys' daily tirade at the news channel about the nation going to hell in a hand-basket, thanks to Grant Henderson's delectable sense of curiosity. She had told him a few facts about the church the previous Sunday, and he had asked if she would meet him before church that Wednesday to tell him more.

Gladys muttered when she told her, but couldn't really object. Now Florence stood with Grant outside the church nursery, feeling delightful bits of freedom floating around her like butterflies. "When the church first started, back in my day some forty years ago, there was no nursery. All the rooms down here were used as a school for the children of this town. This church was full of laughter and the sounds of children singing. I was one of the teachers."

"I saw a bunch of old desks in a storage room down the hall," Grant said. "Were they from the school?"

"Yes. I don't know why they haven't sold them. The church could use the money."

"Why did the school shut down?"

"It didn't shut down as much as fade away. When our original pastor went to glory twenty years ago, we needed a new pastor but had no idea how to get one. So we put ads in several papers and got two responses. We didn't know anything back then about checking references or backgrounds. The two who responded, we invited to come."

"Was one of them chosen?"

"Well, they both came. Each of them was given a service to give their testimony and preach a sermon. We all had a meeting and voted. The first man, Jim Chase, won by one vote. He was asked to become our pastor, and was for five years, until something happened that caused him to leave unexpectedly. That was fifteen years ago, and we've been floundering for a new pastor ever since. We'll get one and he'll stay for a year or maybe two. One stayed as long as five." She patted his arm. "I hope your brother sticks around. He's a gem."

"Thanks." Grant looked in the nursery and Florence noticed new flowers painted on the wall. Who had painted those?

"Mrs. Florence?"

His smile was so charming. "Just Miss, son, I never married."

"Oh. Well, then, Miss Florence?"

"Yes?" She followed him down the hallway toward the room that stored the school desks.

"What happened to the other preacher, the one who lost by one vote?"

"He decided to stay and become head deacon." Florence wasn't surprised when Grant stopped in the middle of the hallway. She let her little fact sink in. "Rod, me and Gladys are the only ones left from that time back then. Over the years all the others have gone on to heaven or moved away. I miss the school children, though I know most would be parents and even grandparents by now."

She looked at him from the corner of her eye. "Well, not all of them. Jean isn't a parent yet." She was pleased to see she'd surprised him again. "Yes, Jean's family arrived during the last year before the school shut down. She was in my class. Fifth grade. She was such a joy those first few months. Always laughing and getting the other children laughing with her."

"Jean?"

Florence sighed. "I know. Hard to believe now that the precious girl is so forlorn. Everything changed that fall."

They had reached the storage room. Grant tried the door. "It's locked." He pulled out the church key and inserted it, but it would not budge. "All the rooms open with this key."

"Maybe you put it in upside down."

He tried again. "No, it's got a different lock. Why would someone go to the trouble to get a new lock installed on an old storage room door?"

She touched the doorknob. "What a puzzle for you to solve." She shot Grant a look. "Do you like puzzles, or do you like for things to be more open and easy to decipher?"

He stared at the door. "Well I don't like doors that won't open with the key I have." He glanced back at her. "Why do I get the feeling you're not asking about the door anymore?"

She giggled like a twenty-year-old. "Well, I was trying to figure out which of our two young, single ladies would suit you better."

"Now, Miss Florence, I'm only planning to be here six months. No need to try to find me a girlfriend."

"Six months is a long time," she countered. "And you're too old for a girlfriend. You need a wife."

His eyebrows flew up. "That's a big jump. I just got here, you know."

She couldn't recall the last time she'd giggled so much. This man was a charmer. "Well, Susan is definitely the prettiest girl at Brookside, with her wavy red curls and those sea green eyes, and such stylish clothes. I noticed her glancing your way a couple of times last Sunday."

"Miss Florence, really..."

"But Jean is a dear, too. She has so much goodness and life locked up somewhere deep down inside her. I know it's there. She just needs someone to..." Florence looked at the storage room door, then smiled up at Grant. "To find the right key."

"Speaking of keys." Grant's red face explained why he was so eager to change the subject. Did that color come when she'd mentioned Susan, or Jean? "What if the key has been lost or thrown away years ago?"

"Hmm. Then I suggest you find some less conventional way to get in. The storage room does have a window..."

She was rewarded with a hug. "Miss Flo, you're brilliant." He headed for the exit door. "Want to come?"

Florence caught herself giggling again. "I wouldn't miss it, but don't ask me to crawl through the window. Even if I wasn't too old for such shenanigans, I wouldn't fit!"

*Why did
he seem
to show up
in every
conversation?*

Grant

Grant had Florence wait at the window while he got a crowbar and several screwdrivers from the shed behind Stewart's house. The window didn't need guarding; he just wanted a minute to think. He wondered if Stewart's meeting with the deacons would be over before church started, or if he'd have to wait to talk with him until afterward.

Running back, he pocketed the screwdrivers, glad he hadn't changed from the jeans and t-shirt he'd worn earlier to work on his motorcycle. He tossed the crowbar from one hand to another. Looking at it made him think of Jean.

Back at the window, as casually as he could, he mentioned Jean while he worked at the ancient, wood-framed window. He had to lay flat on his stomach, since the bottom floor of the church building was half encased in the sloped hill. This window was nearly level with the surrounding ground, which would make it easier to climb into if he could manage to get it open. "You said everything changed for Jean that last year of school. Do you know what happened?"

"Some." Florence slid cautiously to sit on the grass, leaning her back against the brick wall next to the window. "That was the year her parents split up. She had been so attached to her father. When he left, for a time she became quiet and withdrawn. We all tried to help, and after awhile she seemed to be doing better. Rod even chose her to be his special helper that year for the school Christmas program."

"Rod?" The hairs on the back of his neck rose at the man's name. Why did he seem to show up in every conversation?

"Oh, he wasn't always like he is now. Back then he was young and dashing and so friendly."

"Are we talking about the same guy?" Grant yanked a piece of wood from the framing. He'd better be careful or he'd end up with a hand full of splinters.

"Things were different back then. That man could charm a bird from a tree. Jean's mom, Grace, was so lost without her husband, and we could all see how grateful she was when Rod took an interest. Jean needed a man's influence in her life. Rod would go to their house and help with car repairs or whatever around the house needed fixing. Really, you wouldn't believe how helpful he was back then."

"You're right about that," Grant said under his breath, grunting as he leaned his weight against the crowbar until it wedged between the window and the wall.

"Jean's mother had pulled out of nearly everything after her husband left. I think she felt ashamed. Back then divorce was much less common and of course you know how people talk."

Grant grunted again, and Florence must have taken that for agreement. "Rod convinced her to come back to the choir. She had such a lovely voice, and we all welcomed her back gladly. Rod spent that hour every Sunday downstairs working on the props and set for the big Christmas program we'd planned. He'd take Jean down with him for that hour so Grace could enjoy a break. Until Jean got sick."

The window started to budge. He sat up to lean more weight on the crowbar. "Sick with what?"

He wiped his sleeve against his forehead before the sweat could drip in his eyes, and looked back to see Florence shaking her head. "They never did figure out what it was. Jean was violently ill. It would come and go, and lasted for weeks. Grace took her to doctors and specialists. No one ever could find out what was wrong. But whatever it was, it changed her forever. When she was well enough to come back to church, she was extremely thin, and seemed to be only half of herself. She was weak and had no interest in school or play. During choir practice, she'd sit on the floor next to her mother's chair and put her head against her mother's knee. It would break your heart."

Grant did not verbally agree with Florence, but the thought of Jean as a child, sick and missing her father, did hurt something deep inside him. If they never found the cause, it might still be dormant in her system, and reappear at any time. Was that why she didn't play with the children? "Do you think—is it possible that she's still—"

"What are you doing?"

As if thinking about her made her appear, Grant looked up to see Jean standing to his left, staring at his crowbar in the window as if he were committing a crime.

"Where'd you come from?"

Susan Meeks appeared behind her. "We're meeting Candy before church. She called and said she's been reading her Bible and has lots of questions." Her eyes took in his jeans, sweaty shirt and the crowbar still sticking out of the half-open window. "You don't look like you're here for Bible study."

"Hello to you both," Florence said. Grant helped her as she took a great amount of time and several huffs and puffs to get off the ground to a standing position. "Exactly the two women we were discussing. How nice."

Jean's cheeks faded a shade paler. Susan was openly curious. "You were talking about us?"

Florence patted Grant's back, but then pulled her hand away and dug around in her purse for a minute until finally accepting the rag Grant held out. She wiped her hand and he laughed. "She was giving me a lesson in church history."

"And what kind of historian would I be if I did not include our church's two young, pretty, single women?"

At that, Susan blushed, but Jean kept her eyes on the cracked-open window. "What are you doing to that window?" she asked again.

He nudged the crowbar with his foot, wiping his own hands on the rag. "The storage room is locked, but the church key won't open it. Do you know where the key to this room is?"

Her eyes never left the window. "It's...gone."

He nodded. "I figured so. Florence suggested I find another way in."

Florence giggled. It was funny watching her laugh. Her cheeks jiggled.

Grant kept the smile on his face as he turned from Florence back to Jean, thinking of her sickness and wondering if she was in any danger now. "If you're worried about me breaking the window frame, I'd planned to—"

"Hey, everybody. Are we having church outside?"

Stewart joined them. Grant noticed his brother's jaw clenched tight behind his smile. While Florence went back to embarrassing the girls, Grant leaned toward him and asked quietly, "The deacon's meeting didn't go well, did it?"

Stewart angled his body to face the back of the church building, away from the group. "Let's just say I need to preach tonight about controlling one's temper, so I can hear the message myself. He raked me over the coals. That man wants me gone."

"What will you—"

A shriek brought their heads around to Florence. She stood, mouth agape and finger pointed. Jean looked at Florence, then turned around to look behind her. "Oh, no."

Grant felt the air leave his chest. Only Susan seemed able to move. "Oh, Candy," Susan said, approaching the woman whose face was covered in cuts and bruises, who collapsed at her feet. "What have they done to you?"

Jamaica

The sign had been flipped around to say "Closed" for at least half an hour when the man tapped on the door. Jamaica ignored him, wiping the counters down for the final time that night. If he could read, the sign told him the store hours. If he couldn't, his sense of sight should clue him in that the store was closed for the night. If the lights turned out and the chairs set upside down on the tables weren't enough, the fact that the door wouldn't open when he pulled on it should work.

He tapped again. Jamaica hung the washed mugs on their pegs and yelled, "Come back tomorrow!" She turned back to her task. "I'm tired, my feet hurt, and I'm not dealing with one more person tonight." Whoever it was would not hear her mumbling, but it felt good to say it.

Another tap. This time, when Jamaica looked up, ready to give a piece of her mind, she saw what the man held under his jacket, visible only to her. The mug in her hand dropped to the floor. Its handle broke off, but Jamaica did not pick up the pieces. As if in a trance, she walked around the corner, across the room, and opened the door.

"I don't like to be kept waiting." The man was olive-skinned, of average build, with greasy hair. His nose jutted over to one side, as if broken so many times it had given up trying to go back to straight. For a moment, Jamaica could not tear her eyes away from the long scar around his neck, as if someone had tried to strangle him with a wire or cord.

"Who are you and where did you get that?" Jamaica reached for the photograph he held, but he pulled away, tucking the picture into his jacket away from sight.

"Let's not rush things. I brought that to…inspire you to want to help me."

"Help you do what? What do you want?"

"I hear you're the best place in town to get information."

The man's voice was like gravel. Jamaica backed several steps away. "What do you want?" she repeated, hating how her own voice was down to a whisper.

His mouth curved into a satisfied smile. Jamaica knew he was aware that, with that photograph, he would get whatever he wanted from her. "I want information."

"About what?"

"About a piece of property stolen from me today."

"I'm no detective. Why don't you call the police?"

His chuckle came out as a gurgle through his throat and Jamaica fought the urge to gag. "I don't need a detective. Or the police. Just a little information."

He pulled out another photograph and Jamaica frowned. "Isn't that the woman who ended up in the papers last week?"

He snarled. "They took her from me. I want her back."

"A person has the right to go to church if she wants."

His hand was instantly around Jamaica's neck. "Not her. I reminded her of that earlier this evening. She did not seem to agree and now she has left me, the man who provides for her and takes care of her. That is not smart."

Jamaica struggled to breathe. "Why not just let her go?"

He shoved her and she slammed against a table, knocking the chairs off onto the floor. She winced and put a hand to her hip where a bruise would be tomorrow. "She is mine," he spit out. "No one who belongs to me ever walks away. I want to know where she's gone. Who she is with. Who is keeping her from me." He inched forward and she backed around the table to put space between them. "You know everybody in town. Find out where she is and let me know."

Jamaica was shaking but kept her voice firm. "What do I get in return?"

He pulled the first photograph into view again and Jamaica's eyes filled with tears. "You'll get the information you've been seeking. A fair trade. One person's whereabouts for another's."

No words were needed. Jamaica nodded.

"I'll be in touch," the man said. He picked up a fallen chair and placed it back on the table. "Have a nice night."

When he was out of sight, Jamaica sank to the ground and sat staring out the glass door, her mind seeing nothing but the picture he had held so tightly in his hand.

Wednesday evening, July 16

Jean

The pacing was irritating, even to herself, but Jean couldn't get her feet to stop acting like her mind: going back and forth but not getting anywhere. Finally, in a moment of admitted desperation, she went to where Grant stood in the doorframe between her kitchen and living room and asked, "What are we going to do?"

He looked at her and Jean knew her life would never be the same. She had seen the signs, when he didn't back away as every other guy had when she froze up on them. When he followed no matter how fast she tried to get ahead of him. Especially when she saw him with a crowbar prying open that window...

Her life had been one of routine and order. Boring and predictable. Unhappy, but it was a comfortable unhappiness. She knew what to expect.

Ever since he came, Jean felt as she had the day she climbed onto the merry-go-round for the first time. It had whirled and circled so fast she couldn't see anything clearly anymore. She was afraid and wanted to get off, but all the other children were screaming in delight and no one could hear her cries for help. Now, she couldn't get her feelings straightened enough to even know what they were.

Jean scowled. She wasn't even making sense in her own head.

The misery must have shown on her face for Grant's softened and showed deep concern. "Hey, it'll be okay." He reached out and touched her cheek, just with a finger, but it might as well have been a firecracker. Her eyes shot wide and she backed away quickly, banging her head against the opposite side of the door frame.

"Ouch!"

He was close again. "Are you okay?"

"Yes." She rubbed the back of her head. "Candy is the one we should be talking about."

He nodded, perhaps recognizing her silent plea to stop focusing on her. "Last time I went in there, the doctor said there was no internal damage, so we can thank God for that."

"He beat her badly, though." Susan sat nearby in one of Jean's chairs, the picture of everything Jean was not. Calm. Beautiful. Articulate. She looked up at Grant. "Isn't there something we can do to arrest that jerk and put him in jail?"

"Not if Candy won't press charges, and my gut's telling me she won't."

"Does your gut talk to you a lot?"

"In times like this." He smiled. "And whenever I eat pizza."

Jean watched their conversation with something akin to pain. Susan was so comfortable talking with Grant. So unafraid. Jean grimaced. She wanted to bang her head against the wall that she was even thinking such selfish things when Candy had just been brutally beaten.

When Candy had collapsed outside the church earlier that evening, Jean had felt her heart drop. She'd run to her side. "Candy? Candy? Can you hear me?"

"How can I help it?" Candy's voice was ragged. "You're yelling in my face."

"I'm sorry." Jean brushed hair from Candy's blood-stained forehead. "We have to get you to the hospital."

"No!" Candy surprised her by sitting up. "I can't pay for a hospital." She fell back onto the grass. "Just let me rest here for a minute. I'll be fine."

"You're nowhere near fine." Grant had knelt next to Candy on the opposite side. "Your eye is swelling shut, and you have multiple cuts on your arms. You could have internal injuries."

"Nah, I'm okay." Candy's words slurred and Jean knew her look at Grant held barely-contained panic. "I've had worse."

"Worse? This has happened before?" Susan was all business as she approached. She must have run to Pastor Henderson's house, for she was followed by Brenda, who carried something like a bed sheet in hand.

"Not lately, but yeah."

"Can you tell us who did this?" Grant's words were low. "I'll call the police right away."

"No!" Again, Candy tried to sit up. "No police. Promise."

Grant held her down. He looked at Jean and Jean could only shake her head at the question in his eyes.

"Promise?"

Candy reached out her hand and he took it in his. "I promise."

"If you refuse to go to the hospital, we need to get you back to our house so we can clean these cuts," Brenda said.

Candy sat up and held her head. When she pulled her hands away, they were covered in blood. "I need a place to hide until I can get a job and start a new life." She looked at Susan. "You said Christians were God's kids and all part of a family, right? And they take care of each other, right?"

Susan nodded absently, laying the sheet out next to Candy and urging her to roll onto it so they could lift and carry her. "Yes, that's right. We're to bear each other's burdens, help each other in need. Don't worry, Candy, we'll help you find a place to stay."

"No, don't find me a place." Candy's eyes locked with Jean's and her hand pointed. "I want to stay with her."

*"Why is it
so frustrating
to you
that I'm
interested?"*

From the look on the young woman's face, Candy realized she probably could have eased into the idea a little better, but her head was splitting and she could hardly think straight, much less take a lesson in tactfulness. She moaned and rolled onto the sheet. They lifted her and multiple muscles screamed in pain. He had used a cane this time.

Candy went in and out of consciousness, and only once they'd settled her on the long seat in someone's van and they all thought she was out, did she hear them discuss her situation.

"She said she went back to her place and told her roommate about Jesus."

"And some guy named Slash came in, and it sounds like she told him, too."

"He must be the guy she said thinks he owns her."

"I can't imagine what her life has been like."

Candy wanted to pipe up and tell them they didn't know the half of it, but she could not get her mouth to work around the swelling. That wasn't from the cane. That had been his fist.

"I want my money, Slash," she'd said, trying to stand tall and not show how much she was quaking inside. "I'm done with this life. I'm starting over."

He had laughed at first. When she hadn't backed down, he had stopped laughing. In less than a minute she was curled on the floor enduring his wrath. Champagne screamed from the other corner of the room, but Slash didn't care how loudly she yelled. No one would come to help. She was his property. He owned her money, her clothes, her body, her life. How dare she think she had the right to make her own choices? He had shouted that, and many other things, cursing and spitting on her, landing one final kick before shouting to Champagne to clean her up and pack.

"Be ready in thirty minutes. We're moving on." Then he'd slammed the door and the sound had burned through her skull like fire.

Champagne cried as she had pulled Candy, barely conscious, over to her bed. Slash's words echoed through her mind as Champagne put pressure on the deepest cuts. Ten minutes passed. Candy knew she had to make a decision, had to get up, but she could not remember why.

Champagne, still crying, pulled her upright. "Candy, you have to go. Get out of here right now and go someplace where he'll never find you again."

"What—about—you?" It was hard to talk. Hard to think.

"It's too late for me." Supporting her weight as much as she could, Champagne half-dragged Candy toward the side door of the rundown apartment building. She opened the door. "This is as much as I can help you. Go, Candy. Go and live the life your grandmother prayed for you."

Now, being carried from the van into a home, Candy wished she had been strong enough or coherent enough to convince Champagne to come with her. Slash would return and be furious that she was gone. He would take out that fury on Champagne.

Candy didn't want Champagne to die, not before she could know the freedom of accepting Jesus. They set her on a bed, a softer bed than she'd enjoyed for years, and someone mentioned they should call a church member who was a family doctor. As they gathered around her bed and prayed for her, she prayed for Champagne.

God, she doesn't know you. She's so alone, like I used to be. She needs to know You love her and want to set her free. Send someone to help her, like you sent me. Please.

Later, she would try to figure out a tactful way to explain to her new group of friends why she chose Jean as the person she wanted to stay with. Plain Jean, the girl who barely spoke and wore dark colors, was a choice of practicality. Everything about her was safe. Slash would never notice her, much less suspect her of consorting with the likes of Candy. Wherever this girl stayed, it would be the perfect place for Candy to hide for now. Once she healed, she would look for a regular job and earn honest wages. She should have known Slash wouldn't give her any money. He took it the moment they made it, always arguing he needed it to pay their expenses, or to save it so they wouldn't spend it frivolously.

Candy winced when someone touched her. A cool hand rested on her forehead. "It's alright. I'm a doctor. I'm checking to ascertain the extent of your injuries. Relax."

She hadn't understood the long words, but she got the part about relaxing. What an impossible command to someone who hurt everywhere. The worst hurt was inside, the pain of regret for that day so many years ago when a young, handsome man paid attention to her, bought her gifts, told her she was beautiful. He had promised her the world, and when she agreed to go with him, he gave it to her. The world and all its evils.

The doctor pressed on her ribcage and Candy was glad for the excuse to groan aloud. So much pain. Years of pain. She was torn down into her soul, and wasn't sure if God Himself could heal a wound that deep.

Grant

Grant watched his brother pull off his glasses and rub two fingers over the bridge of his nose. "Have you told Brenda about what happened at the deacon's meeting last night?"

"Not yet." Stewart frowned. "She was so concerned about Candy, I didn't want to add to her worries. I feel badly that this has been so hard on her from the beginning. I had no idea inviting Candy to church would cause so much trouble."

"If you'd known, would you not have invited her?"

Stewart considered for a moment, wiping his glasses with the edge of his shirt. "I would still have invited her. It was the right thing to do."

"Then you can let God handle the consequences." Grant had more to say, but the bell from the door to Jamaica's coffee shop rang and Susan Meeks slipped inside, wearing a bright blue dress and a wide smile. Florence had been right about one thing. Susan was a beautiful woman.

"Hello, Pastor. Hello, Grant. Are you out for breakfast or just coffee?"

Stewart held up his cup as answer. Grant held up his pastry. "I don't know what it's called, but it's good."

"I'm glad you're both here." Susan lowered her voice somewhat. "May I interrupt you for a moment to ask a question?"

Stewart pulled a chair from a nearby table and motioned toward it. "Be our guest."

"Thanks." She sat. Grant couldn't help but contrast how confident she was with how nervous Jean would be in the same setting.

"I keep thinking of Candy and that horrible man who beat her," Susan said. "I don't know if you'd heard, but I'm in college right now, majoring in forensics."

"I thought Jamaica had told us everything there was to know about everyone in this town," Grant said loudly enough for Jamaica to hear from where she wiped down the counter across the room. "But she hadn't mentioned that yet."

"Well, you need to come in more often if you want it all, boy." Jamaica waved in his direction. "I can only say so many things in one sitting."

Susan smiled at Jamaica, then focused on him again. "I want to see this man caught and brought to justice."

"Did you always want to study forensic science?" It was off the subject, but Grant was curious. He'd expected someone like Susan to major in music, or... he couldn't think of anything else, but forensics would have been his last guess.

She shook her head. "I started in criminal justice, but it didn't take long for me to realize I wasn't tough enough for actual field work, so I've switched to the analytical side of things. That was my sophomore year. I'm a junior now, and near the top of my class." She smiled. "I hope you're duly impressed."

He nodded. "I am. So what are your plans about Candy, and what does it have to do with us?"

"Well, I'm concerned about a few details. Everybody knows she's been here in town for years, but nobody knew about this guy until yesterday. I'm getting the impression he's a pimp, and not one she chose. Maybe he has some hold on her, like a debt, or information or something, that has kept her under his thumb all this time."

Jamaica wiped the table next to them, then moved on to the table parallel to it.

"I planned to talk with the local police, but I remembered how panicked she got when you suggested we call them. I was wondering if I should go into Charlotte and talk with law enforcement there instead of here. They would definitely have access to more resources, but I've never done anything like this before, so…"

"You need a refill?" Jamaica stood behind Stewart, her usually smiling face grim.

"I'm good, thanks." Stewart wiped his glasses again, targeting one smear on the left lens.

When his glasses were back in place, he looked at Susan. "I agree that Candy's reticence about the local police should be taken into consideration. Remember how she made Grant promise not to contact them? I'd like to talk with her about her situation, but not until she's had some time to recover. For now, I think you talking with law enforcement in the city is a good alternative."

"Then that's what I'll do." Susan stood. "The other day when Candy told me her story, she mentioned a sheriff in Edison, a little town on the other side of the city. I may check in with him also to see if he knows anything. See you both later."

"Great. Thanks for doing that." Stewart finished his coffee and stood. "I'd better get to work. Join in…"

"Or fill in," Grant finished. Susan was up at the counter ordering a drink, so Grant returned her chair to the other table. "Have you found any ministries to join in yet?"

"To be honest, no. I found plenty of ministries the church used to be involved in, but currently there's hardly anything happening."

"So there are plenty of gaps to fill in then." Grant threw away his used napkin and followed Stewart to the door. "As Dad always says, where there aren't opportunities to join..."

"There are holes to fill." Stewart pulled out his car keys and sighed. "I've been talking to people all over town this week. What I hear most is that drugs are becoming a big problem among the teens. They don't have anything interesting or meaningful to do, so they get in trouble." He shifted his glasses. "And you know if there's one thing I'm not gifted at, it's coming up with ideas. I was hoping there would be something already in place that we could contribute to."

"Have you checked with the other churches and non-profits in the area?"

"Not all of them. I'm headed to the shelter today to hopefully get more information on how to help with situations like Candy's, and then to a church across town that used to have an outreach to the motorcycle groups that come through each summer. I'd like to see if they are interested in working together to start that up again. Where are you headed?"

"I thought I'd drive over to Jean's and see if they need anything."

"How considerate." His brother smirked at him.

Grant shrugged. "Yep, just call me the Good Samaritan."

Stewart clapped Grant on the shoulder. "Well, have a nice day, Good Samaritan."

Grant chuckled and stood casually until Stewart was outside, then jogged to the curb where he'd parked his motorcycle. He kicked it in gear and it roared to life. Putting on his helmet, he pulled out into the road, then let it fly. His original plan for the day had been to attack that stubborn window again. It still wouldn't budge over halfway. Grant was entertaining the idea of just breaking and replacing it. Whatever he decided, however, as antsy as he felt, getting through the window and moving into the storage room was no longer first on the morning's agenda.

He was not usually the worrying type, but all morning he had felt an inexplicable need to get to Jean's house and make sure everything was okay. He wanted to check on Candy, of course, but Jean was his real concern.

It took less than five minutes to span the distance from Jamaica's shop to Jean's home. Looking at it in daylight, he was surprised at its size. From what he knew of Jean, he expected she would live in a small apartment with minimal decorations and functional furnishings. Instead, he walked up a stone walkway to a covered porch that wrapped around a wooden, two-story home, backed by trees. Through the trees, he could see the church. Florence had told him the other night that Jean often walked to and from church. When he had questioned the safety aspect of walking alone at night, she'd proudly added that Jean carried a can of mace in her purse.

Grant stood at the door, noting it could use a fresh coat of paint. How did she manage to take care of a house all by herself? He knocked, but softly, not wanting to wake Candy if she was sleeping. He looked at his watch. Eight fifty-five. After last night, Jean might still be sleeping as well. He'd feel like a heel if he woke her up.

"Are you all right?" he asked as soon as Jean opened the door. Her hair was swept up in one of those ponytail-bun things that Brenda liked to do when she was cleaning. She wore baggy jogging pants and a large t-shirt. She didn't have time to smile or answer his question before he asked two more. "Has all this stress made you feel sick? Were you afraid last night, knowing some murderous man was out there looking for Candy?"

"Good morning," she said. Her smile, maybe because it was so rarely seen, somehow made him worry more. "Why don't you come inside for this interrogation?"

Jean

"So you're not feeling sick, then?" Grant came inside, tossed his jacket on the back of her living room couch, and sunk into the nearby recliner.

"Make yourself at home," Jean said. He grinned and she almost returned the expression before she remembered she wasn't the grinning type. "How did you know I took a sick day from work today?"

The worry lines between his eyebrows reappeared. "You took a sick day? So you are feeling badly?"

"No. I called the bank and told them a friend of mine was sick and needed my help. I haven't taken a sick day in the five years I've worked for them, so they didn't have a problem with it."

"You work at a bank?"

"Wait. If you didn't know I took a sick day, why are you here asking if I feel sick?" She walked toward the kitchen. "Want a drink? I can offer you some ice water."

"Sure."

She returned to the living room and handed him a glass. "Sorry that's all I have. I'm not used to guests."

"Thanks. To answer your question, I heard about you getting really sick back when you were a little girl."

Jean felt her face shut down. Her body went numb.

He shrugged, but his gaze on her was sharp. "Since they never figured out what it was, I wondered if you still had trouble with it sometimes as an adult."

She took a long sip of water, then held the cool glass against her heart. "No. No, I don't get sick. Thanks for asking." She moved away from his presence, his gaze, his concern. "But I'm sure you really came to check on Candy. The doctor gave her some pills to help her rest and she's slept the last fourteen hours. I think it will help her heal. Do you want to leave her a message or something?"

"No, I'm good. Thanks for the water." He rose and set his glass on a coaster on the coffee table.

She breathed a sigh of relief as he turned to go, until he stopped and looked back at her. "You know, I can't picture you as a bank teller, chatting with people all day long."

"I'm not a teller. I work in the back balancing the books."

His grin was back. "Ah, I see. Numbers are better than people."

Her chin went up at his teasing. "Of course. Numbers are consistent and logical and non-intrusive. They aren't like you, so—so—"

"Charming?"

"No. So ask-questiony."

"That's not even a word." He sat down again, propped his feet up, and sent her a cocky grin. "I'm going to stick with charming."

"Irritating, then."

His look turned serious. "Why is it so frustrating to you that I'm interested?"

She felt the ridiculous urge to cry and heard it in her voice. "Because you shouldn't be interested. I'm boring and predictable and just Blue Jean."

He put his feet down and leaned forward. "Jean Louise…"

116

"Why do you call me that?" She was nearly shouting and had no idea why. She remembered Candy was in the adjoining room and covered her mouth with her hand.

"Jean Louise is your name." He stood and moved toward her.

She backed away. "No one calls me that. Why don't you call me Blue Jean like everyone else does?"

"Because Jean Louise is pretty, and Blue Jean is sad."

"Call me Blue Jean."

He took another step forward. "Do you like to be called Blue Jean?"

She turned her back to him. "No."

"Then why not like Jean Louise?"

She tightened her arms across her chest, as if it would protect her heart. "Because...I don't know. When people call me Blue Jean, I know what it means. I know how they see me. What they expect me to be."

His breath touched her from behind. "And me calling you Jean Louise means what?"

She whirled on him. "How should I know? You said it. Jean Louise is pretty. Maybe you expect me to be pretty, which is impossible. Maybe you expect me to be—to be—I don't know, something I'm not."

He was too close. She backed against the wall and had nowhere else to go. He put one hand on the wall above her head and leaned toward her. "But you are pretty, Jean Louise. And smart. And funny. And I find you very interesting."

She frowned up at him. "There's nothing interesting about me."

He shook his head, pulled his hand off the wall, and backed away. "I'd think you were fishing for compliments, but I'm pretty sure you actually believe what you're saying." He flopped back into the chair, filling it with his large limbs. "You seem

117

scared of just about everything, yet you walk home in the dark with a can of mace. You live in a house big enough for a family, but you never have anyone over. You wear dark clothes and avoid attention, but you've made friends with a prostitute who used to own a neon pink feather boa. What exactly about you is not interesting?"

She had to smile at him. "Okay, so you are charming. My mother would love you."

He cocked his head. "And you?"

A blush crept up her neck and flamed across her cheeks. She opened her mouth but no good response came, no funny comment, not even a sarcastic one. So she did the only thing that came to mind. She set down her glass and turned to leave the room.

He was laughing. "I like you, Jean Louise. Just when I think I've got you figured out, you surprise me."

She stopped near the door, her hand on the frame, her back to him. "Don't try to figure me out, Grant," she whispered. "You won't like what you find."

Unable to bear the questions that would pour from those incredible dark eyes, she moved forward out of the room, shutting the door behind her.

*A makeover
was about as
appealing as
sucking on
a lemon.*

Brenda

"Really, Candy, you should be resting. It's only been a day." Brenda sat on the bed in Jean's bedroom while Candy riffled through Jean's closet.

"Like I said, I've had beatings worse than this before, and nobody let me rest then. One guy broke a couple of ribs once." Her voice came muffled from inside the walk-in closet. "I need to find an outfit to wear so I can go get a job."

"A job?" Brenda bit her thumbnail. "Pardon my frankness, but you have bruises all over your face. Who's going to hire you?"

Candy stuck her head out from the closet. "You'd be surprised how good I am with makeup. Could you come in here and help me find something? I don't think this woman owns one outfit that isn't boring, depressing, or shaped like a balloon. Where'd she get these things—the Salvation Army?"

Brenda was surprised at the spaciousness of Jean's half-filled closet. It didn't seem to fit her at all. She looked around at the dark skirts, stacks of jeans and plain blouses. "Actually, I shop at the Salvation Army and find some great clothes there. Jean's clothes..." She pulled a dull grey dress toward her, then let it fall back in its place. "Maybe we should go shopping."

"I can't go shopping. I don't have any money. When I do get a job, I'm going to start out in debt to Jean already for staying here and eating her food, and—wait a minute."

"Did you find something to wear?" Brenda asked. Even Jean's shoes were dark and nondescript. Practical.

Candy leaned toward her and whispered, "You couldn't pay me to wear anything in this closet. What's the deal with this girl? Is she colorblind? No, never mind. I have an idea."

"What is it?"

"Jean!"

Brenda nearly fell into a pile of tops. "Candy, you've got to stop yelling without warning people."

"Okay. Warning you...Jean!"

"What? What it is?" Jean appeared in the doorway, breathless, a spatula in one hand and a pan of partially-scrambled eggs in the other. "Are you hurt?"

"Of course not." Candy threw a pair of black pants onto Jean's bed. "I can't wear your stuff. It doesn't fit. Can we go shopping? I'll trade you a trip to the store for a makeover."

Brenda looked at Jean. From the purse of her lips, a makeover was about as appealing as sucking on a lemon.

Candy must have thought something similar, for she said, "You know, whenever a new girl came around, Slash gave her a name. Usually the name of a drink. I was already Candy when he met me, so he kept that name for me, but he re-named Champagne, and Brandy, and even named one girl Whiskey because she could knock a man flat in half an hour."

Jean's eyes were huge. She nearly dropped her pan of eggs.

Brenda followed Jean back into the kitchen, Candy talking behind them. "I think he'd name you Lemon Water. Right now you're kind of sour, and you wouldn't be any good at attracting customers. But add a little sugar, and you'd be a tall glass of Lemonade. All you need is that added sugar."

Jean was back at the stove, fervently scrambling her eggs. Brenda wondered if she should intervene. Imagine living alone for years then having Candy for a houseguest!

"I'll drive if you want to go shopping," Brenda offered. "We could start at thrift stores and see what kind of deals we find."

"Fun!" Candy wolfed down half the scrambled eggs that Jean dished out. "Say, you're a good cook. Maybe I can think of something else to teach you in exchange for cooking lessons."

Jean seemed to be having a hard time getting her first bite of eggs into her mouth. Brenda had her own mouth covered by her hand, trying not to laugh.

"Hurry up, Lemon Water!" Candy was up and nearly at the door already. "I'm dying to get a new outfit. I don't know about you, but I could go for something red. With a scarf. And heels."

Jean slowly rose to her feet. She picked up her plate and Candy's and took them to the sink. When she turned around, Brenda wondered if they would make it through the day without her fainting.

"Don't look at me like that," Candy told Jean, nudging her toward the door. "Whatever clothes I buy, I'll let you borrow them!"

Friday Afternoon, July 18

Sheriff Ian Craig rubbed his eyes with a weary hand. It was going to be a long Friday. Two drug-related robberies and one homicide already. Some days he hated living near a big city. When he retired, he was going to move way out in the middle of nowhere, and sit on a porch and watch horses. Or maybe cows, they were slower.

The knock on the door to his office reminded him he was at least twenty years away from retirement. He sighed. "Come in."

Wow. Now that was something he didn't see every day. The woman who entered was a knockout, with red, bouncy curls and bright eyes and a smile worth a million bucks. Her navy suit and the way it fit was no chore to look at either.

He stood and put a hand out. "Ian Craig. How can I help you?"

"Susan Meeks." Her grip was firm. "I'm hoping we can help each other."

He gestured toward the chair across from his desk. "I'm all ears."

She settled comfortably and crossed her legs. He waited to hear she was a reporter and wanted a story. Or maybe she was a neighborhood watch coordinator and had some complaint about suspicious activity in her suburban neighborhood.

"I'm here about a pimp who I believe is involved in human trafficking and exploitation. I want him behind bars, and I want you to help me put him there."

Ian sat up straighter. Beauty and substance. "Tell me more."

She opened her purse and pulled out a newspaper clipping. "Do you recognize this woman?"

He noted the paper was not local, but from the small town of Oakview about thirty miles east. He looked at the woman in the photo. "Is this . . ?" He skimmed the article. "It is. Candy. I wondered what happened to her."

He handed the newspaper back with a chuckle. "She ended up in church? That's something I never expected to see."

The woman across from him flashed that megawatt smile again. "She did. She also gave her life to Jesus."

His smile lost its amusement but none of its sincerity. "I am genuinely glad to hear that."

"You're a believer?" Now it was her turn to sit up straighter.

"I am. Not the best one I could be, but I try to represent God's desire for justice in this world here in my little patch of it."

She beamed. "I knew God sent me to you. Candy said you used to help her contact her grandmother when she was still living."

His nod was sober. "Sweet, elderly woman. She never gave up. I used to dread her calls every week, asking if I'd had any leads, any news. I started hunting for Candy on my own time just to try to find something that would give her some hope."

"Did you ever come across information that led you to believe Candy was being prostituted against her will?"

Again, he was impressed. Most young women would stumble over that word, embarrassed to talk about the topic with a man, even if he was the county sheriff. This woman intrigued him more than any had in a long time. "Definitely. I followed Candy's trail and it always intersected with a guy I've been tracking for years."

"Does this guy go by the name Slash?"

Ian stood, suddenly wary. "Who are you? It took me two years to uncover his title. How do you know so much?"

The moment he stood, she had as well. She faced him, clearly not intimidated by his uniform, badge, or bulk. "I'm a friend of Candy's. She left Slash, but not before he beat her senseless. She's hiding out now, but how long will it take before he finds her? I want to stop him." For the first time, her confident aura wavered. "I just don't know how."

Ian felt himself grinning like a fool. He would have to do a background check, but if this woman's story cleared, he would be happier than a kid with a new toy tractor. "Would you want to walk down the street with me and grab some lunch while we talk this over? I have a feeling you might be the answer I've been looking for."

She cocked an eyebrow at him and he cleared his throat. "That is, I've had an idea I've been working on for several months, but couldn't implement it because I couldn't find

Slash's home base. If we can plan this and execute it while he's still looking for Candy, before he leaves that area, we might nail him. And not only him, but the guys who work for him all around this town and a few others. We might even hit some of the heavier pockets in Charlotte."

"More guys who work for him?"

"No, the guys he works for."

"Sounds big."

"It is. And it could be dangerous."

If anything, her smile broadened. "I'm in."

Friday Afternoon, July 18

Brenda

It was easy to see Candy was as pleased with her purchases as Jean was not. Candy sunk another chicken nugget deep into her puddle of sauce and popped the entire thing into her mouth. "Mm, I used to love these things when I was a kid. We'd celebrate the day grandmother got her social security check each month by going out and splitting a happy meal. I feel kind of selfish getting all of these to myself."

Brenda did not realize how much she assumed about Candy until comments like those stripped away her preconceived notions. *Lord, please forgive me for judging her. Help me to see her as You do, as a precious child who needs Your unconditional love. Help me to represent You to her.*

"So I have a question."

Jean had been quiet through most of their meal, taking dainty, feminine bites, which looked a little odd since she was eating a McDonald's dollar burger. She finished chewing, then looked at Candy. "A question about what?"

Candy dipped another nugget, but this time only bit off half. "Last night I found that section in the back of the Bible, where you can look up words and it tells you where to find them in the Bible."

"The concordance."

"Is that what you call it? Well, anyway, my cuts were itching and that lump on my head hurt, and I thought about Slash and got kind of scared. So I looked in the back and found the word, 'fear.' There are a bunch of verses with that word, did you know that?"

Brenda nodded. "God tells us not to fear over three hundred times in His Word."

"So how do you know which things don't work in the Bible and which do?"

Brenda stopped with her forkful of salad in midair. "What do you mean?"

Candy looked at her, then looked at Jean. "Well, God talks about us not fearing because He's with us forever. And in one place it said if we were afraid, that wasn't from God, because God gave power, and love, and...and something else..."

"A sound mind," Jean added.

"Yeah, which means thinking straight about things, right? So, if those verses don't work, how do I know which other ones don't work either?"

Brenda set her fork down. "All the promises in the Bible work, Candy. God never lies. What makes you think they don't work?"

"Because of you."

Jean set down her hamburger and visibly shuddered. Brenda took in a deep breath. "What do you mean?"

Candy looked from one to the other. "Both of you. You've probably been reading the Bible your whole lives. You know more about God than I ever will, not even if I try for a hundred years to catch up. But you're both so scared you can hardly stand it. Brenda, you bite your fingernails in church like I used to suck my thumb whenever my parents started shouting at each other. And Jean, I've seen women held at knifepoint less scared than you look whenever somebody at church just tries to shake your hand."

She shrugged. "So if God says you don't need to be afraid, but you still are all the time, then it doesn't work. I want the stuff that works, so how do I know—"

Oh, God, what kind of woman am I? My lack of faith in You is so obvious, even a brand-new believer sees it. Brenda started crying. She tried to hold it back. A passing woman glanced her way and Brenda lifted her hand to bite a nail. She stopped and stared at her fingers, at all the nails bit down to the quick, and the tears burst free.

"Oh, man, I wasn't expecting that." Brenda heard Candy's voice over her own sobs. "Jean, you aren't going to start crying, too, are you?"

"No, I won't cry." Jean's voice was leaden. "I never cry in front of people."

"What'd I say? She's really going at it."

Brenda cried harder. "You said—you said." She had a hard time forming words through her tears. "You said we aren't living by what the Bible says. We know the Bible is true—I know it's true—but I still let fear have my heart so often. I worry so much about what other people think."

"Well, that's a way to make yourself miserable if I ever heard one." Candy grabbed a French fry and munched on it. "I don't get it. You've got a book from the God who made the whole universe, and it says He loves you so much He sent Jesus to die for you. And you're worried about what a few piddly little people think of you? Who cares what anyone thinks? All that matters is what Jesus thinks."

Candy waited awhile, but when Brenda continued crying, she finally said, "So you're saying all the stuff in the Bible is true, and it does work, you're just not doing it?"

Brenda felt the shame wash through her. She nodded.

"Well, who'd have thought that? I figured a preacher's wife would be smarter than I am at least."

Brenda found a napkin and wiped her nose. "Apparently not," she said, leaning her head onto her propped up hand. She felt smaller than the French fry crumbs Candy had left on her tray.

"Let's fix that, then." Candy grabbed Jean's half-eaten hamburger. "You done with that? Let's get going. I want to go home and let's read all those verses under the word 'fear' and figure out how we're supposed to live."

"And you shall know the truth, and the truth shall set you free."

Candy and Brenda both looked at Jean. Her voice was soft, her eyes distant. Brenda's hurt and shame was open. Jean's seemed to sink deep inside.

"Is that from the Bible? Who said that?"

Jean focused on Candy. "Jesus said it."

"I like that! That needs to go on a wall somewhere so I can see it every day. Let's go back to Jean's house and write down all the truth we can find, and decide to live by it." Candy tossed their trash into the receptacle. She took Brenda's hands and gave them a little shake, her face lit up. "I've wanted freedom from fear more than anything else for the past fifteen years. Now I'm going to get it, and nothing in this world is going to stop me."

He marveled
at the change
in her when
she thought
no one was
around.

Gladys

"Every other day of the week, we go where you pick, Gladys. Once a week, you can come here for my sake."

Gladys sat on one of the modern, hard, uncomfortable chairs. She folded her hands on the small, round table with silly little coffee cups painted on its surface and let a long sigh assure Florence of her disapproval. "I don't like that foreign woman always standing over our table every time we come here."

"Gladys," Florence said, her eye roll grating on Gladys' nerves. So immature. "She has to come to the table to get our order for lunch. And she isn't foreign."

"I order exactly the same thing every Friday. She should just fix it without having to ask." Gladys folded the paper menu; they didn't even have decent laminated menus.

"If she did that, you'd decide that this time you wanted something different and she shouldn't presume to know you so well."

"Humph. As you presume to know me so well."

Florence's shoulders sagged in that defeated way of hers. "Gladys, I've lived with you all my life. If anybody knows you, I do."

"Well, I for one—"

"Hello, ladies. What can I get for you today?"

How did that woman sneak up on them like that? "I'll have what I always have," Gladys declared.

"Me, too," her sister added, smiling at Jamaica.

Jamaica. Who named their child after an island?

"One club sandwich on wheat, one on white. I'll have them up in a jiffy."

"You shouldn't eat white bread, you know. It'll clog you up and all those preservatives will probably give you cancer."

"Oh, Gladys, let up for once."

"This place bothers me. Too many different people are moving into our town. It's the reason we have things like coffee shops."

"Which are nice."

"And motorcycle gangs coming through every summer now."

"They're not gangs. Just groups of people who like to ride motorcycles."

Gladys sniffed. "Well, they drink and carouse and turn the town into a saloon for two nights a year. I'll bet if our new pastor hears about it, he'll be inviting all of them to church to join the prostitutes."

"Just one prostitute."

"So far. Who knows how many will show up next week?"

Jamaica brought the sandwiches. "I saw in the paper about Candy coming to your church. That sure caused a stir, didn't it?"

"Humph. It was scandalous." Gladys pulled a pair of small scissors from her bag and notched the corner of one mustard packet. She spread one line of mustard on each section of sandwich.

"I heard she had some trouble because of it. Got beat up pretty bad."

"That's terrible!" Florence was lavishing blobs of mayonnaise on her plate to dip her sandwich in. "I hadn't heard. When did that happen?"

"Wednesday." Jamaica refilled their glasses of iced tea. "Didn't you see her? I heard she came to church covered in cuts and bruises."

Gladys scowled. Would the woman ever go away so they could eat? "My arthritis flared up. We weren't at church Wednesday."

"Oh." Jamaica collected empty straw wrappers from a nearby table. "So you don't know where she's staying now?"

"I'm sure someone took her to the hospital, if she was that bad."

"No, she's not at the hospital."

Gladys narrowed her gaze at Jamaica. "Are you looking for her? Does she owe you money or something?"

"Nope. Just curious." Jamaica quickly backed away. "Enjoy your lunch and let me know if you want dessert, okay?"

"Thanks, Jamaica." Florence waited till she was out of earshot, then said, "She's so nice."

"Hmph." Gladys wasn't so sure.

"Poor Candy. Who do you think beat her up?"

"Probably someone she'd stolen from."

"Gladys!"

"I said it before and I'll say it again. I do not like the direction this town is headed. And our church now seems to be going with it."

Grant

She was painting flowers again. Grant took advantage of Jean's concentration and enjoyed watching her a moment before alerting her to his presence. She used soft, wide strokes and hummed as she worked. He marveled at the change in her when she thought no one was around. Her gestures, her voice, the sway of her lithe body to the music, all were comfortable and serene. Things he never saw when she was with him.

She intrigued him, but man, was she bad for his ego.

His soft tap on the lower half of the nursery door had her frozen in a moment. She turned and, was he imagining it, or did her face register relief—perhaps even a little pleasure—when she realized it was him?

"Hi." He said it casually, wanting that comfortable feeling to come back to her, so it could spread to him again.

"Hi." She looked down at the cup of paint in her hand. Carefully, she set her paintbrush back down in it. "Thanks for not inspiring me to paint the carpet again."

She actually smiled, right at him, and he sucked in a breath. It made her beautiful.

Her smiled faltered as he stared. "Is everything okay?" She set her cup down.

"Yeah. Great." He removed his helmet and held it under one arm, shoving his free hand through his mass of unruly hair, telling himself not to feel self-conscious about it. Girls in college had always said his hair looked best after he'd been riding around on his bike. Something about it curling up.

"Guess what I did this weekend?"

Was she actually initiating a conversation? He told himself not to grin; it might scare her back into silence. "Um, let's see, you went to the circus, ate three bag-fulls of cotton candy, and got a stomachache from riding the Ferris Wheel."

"We don't have a circus here." She put her hands on her hips. "And three bags of cotton candy would much more likely cause a stomachache than a ride on a Ferris Wheel anyway."

"Okay, then I guess you—"

"I didn't actually want you to guess," she said, her mouth hinting of that smile again. "It was just an introductory statement."

"Oh, well I've been 'introducted' then." He leaned onto the lower half of the nursery door and smiled. What had happened to her? "So what *did* you do this weekend?"

"Candy decided we needed to go shopping. She and Brenda looked through my closet for something for her to wear. For some reason, she hates all my clothes." Jean tilted her head to the side, a puzzled frown on her face. "Why do you suppose that is?"

"Um...well..."

She looked at his face and laughed. "I'm kidding. I know why." She seemed to enjoy his look of shock. "You should have seen the things she bought—well, I bought and she's supposed to pay me back. Or at least that's what she told me. I heard her telling Brenda in the dressing room that it was partly a ploy to get me a new wardrobe." She looked down at her broom skirt and faded blouse. "As if I would ever wear the things she picked out. Candy is addicted to outfits that make her look like a bowl of rainbow-colored sherbet."

He stood there, grinning at her, until she looked away and shrugged, saying, "So what are you doing here this early anyway? Church doesn't start for another hour."

"I came hoping you'd be here."

All the comfort and ease he was loving evaporated in an instant. She turned and meticulously started cleaning her paintbrush with a wet wipe. "Why?"

He wasn't sure if he wanted to shake her or kiss her. Since there was no sense contemplating either option, he got right to the point. "I met your uncle today. The one who works in town at the mechanic shop."

"Uncle Doug?"

"That's the one. I was there today asking about a job. I need to work while I'm here. Stewart's busy full time with ministry, but I'm not. Your uncle said they had a position open due to some guy named Bob having an accident."

"Yeah, Bob fell asleep and fell out of his deer stand a couple of weekends ago. Broke his arm." She was still wiping her completely clean paintbrush, her back to him. "I didn't know you were a mechanic."

"I've been tinkering on things since I was a kid. Drove my dad crazy when I was five and disassembled all his watches to see how they worked. In high school, when I wasn't playing sports, I worked on an old scrap of a motorcycle I'd gotten super cheap. It was mostly worthless, but whenever I could, I'd get another part for it till I had something worth riding."

"So is that why you were looking for me, to tell me my uncle gave you a job?"

"He didn't give me the job, not yet. There was a condition."

She took the bait and turned to face him. "A condition?"

"Yep." He tried to keep a straight face. "He said I could have the job if I could get you to ride to his shop with me on Chachie."

"Chachie?"

"My motorcycle."

"You named your motorcycle?" She almost smiled, then shook her head. "Wait, did you say you wanted *me* to ride on your motorcycle?"

"I'll drive. All you have to do is sit there." He grinned. He couldn't help it. "Doug even let me borrow an extra helmet." He lifted the pink helmet he'd stashed on the floor out of sight and showed it to her.

"You've got to be kidding."

"Please, Jean. I'd really like this job. This is what I'm good at. I don't want to have to ask Jamaica if I can wash her windows or pour whipped cream into people's coffee."

"I've never ridden a motorcycle in my life."

"I know. Doug told me you're deathly afraid of them."

"Not deathly afraid. Just...almost deathly afraid." She had her hands on her hips again. "This isn't fair. You want to get me on a motorcycle. Candy wants me to wear fire-engine red. What is wrong with everybody lately?"

He laughed. She was trying so hard to be mad at him.

"I promise I won't let you fall off. And see, the helmet is pink, not red, so I'm not as bad as Candy." He held the helmet toward her. "Please? Pretty please? With sugar on top?"

She looked up at the ceiling. "Sugar. Oh great. Just call me Lemonade."

"What?"

"Nothing." She grabbed the helmet. "You're going to hound me until I give in, aren't you?"

"I told you I really want this job." *And I really want to see you in a pink helmet on my motorcycle, actually having fun.*

She let out a longsuffering breath. "You are hopeless."

Grant watched her look the helmet over as if she'd never seen one up close before. *On the contrary,* he thought with a smile. *I'm actually starting to feel some hope regarding you.*

"The shop isn't open this late, and we have church soon anyway, so I'll pick you up at the bank tomorrow. When do you get off work?"

She peered up at him all round-eyed. "F-five o'clock?"

"Is that a question?"

She looked at the helmet in her hands. "No."

He let his voice sound as happy as he felt. "See you at five then." He grabbed his own helmet and quickly walked away before she had the chance to change her mind.

"If you want
to live,
you say
what he tells
you to say."

Champagne

The ride into the city was made in silence. No radio. No talking. Champagne kept her eyes on the bright lights and tall buildings sliding by, avoiding any glance at Slash. A quiet anger simmered beneath his surface. His appearance looked non-threatening, but so was a panther's to someone who didn't know a silent crouch meant it was ready to pounce. Champagne planned to give him no reason to pounce at her again.

She had never been to this part of Charlotte. Slash's route took them from a four-lane road to a two-lane, then down narrow rows of pavement with no lines at all, striping the ground between rundown buildings covered in graffiti and bordered by trash. Champagne lowered her eyes when they neared a group of young men with guns in full view. Slash turned left, obviously familiar with the area. He parked in front of a chain-length fence topped with barbed wire. A flash of his headlights brought someone to the gate. Once unlocked and opened, Slash drove through, speaking for the first time since he had ordered her into the car with terse instructions for her first job of the night. "You remember what to do?"

"Yes."

"Nothing but what I told you to say."

"I remember."

"Good girl." He ran his hand across her shoulder, under her hair, around the back of her neck. A light squeeze—an affectionate gesture from some, a threat from him—accompanied his soft words. "I know I can count on you. You'd never leave me like she did, would you?"

"No."

"You have five minutes. Go."

Champagne opened the car door and her weak knees barely held her up when she tried to stand. *You're confident. You're not afraid. Fake it.* The words did not work, so Champagne resorted to humming to herself as she picked her way across the uneven driveway toward a door on the side of the building. She heard a car door shut behind her and forced herself not to look back. She hadn't done anything. He wasn't coming after her.

She heard Slash's voice give a greeting and several voices murmur in response. She had to hurry. The moment he finished the drug exchange, he would want to leave, and fast. Champagne felt blindly until she reached a doorknob. Rusty hinges complained as the door creaked open. She stepped inside, hearing the click of her heels on linoleum, looking for the lighted room. There. To the right.

Her soft knock was answered by a young voice. "Come in."

Champagne entered the tiny room, empty except for one twin bed, a small bedside table, and two pairs of shoes flung near the door. "Slash sent me."

The girl was young, dark skin on display in a dress that left nothing to the imagination. Champagne felt the girl's fear, but the pain shooting through her was not from the girl's pain, but rather the meager look of hope still in her eyes.

"My name is Pansy," the girl said. "I'm fifteen. Are you—"

"Don't tell me your name. Don't tell me anything," Champagne ordered, the words coming out tight and hard. "You've got to shut yourself away, become someone else, never reveal who you really are."

The girl sat on the small bed and pulled her knees up to her chest. She tucked her head into the curve between her knees. "I want to go home."

Her whimper ripped through Champagne. "Listen, I don't have much time." She sat next to the girl on the bed and grabbed her arm. "Look at me." When the girl raised her eyes, Champagne spoke with urgency. "My job tonight is to help you stay alive. Slash wanted me to tell you that, if anybody comes here looking for you, if anybody finds you and asks you questions, you must tell them you want to stay here. Tell them you want to be doing what you're doing, that it's your choice to be here. Do you understand?"

"But I *don't* want to be here."

Champagne shook her. Better to hurt her a little than have Slash destroy her completely. "It doesn't matter what you want. If you want to live, you say what he tells you to say."

"He said I could go free once my debt was paid for my bus ticket here."

"He lied." Shutting down all emotion, Champagne lifted her hair and turned so the girl could see the back of her neck, the raw, red line below her hairline that had not yet begun to heal. "Do you see it?" The girl started crying but did not answer. "Do you see it?" she asked again.

"Y-yes. What happened to you?"

"Slash will do the same to you if you try to get away. If you help someone else get away. If you cross him at all. It's his trademark, the way he brands us as his. He loves doing it, so don't give him any excuse to do it to you. Understand?"

Someone knocked on the door. Time was up. Champagne gripped the girl by the shoulders. "You say what he told you to say. If you want to live, you do what you're told. Don't think. Don't feel." She felt her voice catch. "Don't hope. Do you understand me?"

Her eyes full of despair, the girl nodded before curling up into a fetal position on the bed and pulling the one flimsy sheet over herself. Champagne wanted to say something that would help, something that would ease the heartbreak. But there was nothing to say. She backed from the room, shut the door, and walked away.

Monday Morning, July 21

Jean

"I can't believe I'm doing this."

"You're not doing anything. I'm doing all the work." Candy put another bobby pin into Jean's hair. "Hand me that clip, will you? Your hair's fine; I want to make sure it stays through the work day till your date."

"It's not a date." Jean shifted uncomfortably in the dining room chair.

"Oh, right, you're helping him get a job." Candy talked around three bobby pins held between her lips. "You just fell off the turnip truck, didn't you?"

"I don't know why you're bothering. It won't last through ten minutes with a helmet on anyway."

Candy gave her a small swat on the shoulder. "By then it won't matter. It's the first minute that makes all the difference."

"You're wasting your time."

"I offered to trade you a makeover in exchange for you letting me borrow money to buy clothes. So shut up and enjoy it."

Jean bit her lips closed and endured Candy's makeover. When Brenda dropped by for their short Bible study before Jean went to work, she whistled. "Wow, Jean, you look fantastic."

Candy gave Jean an appraising look. "I'm pretty proud of myself," she said. "I knew Jean would panic if I put on too much color, so I just gave her a subtle bit of peach blush, some cream eye shadow, and lip gloss instead of lipstick. Go look at yourself, girl." She playfully shoved Jean toward the small bathroom adjoining the guest room.

Jean trudged toward the bathroom. Her first glance inside had her smiling. All across the large bathroom mirror were the words, "You will know the truth, and the truth will make you free," written in bright red lipstick.

"Nice," Jean said.

"It's better than nice!" Candy shouted from the dining room. "I did a great job."

Jean ducked her head under the verse and saw her own reflection staring, wide-eyed. Was that her? That girl who looked...who looked...

She looked like a Jean Louise.

Not a Blue Jean.

"Now on to your outfit." Candy found her and tugged her toward the stairs. "I have a surprise for you."

"I'm not wearing any of your clothes, Candy." Makeup was one thing. Red ruffles and purple heels were another.

"We're not living in fear anymore, remember?" Candy lavished clouds of hair spray on her as they walked. "Don't you trust your friends to have your best interests at heart?"

"And today," Brenda added, leading the way up the stairs. "We believe your best interests would be impressing that brother-in-law of mine."

Jean entered her room and gasped. Lying on her bed, covering over the dark slacks and top she'd selected to wear, was a silk cream shirt and soft camel-colored slacks.

"See, we didn't go overboard," Candy said, her face smug. "Brenda snuck these into the car while you helped me pick out clothes at the store." She added, "But she paid for them first!"

Jean had the silly urge to hug them both. She touched the soft material. "Thank you."

"Well, get dressed, girl! We've already missed half our study time making you look date-worthy. I'll ask Brenda my questions for today while you get this on. Don't forget the shoes."

Candy continued talking as she followed Brenda from the room, closing the door behind her. Jean bent over and picked up the low-healed, beige pumps. They had thought of everything.

Ten minutes later, Jean exited the room. Candy and Brenda clapped, and she blushed. "I'm not used to feeling so..."

"Pretty?"

She smiled at Candy. "Yes, thank you. And comfortable, too. Everything feels so soft."

"Mm-hm. Huggable."

"I'm not the hugging type."

"I didn't say *I* wanted to hug you." Candy looked her over, tucking one stray strand of hair back where it belonged. "I'm talking about that big football player you'll be seeing tonight."

Jean went silent and sat.

"Don't sit down like a block of cement. Be feminine. Soft."

How could she explain the sense of terror rising in her chest? "You don't think he'll actually hug me, do you?"

Brenda sat next to her and put a hand on her shoulder. "I don't think it would be a terrible thing if he did, Jean."

"No living in fear, remember?" Candy stated. She stood over them and waved her arms like a choir director. "You." She pointed at Brenda. "You are going to live this day trusting God and not putting even the tip of a fingernail into your mouth."

"You said that last week."

"Bad habits are hard to break. You wouldn't believe how long it took me to get off beer. Now you." She pointed at Jean. "Remember what your assignment is? You will live today without fear. You will smile at people and even start a conversation if the opportunity arises."

Candy marched around the table and finished her speech with, "And I will stay here and study the Bible some more. This has been the best week of my life. I never thought getting beat to a pulp would turn out so good." She smiled and announced loudly, "All of us today will think more about helping and loving the people around us, instead of worrying what other people think about us." She chuckled. "It'll be easy for me to keep from blowing it, since I'll be here all by myself!"

Brenda rose and hugged Candy. "I think you already succeeded for today." She gestured toward Jean. "Are you ready for work? It's about time to go."

Jean nodded and rose with slow, measured movements. "Are you sure this is—"

"You really do look wonderful," Brenda assured. "Not ostentatious at all."

That was the answer Jean needed. She took in a deep breath. "Okay then."

"Remember, no fear!" Candy shouted from the doorway as Jean and Brenda walked toward their parked cars.

No fear, Jean told herself. *No fear.*

How was she supposed to have no fear when she was wearing clothes that would probably make people look at her? Not to mention in exactly eight hours she would be riding on the back of a motorcycle. Behind a man. A man Candy wanted to inspire into hugging her. Just the thought had Jean trembling, but she realized something odd as she drove toward work. The trembling she felt was not entirely out of fear.

What did that mean?

Monday Afternoon, July 21

Stewart

"I'd like to help." Stewart looked up from the newspaper clippings to where Susan Meeks and Ian Craig sat across from him in his office. "How does something like this work?"

Susan was the first to speak. "As you can see from the paper, that city successfully apprehended nineteen people who were either involved in selling or buying drugs. Sheriff Craig thinks we could do that here, but combine it with his town and even parts of the city, too. All the places Slash is working. Sheriff Craig has jurisdiction over his county and the next, but not Charlotte, so he's been in touch with the Charlotte-Mecklenburg police department and the FBI about that area, and with our county sheriff about Oakview."

Ian nodded. "I've been training my men to be prepared for this if and when I got the opportunity. Susan provided it to me when she told me Slash was based here in this town. If we can get enough deputies and volunteers, I think we could clean up this area."

"I've been hearing about drugs being a problem around here."

Susan nodded. "It's gotten much worse over the past few years. I'm guessing that's around when Slash must have come with Candy and whoever else he brought. Just think, if we could get rid of the drug trade, how much that would help this town for good."

"I agree. But how does this end up helping Candy?"

"Don't you see?" Susan edged forward on her seat. "If we can arrest Slash, she's safe. We can help whoever else he's trapped here as well."

Ian Craig handed him a page covered in statistics. Stewart skimmed over them while the sheriff explained. "Here's how it works. The volunteers get online or connect with our known sellers about buying drugs or hiring prostitutes. Everything happens on one night. The best night would be during an event, like something from out of town, because crimes like trafficking and drug selling rise when there are people away from home. That night the volunteers pose as drug buyers or johns—guys who use prostitutes. We equip them with cameras and recorders, and once they have incriminating evidence, we intervene and land the perpetrators in jail."

"Just like that?"

The sheriff shrugged. "It's a little more complicated, but that's the main idea."

"You know what would be the perfect time? Friday, August first, the weekend when the bikers come through!" Susan clapped her hands together. "It's an event with people coming from out of town, so some of your volunteers could pose as bikers. It would be the perfect cover."

Stewart nodded. "I was thinking of that weekend as well." He shook his head. "I had hoped to do an outreach that weekend, maybe passing out tracts with free water or something, but…"

"But let me guess." Susan frowned. "It got voted down."

He did not even need to nod. Susan sighed. "Well, maybe we can witness to the guys we arrest instead!" She grinned at Stewart. "Don't put that up for a vote, okay?"

He smiled. It was nice to know not everyone was against him. "You got it."

"Ian," Susan said, then blushed. "I mean Sheriff Craig, I know Candy is concerned about the girl who is her roommate. She was trafficked into prostitution by her dad, and Candy is worried if we go after Slash, she'll be in danger. Is there some way we could get to her before this all happens?"

"It would risk Slash getting suspicious if we did anything outright," the sheriff responded. "If you knew someone not well known in town, who could go visit her as, say, a customer, that might work. And Ian's just fine, by the way," he added with a smile.

"Fine for—oh." Susan blushed again and looked away. "I'll have to think on that for awhile. The-the situation with Candy's roommate, that is."

Stewart focused on the sheriff. "August first is two weeks from tomorrow. That doesn't give us much time."

"No, and that's a good thing. Like I said, I've been preparing my men for some time now. For volunteers, we don't want them to have a lot of time to let information slip out. One misplaced word and the whole thing is over. Guys like Slash have a wide network. Any kind of threat, and they disappear like cockroaches when you turn a light on. And if they got wind of this and went into hiding, we'd probably never have another chance. This is it. So choose people you trust."

Stewart stood when the sheriff did and they shook hands. "I'll be in touch," Ian said. He turned to Susan. "Maybe Susan can be our go-between so I don't raise suspicion by calling or showing up here too often. I'm known in these parts, so a low profile would be best."

"You can call me anytime," Susan offered. "When-when you want to get a message to Pastor Henderson."

Ian nodded and half-smiled. "I'll do that." He nodded toward Stewart. "Pastor."

"Sheriff." Stewart sat back down as Ian left the room.

"Oh, I need to give him my phone number." Susan started toward the door. "My, but that sounds forward, doesn't it?"

Now alone, Stewart studied the newspaper clipping again. It spoke of success, of drug dealers being put behind bars. *Lord, I've been asking You how we should start to get involved in this community. Is this from You, or am I jumping ahead of Your will? He said to choose people I trust. How do I know who to trust, Lord? We haven't even been here a month. People in the church already think I'm a renegade. I already brought up the idea of ministering at the motorcycle event and that was shot down. What will happen when they find out I'm going undercover to bust drug dealers and pimps instead?*

Stewart put his head in his hands and prayed aloud. "What You want is more important than what anybody else wants. I thought what I wanted most was to have my own church, but that wasn't the right goal." He looked up. "What I want most is to follow You. Give me the courage to do that, whatever the cost."

He finished his prayer, then stood. Where was that little paper shredder? He needed to destroy this newspaper article, then go find Brenda. They had a lot to talk about.

He'd never
in his life
met
a girl
so distant.

Grant

Grant knew he should stop staring. It was making her nervous. But every time he pulled his eyes away, they went wandering back.

"You look..." He had to find a word that was minimalistic. That wouldn't scare her away. "Pretty."

Her hair was up in some fancy style and some kind of shimmery stuff kept drawing his attention to her lips. She wasn't wearing black, or even dark brown, and her blouse slipped and shifted when she moved, begging to be noticed.

He was noticing all right.

"So, can we go?" She put the pink helmet on top of the papers on her desk. "If I'm going to do something I'm almost deathly afraid of, I'd rather get it over with."

He had come a little early, wanting to see where she worked. A receptionist raised her eyebrows when he mentioned Jean's name. "Oh, so that's why," she said, which made no sense until he turned the corner and saw her sitting at a small desk punching numbers into an oversized calculator. He stopped mid-stride and gawked, embarrassing himself when the receptionist chuckled and said, "Well, what do you know." She wandered back toward her desk. "Never thought I'd see the day..."

Grant had not gotten over the change when she glanced up and noticed him. She froze, then seemed to force her face into a smile. "Hello," she said, her voice as soft as her shirt looked.

Was she dressed up for him? Should he even hope such a thing? "Nice outfit." *Great job, Grant. You should write romantic cards for a living.*

She pressed her lips together and the shimmery stuff caught the light. "Thanks." She picked a miniscule piece of lint from her pants.

He wished he could say something to make her less nervous. He was suddenly feeling rather nervous himself, as if he were in middle school waiting for a girl at her locker.

"So, not being a teller, I guess you don't have a stash of lollipops to give away."

She didn't look up at him, but she did smile. Her slim hand opened a drawer to her right. She pulled out a lollipop. "I stay supplied, in case little boys wander my way."

"I'm glad I wandered your way." That was better. That would work in a card. He took two steps closer and reached for the lollipop.

She pulled it out of reach. "What's the magic word?"

Dressed up, smiling, and teasing? He wasn't sure if he could handle all this at once. He leaned onto her desk and grinned. "You're beautiful?"

She frowned and looked down. "Nope."

He bent down until he caught her eye. "You're beautiful, please?"

Grant could see she tried to stop it, but a smile peeked through. She handed over the lollipop and he pocketed it, for some reason feeling he had just won something important.

He led the way outside toward his bike. "Meet Chachie," he said with pride.

"Is this the motorcycle you worked on when you were younger?" She ran a hand over the leather seat.

"Sure is." He clipped his helmet strap under his chin. "Need help with your helmet?"

154

"I don't think so."

She put it on while he threw a leg over the bike, balancing it so she could get on behind him. "Hop on."

She stood next to it, staring at the seat. "Um…"

"All you need to do is sit and hold on to me. If I turn, lean with me." He smiled. "Just don't yank us both off or anything."

With slow movements, she sat behind him. He waited for her to slip her arms around his waist, but she didn't. He looked back. She had gone pale. "You'll want to hang on to me. Doug's place isn't far, but I don't want you falling off."

He turned around and shook his head. He'd never in his life met a girl so distant. When her hands sneaked under his arms and clutched the sides of his jacket, Grant kept his disappointment silent.

"Here we go." He pulled slowly out of the parking lot and onto the road. He crept through the first few miles to help her relax. At the first red light, he looked back. "You okay?"

Her cheeks were devoid of color, but she nodded yes.

He probably shouldn't, but decided not to resist. "Then let's give you a real ride." The light turned green and he shot forward. Jean squealed behind him and he grinned when her arms wrapped tight around him and clung. She did not loosen her grip through town, or even when he pulled into the parking lot of Doug's shop. Only when the motor was off and he touched her hand did she pull away.

"Would you look at that."

"Hi, Uncle Doug." Jean unclipped the strap and pulled her helmet off. Whatever had been holding her hair up, some kind of little brown things, fell down onto the pavement. She picked them up, then shook her head and more fell out.

"Hey, Blue Jean. Hey, Grant." Doug shook Grant's hand. It looked like he would pull Jean into a hug, but she took a step back and he tugged a section of her hair instead. "Good to see you. I didn't think he could do it. What kind of magic does this guy have that he convinced you to get on a motorcycle?"

She smiled and shrugged.

Grant's chest swelled with victory. He had won. "No magic. Just charm."

Jean rolled her eyes and looked at her uncle. "He begged me. Told me he wouldn't get the job if I didn't."

"Don't tell him that." Grant held a hand to his heart and pretended to look wounded. "My charm is the only appeal I've got."

"Oh, you've got plenty of appeal..." Grant watched in delight as Jean covered her mouth with her hand and blushed furiously.

Doug chuckled. "Well." He slapped Grant on the back. "The job is yours. You can start tomorrow morning. If you can get that girl on a motorcycle, I figure you can handle anything I send your way. I've never worked on a car yet more stubborn than Jean."

Tuesday Afternoon, July 22

Don't fear, Jean told herself. *Don't fear.*

Was he trying to scare her to death? They'd stop at a red light and she'd just start to breathe again, when the light would turn green and he'd zoom forward as if the devil himself was chasing them. She never knew the phrase, "hanging on for dear life" had such a literal meaning.

"Isn't this great?" he yelled back as they pulled onto a long stretch of straight road. The wind rushed around them and Jean buried her head into the back of his jacket.

God has not given us the spirit of fear, but of power, and of love, and of a sound mind.

She wasn't sure God had given Grant a sound mind. Who in their right mind could be enjoying this?

The motorcycle slowed and she lifted her head. He had pulled into her driveway, but then veered off onto the grass toward the trees. At the small brook that divided her property from the church, he breaked and turned off the motor. Jean had a hard time uncurling her fingers from his jacket.

"Well?"

He looked like such a little boy, so eager to hear she had enjoyed the ride. She pulled off the pink helmet and reached to smooth her hair down. "Well..." she stalled. "I'm not sure if I'm less deathly afraid of motorcycles now or more." She smiled at him. "But I'm glad you got the job."

"You honestly didn't think that was fun?" He reached for her helmet and hung it by its strap from one handlebar, doing the same for his on the other. "Maybe you should try it a few more times till you're used to it."

The thought had her heart pounding again. "Candy is teaching us to not live in fear, but I'd rather start with smaller things, like starting conversations."

He lowered himself to sit on a log near the water and invited her to join him. "Did you say Candy was teaching you? I figured it would be the other way around."

Jean sat beside him. "I did, too, but Brenda and I are learning from her instead. She is showing both of us that we know a lot of Scripture in our heads, but aren't actually living it.

So we've been meeting in the mornings sometimes and writing down verses and how to live them."

"I've noticed you are different, not as...hidden away."

Jean ducked her head, but she nodded. "Candy gives us assignments. Well, they're more like commands. Brenda is supposed to make it through the day without biting her fingernails."

He picked up a fallen branch and tossed it into the water. "Now that I think about it, she has been doing that less. Good for Candy. What's your assignment?"

She felt herself blushing again. "I'm supposed to smile at people. And start conversations if there is an opening."

"Ah, I see." He threw in another branch, then pulled the lollipop from his pocket and opened it. "And here I thought you'd been smiling at me lately because you were actually glad to see me."

She snuck a glance to see if he was joking or not, and could not quite tell. He had the lollipop in his mouth and was watching the water. "This is the reason our church is called Brookside," she said. "I used to run away and come here. I'd stare at the water, wondering where it came from, where it was going."

He turned to her. "Were you running away from home?"

She looked across at the church. "No."

Jean felt his gaze on her, but put hers on the water drifting by their feet. He spoke into the silence. "Is your mom still around? I don't think I've met her."

She shook her head. "She moved to Virginia when I was about eighteen. Said she couldn't live in this house anymore. Too many memories. She wanted a new start."

"Why didn't you go with her?"

Jean kept her gaze on the ground. "I was needed here." She picked up a wildflower and twirled it between her fingers. "The house was paid off—my dad built most of it—so she left it with me. I think I expected her to come back after awhile, but she surprised me by getting a job and settling there. She comes back for a visit a couple times a year." She rubbed her hands up her arms, the softness reminding her of her new clothes.

"So." Grant brushed branch particles off his knees and stood. She had felt his gaze as they sat, felt the questions he wanted to ask. He surprised her when he did not ask them, but instead reached out a hand to pull her to her feet. She almost took it, but managed to reach out and stand at the same time, getting to her feet before their hands actually touched.

He sighed, but then pulled the lollipop from his mouth and smiled at her. "So," he said again. "This smiling thing. You're supposed to practice smiling at people, right?"

"Right."

"Give it a try."

She looked down, self-conscious. "What do you mean?"

"I'm helping you do your assignment." He was grinning now and she felt a blush creep up for about the tenth time that day. "Go ahead, smile at me."

She smiled.

"Not down at the ground." His tone was exasperated, brotherly. "The caterpillars don't care. Smile at me."

She kept the smile, widened now, and glanced up at him.

"No, no. That won't do." He came to stand directly in front of her. A finger lifted her chin. "Look at me, Jean Louise." His voice had changed, softened. She looked at him. "Smile at me. Please."

Her heart started racing again, but it didn't have anything to do with his motorcycle. She swallowed, breathed, tried to get her mouth to move, but it would not obey her command. His eyes filled with the same kind of confusion rushing through her. Everything seemed to slow to a stop. His face was clear and the world behind and around him grew hazy.

"Jean..." he whispered.

This was a totally different kind of fear. She took a step back.

He kept his hand out toward her for a moment, then pulled it back and shook it a little, as if shaking the feel of her skin away. "Okay," he said, looking away from her face, his tone carrying a forced casualness. "Did she give you any other assignments? How about shaking hands? You don't shake hands. Oh, wait, you said it was starting conversations."

She clenched her hands and smiled at the ground. "I take it you'd like to help me face those fears, too?"

"Indeed I would." He approached but stopped a safe distance away. She glanced up enough to see his smile was chagrined. "But I think we'd best save those lessons for another time."

*"I wonder
why he's being
so helpful."*

Susan

"This was a great idea. I feel like a teenager again." Susan grabbed two pieces of extra-cheese pizza and flopped them on her paper plate before making her way toward the fellowship hall's longest table.

"I figured this was the easiest way for us all to meet and discuss our plans for the weekend." Pastor Stewart had already prayed and was enjoying his pizza when Susan sat down. "Thanks for being willing to be Sheriff Craig's spokesperson today."

"Oh, I doubt she minds at all," Brenda teased, taking a seat next to Stewart. "I hear they've been talking on the phone every night getting everything ready."

Susan picked up her first piece of pizza and used a bite as an excuse to not have to respond.

"I think she's blushing." Grant sat on the opposite end from Stewart and grinned. "Yep, definitely blushing."

Susan looked across to Jean, who thankfully took pity on her and changed the subject. "Candy came with me to children's church today," Jean said. "I planned to teach the story of the prodigal son, but Candy kept interrupting with questions."

Susan noticed how Stewart sent Jean a look of gratitude. He probably enjoyed getting to preach an entire sermon without interruptions for a change.

Candy, the last to sit down, chimed in, "Yeah, and next thing you know the kids were telling the story, and even acting it out. It was great! I decided I'm the prodigal in the story who ran away and got accepted back, and Rod Carson is the big brother, who is mad that I get to have a party with a fat cow."

"Fatted calf," Stewart corrected, and got an elbow from his wife. "If you care about details like that."

"Speaking of Rod Carson," Grant said, setting his pizza crust down on his plate and wiping his fingers on a napkin. "Now that I have a job, thanks to Jean…"

Susan watched with interest as Grant smiled at Jean and she ducked her head away from his gaze. Was something happening between those two? Was that why Jean was wearing better colors? Well, everything on her was still neutral, rather than actually colorful, but nothing was black or dark brown, which was an improvement. And was she actually wearing lip gloss?

"I keep putting off trying to get that storage window open. But I think I've figured out an easier way to get in the room." Grant reached for another piece of pizza. "So I think I'll have it open soon, which means I need to talk to Rod and the deacons about the desks."

"What about the desks?"

Susan looked up to see Rod standing in the fellowship hall doorway. How long had he been there? Jean did not turn to look behind her, but Susan noticed she stiffened at his voice. She noted Grant had seen that as well. His eyes did not leave Jean's face.

Stewart spoke up. "We wanted to ask you about the desks in that storage room. We'd like to use the room and wondered if the desks needed to be kept, or if—"

"Sell them," Rod said without preamble. "All of them."

Grant's eyebrows went up. "Are you sure? Should we meet with the other deacons and ask if—"

"Sell them," Rod repeated. "They should go right away. I'll make some phone calls. I know a few people who would be interested. I'll have someone come pick them up by the beginning of next week. You'll have the door open by then?"

Grant seemed rather stunned. His one-word answer dragged out as if it were two. "Y-yes."

Rod nodded, then left.

"That was a shock. I wonder why he's being so helpful," Brenda whispered. This time it was she who got a gentle elbow nudge from her husband. "Sorry. Shouldn't judge. Hit the backspace button on that comment."

"Jean, are you okay?" Susan's curiosity about Jean's response turned into concern. She had gripped the table with both hands.

"Jean?" Grant's voice was soft. He reached out a hand and almost touched her. There was definitely something going on between them, with him at least.

Jean's head lifted. She looked at him. Looked at Susan. "It's a good idea to sell the desks," she said, her gaze absent. Susan never could figure out what she was thinking.

The silence lengthened until Brenda broke it. "So Candy, whatever happened with your job search? I see that big bruise around your eyes is almost gone."

Candy touched her face. "Yeah, I only had to put on two layers of powder today instead of four. Jean took me to the shelter. I thought it would be great to work there, helping people escape abuse, but the only work they had available was volunteer. I'm all for helping, but a girl's got to eat, so I'll have to keep looking."

"Any other ideas?" Susan tried to keep her bites dainty but the pizza was so good. While everyone's attention was on Candy's answer, Susan opened wide and filled her mouth with incredible, cheese-filled calories.

"Oh, lots, but your Ian guy told me I had to stay put until after this big bust you've got planned on Friday."

"He's not *my* Ian." Susan covered her mouth with her hand so she could protest despite her mouth being full. "But that was smart of him. You need to stay protected. If Slash finds you, this whole operation is at risk."

She swallowed. "And speaking of, that's the first item on my agenda for this meeting. Candy has to move."

Tuesday Afternoon, July 22

Grant

Grant could see Susan's announcement caught Jean's attention. "Move?" she asked. "Why?"

Susan pulled her notebook from her large, blue purse and opened it to the first page. "Jamaica contacted me yesterday. Some of the ladies from church were in for coffee, and someone let it slip that Candy is staying with Jean while she recovers from the beating."

"Oh no." Brenda bit on her thumbnail. "Didn't they understand the danger Candy is in?"

"No nails," Candy said.

Grant was impressed when Brenda clasped her hands back in her lap. "Thanks," she told Candy. "What are we going to do?"

"I was brainstorming ideas, but Jamaica already had a suggestion. She said Candy could come and stay at her place. She lives above the coffee shop. There's a window that overlooks main street. The more I thought about it, the more perfect it seemed." Susan tapped her pen on her notebook. "Especially since, if we take her over secretly, no one would know where she

166

was, so there'd be no danger of anyone sharing her location with the wrong people. So—I hope it was okay—I told Jamaica everything. Our plan for Friday. How Slash needs to still be looking for Candy for it to work. Even the risk she would be accepting by opening her home this weekend."

Grant edged his chair forward. "And she agreed to help us?"

"Yes."

"I think it's a great idea," Grant put in. "Jean will be at Stewart and Brenda's with Brenda, monitoring the internet responses and giving locations. Let's plan to take Candy to Jamaica's early Friday morning. I'll talk with the sheriff about setting up a couple of men at Jean's house from now until then." He looked at Jean. "Just in case. If Slash hears Candy was there, your house becomes a target." *And so do you.*

The thought of Jean being beaten as Candy had been was more than Grant could stomach. He turned to Stewart. "Where will you be Friday night, Jimmy?"

"Jimmy?" Susan looked from one to the other. "Where'd you get a nickname like that? Wait...Stewart. Jimmy. Ah, I get it."

Brenda grinned and patted her husband's shoulder. "Stewart's mom was a big black-and-white movie buff back in the day."

Susan turned back to Grant and he knew it was coming. "Let me guess. Cary Grant?"

"Ding, ding, ding. She's right again." Stewart tossed a crumpled napkin at his brother. "But don't ever call him Cary."

"Not if you value your life." Grant threw the napkin back, his smile intact. "Thanks for the pizza. Here's for my part." He pulled out his wallet and tossed a bill onto one of the empty pizza boxes. "Let's get to the rest of that list of yours, Susan, so I can go exploring in my future apartment."

"A very small apartment," Stewart pointed out.

"I don't need as much room as you old married men do."

This time, an empty water bottle went flying across the table. Grant caught it.

"All right, you two." Brenda started piling up the pizza boxes. "Jean, what do you do when the boys in your class get unruly?"

"Feed them."

"Well, we already did that. What else?"

"Send them to play outside."

"Okay," she teased, shaking a finger at the group around the table. "You all behave or I'm sending you outside."

The empty water bottle bounced off her shoulder. "Grant Henderson!"

Jean finally smiled and Grant felt his shoulders relax. "Okay, I'll be good."

Susan leaned back in her chair. "You'd better be, because you're the next person on my list."

"Me? What'd I do?"

"It's what we need you to do." Susan passed the notebook to Candy. "I'm not the only one spending time with Ian on the phone."

Candy took the notebook, shooting Susan a look. "Except I call him Sheriff Craig."

Grant chuckled at the blush that flared across Susan's face. He braved a glance at Jean, wishing her face was as easy to read. "So what do you need me to do? I thought I was already set going with Ian on Friday."

"This is a need before Friday." Candy leaned forward, putting both arms on the table.

The tense lines on her face caught his attention. He sat up. "I'm listening."

"I can't let them arrest Champagne, not without giving her one more chance to get out." Candy's eyes were grim. "I wanted to go myself to talk with her, but the sheriff said that would blow everything, not to mention likely get me killed."

Heads around the table nodded. Grant was getting a bad feeling. "Where do I come in?"

Susan answered when Candy lowered her head and looked away as if she was …embarrassed?

"Thanks to a great new law, if Champagne was under eighteen, she'd be treated as a victim even if she was arrested, but Candy thinks she turned eighteen earlier this year. We know she was trafficked into prostitution against her will, so Ian is willing to let us risk contacting her and offering her a chance to get out." She shifted in her chair in a way that could only be described as a squirm.

His bad feeling was growing. "Again, where do I come in?"

Brenda stopped cleaning up the leftovers. Jean stared at her empty plate. Stewart leaned forward. He had the freedom to be curious.

Candy finally spoke. "Ian said the only way is to have a man pose as a john and hire Champagne to come meet him in a safe place, like a hotel. If you look around the table, you'll notice that you're our only option."

Not a chance. "Tell Ian to do it."

"He can't. He's had a run-in with Slash before, so his face is recognizable."

"Get somebody in law enforcement."

Candy's voice lowered to a more serious tone. "There's a reason Slash chose this little town after years in the city. The police were after him in Charlotte, but he found certain officers here willing to turn a blind eye in exchange for free visits, so he runs everything from here now. On nights he has people bringing in money or drugs, he makes Champagne and I stand out on the street corner. If the policemen on watch that night are on his side, we keep them distracted. If they're not, they arrest us and we keep them distracted that way. I know a name or two, but I don't know how far into the system it goes, how many in the department we can't trust. Which means we can't trust any of them."

Susan put her hands out. "Believe me, Grant, we tried to think of other options. There aren't any."

Grant glanced again at Jean. What did she think about all of this?

He knew for sure he hated it.

Friday Night, July 25

Jamaica

Jamaica determined not to let him see her fear. The man seemed to enjoy holding the gun near her, gesturing with the weapon as he talked. The whites of his eyes seemed glassy. If he had recently done drugs, his reflexes would be unpredictable. She was not afraid he would intentionally kill her, not that night, but the wild edge to his actions suggested he might trip or fall, pulling the trigger without realizing it.

If that happened, so close to her, there was no way she would survive.

"You did good, coffee lady." She stared at the jagged scar marks around his neck as he moved close and ran the gun barrel up her arm and across her shoulder. He smelled of alcohol and possibly weed.

"Next Friday then."

Jamaica trembled. "Yes, she'll be here next Friday. Now tell me where my daughter is."

"Your daughter, is she? Cute little thing. A friend of mine found her hanging out at the mall with her little friends. They all had to go home, but she wanted to stay. He said he'd give her a ride. She was real happy about that. All the other girls were jealous, wishing they needed a ride, too, so they could get some attention like that from a guy old enough to drive."

"Where is she?" Jamaica considered grabbing for his gun. Would she have a chance? She dug her hands into the folds of her apron. No, she had to wait. He hadn't given her any information yet. If either of them died in the struggle, Jamaica would never find Pansy.

"Don't worry. One week from today, when I have Candy back, you'll be told all you need to know."

"I want to know now."

The gun was instantly up under her chin. "You are not in a position to tell me what to do." He swayed, his body falling against her. "Pardon me," he said, stepping back and giving her a mock bow. "As I said before, one person's location for another's. You don't get what you want until I get what I want."

He stumbled backward. "Make sure she's here Friday night. At midnight. Just like you said."

Jamaica nodded. She bit her lip until she tasted blood. "Friday. We'll both be here."

He walked in a slithering kind of way to the back and she heard the door to the back entrance click shut behind him. Running to the door, she bolted it tight, then did the same at the front. It was pointless. The entire storefront was glass, floor to ceiling. One bullet through it and anyone could walk right in. On Friday, he would get in, whether she opened the door to him or not.

A distinctly female voice screamed.

Grant

"Gotcha." Grant extracted the final screw and the doorknob started to give way. He had begun disassembling parts of it when the downstairs lights went out. "Oh, great. Perfect timing." He should have asked Stewart who locked up at night so he could tell them he would be down there.

Grant pulled his flashlight from his back pocket, glad he'd gone back to Stewart's house after church to change and grab a few tools. Clicking it on, he got back to work on the doorknob. When he heard footsteps coming down the stairs, he quickly turned the light off and listened. Was it someone just locking up, or was Rod snooping around for some reason? Grant never had been able to figure out why Rod had been standing outside the church building that Sunday night, or who the crying woman had been. Maybe the person coming down the stairs was her. The steps were light, possibly feminine.

Standing, Grant decided to do some sleuthing. There were way too many strange occurrences at this church. At least tonight, he would be able to solve this mystery, as the steps were coming down the hallway right toward him. A tiny light—a keychain flashlight from the looks of it—swung from one side of the hallway to the other. It would shine on him in about three swings.

One…two…

A distinctly female voice screamed when the light found him. The child in Grant found that satisfying, but the man in him heard the real fear in the woman's voice. He was lifting his flashlight to turn it on and see who the person was when she spoke.

"I will use this can of mace on you."

The voice was shaky, and familiar. "Jean?"

Grant heard the sound of papers falling. "G-Grant?"

He'd planned to shine the flashlight on her, but pointed it to himself first. The light hit his face, ruining whatever night vision had kicked in and given him an advantage.

"Grant." He couldn't help but be pleased at how much relief she communicated in that one word. "What are you doing here?"

He swung the light toward her. She still had a can of mace in one hand, pointed toward him. "Hey, you can put that thing away now. I'm not here for you." Though he would have been, if he had known she was staying after church. Should he ask her out tonight? Brenda always said candlelight was romantic. Did flashlight count? From the way Jean still held the can of mace, he decided it must not be. "I'm sorry I scared you. I wasn't sure if you were a good guy or a bad guy." He chuckled. "Come to find out, you aren't a guy at all. What are *you* doing down here?"

She dropped her can of mace into the purse hanging on her left arm, and bent to the ground. "Could you shine your flashlight down here?" she asked. "Mine is small and not terribly useful."

"You should get a bigger one if you're going to be wandering around the church at night. Just don't use it as a weapon if you come across someone until you're sure it's not me."

He could not see if she was smiling. It probably wasn't a good night to ask her out, not after scaring her like that. Now that he thought about it, he should probably wait until after the big weekend, or at least until after his unfortunate trip to see Champagne on Thursday. He was already dreading that.

"Grant? The light?"

"Oh. Sorry."

He tipped his flashlight down and over, finding her hair. It looked silky in the light. He let the beam lower over her shoulders, down to where she knelt on the floor. The papers she gathered...

"Jean." He knelt across from her. "Are those church bulletins?"

She did not look up at him to answer. It would have done no good, since the light was on her and he was in the dark. In more ways than one.

"I gather up the unused bulletins every Sunday night, along with ones people leave in the songbook racks or on pews. Then I turn out the lights and make sure everything is locked up."

"What do you do with the bulletins?"

She went still. "I...throw them away. In the office."

"Let me walk you there, then." He picked up the rest of the fallen bulletins and led the way with his light. "I just realized I never told you why I'm here. I was working on getting the doorknob of the storage room off so I could get into the room. I need to see what all has to be done so we can get those desks out tomorrow."

She said nothing. Grant wished the lights were on so he could see her face. Tension radiated from her, he knew that much. He just didn't know what to do about it. Should he mention the shredder?

They reached the office. "Thanks," she said. She stood in the doorway but made no move to go in.

"I'm sorry I scared you," he said softly. *Were you here the other night, crying? Did you know Rod Carson was standing outside spying? Is that why you carry mace?*

"Don't worry about it." She still did not move forward.

"Do you...is this something you do every Sunday night?"

She turned her head toward him, though he knew she could not see his face, then turned back to stare into the dark room. "Yes."

It had been her. But why? Jean was stoic. He could not imagine what had happened to make her cry like that.

"You can get back to your task now," she said, bulletins in her arms. "I'll flip the lights back on for you on my way out. Just turn them off when you leave."

He knew he was being dismissed, but did not want to go. He wanted to ask questions. Jean stepped into the room and turned on the lamp stationed on the secretary's desk. She glanced toward Rod's office, then at the shredder on the desk, but gave no other hint of what she was thinking.

Grant could barely see her. She stacked the bulletins into one neat pile and laid them on the desk near the lamp.

Then she turned toward him and reached out her hand. He took two steps toward her. Almost took her hand in his.

"I'll take those other bulletins, or you can just toss them in the trash."

He was glad the lamp wasn't strong enough to reveal his embarrassed face. "Okay." He threw his haphazard stash of papers into the trash can next to the desk. She added her own organized stack. With one more glance at Rod's office, she flipped off the lamp.

"I'll walk you out," he said.

"No need."

"I wouldn't feel like much of a man knowing I'd left you to wander in the dark." He smiled. "Even if you do have an intimidating can of mace."

They walked in silence past the storage room and toward the stairs. "Jean?"

"Yes?"

"What do you think about me going to try to get Champagne?"

He kept the flashlight shining in front of them, counting steps as he waited for her to answer. Fourteen steps later, she spoke.

"I don't think it's my place to have an opinion."

Grant chuckled at that. "That doesn't stop most people from forming one anyway. Just ask Gladys."

He wished he could come up with some magic formula that would make her laugh. Or giggle like Florence. *What keeps joy away from you, Jean? Where does your heart hide? I want to find it.*

They started up the stairs. "Well, if you really want to know…"

"I do."

"I felt badly for you when they asked. It doesn't sound like something anyone would want to do. Particularly a man who values his integrity."

He nodded into the darkness. "I appreciate the understanding."

"I won't say I haven't thought of it since the meeting Wednesday, tried to think of another plan. Unfortunately, like Susan and Candy, I can't come up with any other way to help Champagne get out without compromising all we hope to do this weekend. I can only imagine you hate the whole idea and don't want to do it, but it seems necessary."

Grant nodded again. "That's the conclusion I came to as well, but it helps knowing you think so, too."

She stopped at the top of the stairs. "Let me turn on those lights for you."

"Don't bother. I'd probably forget to turn them off and then get in trouble with whoever pays the bills." He swung his flashlight and watched the light dance around the foyer. "I'll pretend I'm Sherlock Holmes and go sleuthing in that room to see what clues I can find."

"Maybe you should save the sleuthing until after the desks are gone." She walked across the foyer to the door. "It will be impossible to maneuver in there while they are still piled three high across the room."

"Point taken. Maybe I'll go clean up my mess of doorknob parts and leave the rest for tomorrow."

He let the light drift near her face, which seemed relieved for some reason. "Goodnight, Grant."

"Goodnight, Jean Louise." She closed the door behind her and he sighed.

Monday Morning, July 28

Rod arrived at church early. He knew Grant wouldn't be the type to let something wait, and he was right. Grant was already kneeling in front of the storage room, fiddling with the door. Parts and pieces of the doorknob lay piled next to the hallway baseboard.

Rod cleared his throat to get Grant's attention. "Why don't you let me handle the desks? I've got a guy coming soon with a truck to pick them up and take them to another school. There's no need for both of us to be here."

Grant pulled the door open. He didn't know when to take a hint, or he deliberately ignored it. "Thanks, but I've been wanting to get in this room for weeks now. I'm curious. Besides, some of those desks might be heavy."

His teeth grinding, Rod followed Grant, but only to the doorframe. Grant had stopped one step inside and just stood there.

"Is something wrong?"

Grant's head shook to the negative. "I just remembered something," he said, still facing inside the room. "Jean mentioned the desks were three high across the room. From the window outside, it's impossible to tell how the desks are stacked. All I could see from there was the top desks of the pile."

He reached out and touched one of the desks. "She'd been in here, before it was all locked away," he said quietly.

"Standing there isn't getting any of these desks moved," Rod reminded him. This job needed to get done. Should have been done years ago. He should have sold the whole lot of them once the talk died down instead of having Florence lock them away.

Grant looked back at him. Rod had no intention of leaving space for whatever questions he wanted to ask. "I've got a lot of things to do today." He forcibly moved Grant aside and reached for the line of desks in front of him. He hefted the top one down and eased it out the door. "Let's get them upstairs and out on the front walkway for when the truck comes."

"Okay."

Rod carried the desk to the stairs, but he stopped and waited for Grant. "Are you coming?"

A desk appeared through the door, Grant behind it. "These things are heavy," he said.

What had he been doing in there? Rod's patience was wearing thin fast. "I'm sure you can keep up." He stood at the bottom of the stairs until Grant caught up, then he led the way up the stairs.

"So..." Grant seemed to have a need to small talk. "I hear the school was a good one when it was around."

"It was." Rod exited the church and walked down the front steps to the edge of the parking lot, setting his desk far enough from the church steps to leave room for the others.

Grant deposited his next to it. "I hear Florence used to teach there."

"She did."

"Was she a good teacher?"

Rod sped his steps. If he trusted Grant in that room alone, he would leave now and be done with this whole thing. "She was flighty. Emotional. Always worried about the kids. Cared more about their feelings than about discipline. You can't run a school that way."

Back at the room, Rod took another desk from the pile. He looked it over, then handed it to Grant, choosing the desk next to it to carry himself.

"Who ran the school?"

Rod waited until they were in front of the church again before he answered. "I did." He turned and hurried inside the church before Grant could ask any more nosey questions.

At the room again, Grant arrived before Rod could get his desk out. "You were the principal?"

"Are you going to work, or just ask questions all morning?" Rod passed Grant and left him behind. He marched up the stairs at the quickest speed his body could handle, and stopped to rest, heaving, after setting the desk down in front of the church. He geared up for another intrusive question, but Grant did not come.

"Hey, Mr. Carson. Is this what I'm supposed to pick up?" Some teenager in a truck pulled up beside the line of desks and yelled out the window. No manners. "Pastor Jack from First

Baptist asked me to bring some stuff to the school from here. Was he talking about these old things?"

Refusing to respond to that remark with actual words, Rod simply nodded. The kid jumped out of the truck and started hauling desks toward it. "Man, these things weigh a ton. What'd they do back then, fill them with lead?"

Rod needed to get downstairs and make sure Grant was not snooping around where he shouldn't. "You go ahead and load these. I'll get more."

"There's more? I'll have to take two trips, man."

"You might have to take three, boy."

The kid laughed as if he had said a joke. Rod turned and hurried toward the church building, stopping just outside when Grant opened the door with his foot and brought another desk out.

"Took you long enough," Rod remarked, careful to keep his voice neutral.

Grant's face was as white as the church steeple. "I found something." He set the desk down and ran two fingers across the top. The words were carved into the wood, in childish print.

"Why would a child write, 'Help me' on a desk? Who were they trying to ask help from?"

Rod covered over the words with his hand. "Probably some jokester kid like the one who brought this truck, trying to get attention." He hefted the desk and started toward the truck.

"Wait. There more on the side, underneath."

"It doesn't matter."

"It does matter." Grant reached out and grabbed the desk. Rod pulled back until his strength ran out. Grant looked at him with suspicion, but when he peered under the desk, he seemed to forget Rod was even there, whispering, "Oh no."

Rod's heart started to thunder. "What does it say?"

"He hurts me." Grant's voice was full of pain. Emotional. Like Florence and the other teachers. Grant picked up the top section to look in the drawer underneath. He pulled out a sheet of scrap paper. What was a paper doing there after all these years? Why hadn't someone cleaned out all the desks and sanded out words carved into them? Rod's eyes narrowed. Grant put a hand to his stomach and then to his mouth. Was he going to throw up?

"What is it? You're getting pretty worked up over some kid's imaginative drawing." Rod snatched the paper from Grant's hands. He looked. Felt the blood drain from his face. He fisted both hands and tore the paper into shreds. "Like I said, some kid's imagination."

"Kids don't imagine things like that." Grant's voice was low as he responded. "They only know things like that if they've seen or experienced them. If you've worked with kids, you know that."

Rod turned his back and tried to catch his breath. "So some kid walked in on his parents and thought it would be funny to shock a teacher. You're getting worked up over nothing."

Grant dared to grab his arm and pull him around. "That paper came from the same desk that said, 'He hurts me.' Was that some kid's imagination, too?"

Yanking away, Rod stood his ground and looked Grant in the eye. "What do you want me to do about it?"

"Don't you care that something terrible must have happened here? If all the facts add up, it looks to me like a child in your school was abused. Don't you want to know who?"

"Frankly, no." Rod kept his voice calm, in control. "Whoever it was, it was years ago. Digging up old problems only makes new problems. Let it go."

"Let it go? How can you say that?"

Enough. Rod stopped at the church door. He turned and found Grant behind him. Standing head to head, he leveled his gaze and let the threat coat his words in black. "Let it go. You don't know what happened here, and you don't want to. All you'll find is more trouble than you can handle, boy." He pulled the door between them, making it clear Grant was not to follow. "I'll bring out the rest of the desks myself. You've helped enough for today."

"I should have stood up fifteen years ago, but I was afraid."

Stewart

Stewart smiled over at the trash can. It served as a good visual for his message tonight, about putting the past behind and becoming a new creature in Christ. "As 2 Corinthians 5:27 says, *Old things have passed away, behold all things have become new.*"

His goal had been to make his point and be finished in ten minutes. He had actually done it, a pleasant surprise. He left the podium and made his way down to pew level, wearing khakis and a polo shirt, purposefully initiating a more casual atmosphere. He hoped to get some ideas, and also to give Grant something else to think about besides his confrontation with Rod and concern about the child Grant was convinced was abused. It was something that needed looking into, but not until after this weekend. Between going to see Champagne tomorrow night and then the bust Friday night, it would do Grant no good to be distracted by a mystery that had been locked away for years. It could wait a few more days.

"I know I'm asking for something new and strange," Stewart announced. "But could you all come over and fill in the first few rows here on the left side? I want us to have a talk."

It was slow going. Brenda came first and he smiled his appreciation. She'd been the one smart enough to suggest that he choose the left side so Gladys would already be in the right spot, as she would likely not only not want to move, but have no qualms about saying so.

Gladys did not move from her place on the fourth row, but her sister, Florence, did. She came to the second row, along with Candy, Jean, and Susan. Grant chose the third row and Rod and Alice joined Gladys at the back. A few others filled in the spaces. Gladys muttered a complaint and Rod nodded.

"Tonight is an important night, at least in my opinion," Stewart began, making sure everyone was settled before he continued. "Since my arrival about a month ago, I've been asking God's wisdom and looking into different ministry possibilities for our church to do. However, over the past week or so, I've been thinking that me choosing a ministry, then letting everyone know and asking them to come on board, isn't the best way for our church right now. Instead, I've decided that, since I believe the pastor shouldn't be the only one doing ministry, the pastor shouldn't be the only one choosing ministry. I want to know what ministries God has given you a heart for, what ideas you have. If we're going to be working together for the kingdom as a church family, then let's consider ministries the church family cares about."

He looked around to gauge the response. Several faces brightened. Others seemed confused. The back row was resistant.

Good enough. "So does anyone have ideas that they've wanted to do over the years, or something you've seen a need for in the community? If you have an idea, please share it. I'll write it down and we as a church can pray over the list of ideas and see which ones God would have us do."

Silence. Stewart told himself not to fidget as he waited.

He was pleased when Grant stood and addressed the group. "I think it would be great to start an after-school basketball outreach. I've heard that drugs are a problem in the community with the teens, and if they had something to do after school, it would not only keep them out of trouble, but be a way for them to interact with believers in a setting they are comfortable with."

"That's not ministry. That's having fun dressed up to look like ministry." Gladys had her fan going already. "I don't see how basketball is going to get anybody saved."

"That's an important point." Stewart admired Grant's ability to look calm, even if he didn't feel it. Gladys and Rod seemed to play on the same team. "If we were only playing basketball, then it wouldn't be ministry. But we would be building relationships, and as the teens get comfortable, they would open up about their lives and we would learn how to invest in them and their families. When they had needs we could pray with them. We could also include special events where the gospel would be given."

Candy had her hand up. "Yes, Candy?" Stewart said, trying not to let his hesitation show. What would she come up with?

"I think we should volunteer at the shelter."

Stewart let out a relieved breath. "Great idea."

"And I'd love to start a strip club ministry."

There could not have been more than twenty-five people in attendance, but the gasp sounded like it came from a hundred. Gladys' fan sped up. Rod clenched the pew in front of him as his face turned red. Brenda put a hand to her mouth and started to bite her thumbnail, but then stopped and put her hand back in her lap.

Stewart geared up his nerve and asked, "Can you explain?"

"Sure." Candy stood up and added gestures to her words. "I think women—not you men—should go into the strip clubs in the city and talk to the girls about Jesus. A lot of them are depressed and lonely and desperate. They're looking for something they'll never find in those places. I know. They need to know that Jesus loves them and they can start over. Trust me, it'd be a big deal to have someone come in and treat them like they matter."

"Absolutely not." Rod stood, his face tight. "We will not have the name of this church dragged into the sewer by associating with that kind of people. Our reputation in this town would be blackened forever. God's name would be sullied."

"Well, that's a lot of big, fancy words." Unruffled, Candy looked around and her eyes went round. "You're just like those—those Pharies—those—"

"Pharisees?" Grant offered.

"Yeah, them! Jesus didn't have a problem being around sinners, and the prostitutes and tax collectors liked being around Jesus. I figure that's because He treated people with love and gave them worth, when they were used to being treated like trash. But the Pharies—whatever they're called, the religious guys—they hated that and said Jesus was being bad."

She flung her arms wide. "That was, like, thousands of years ago and here you're still doing the same thing. Don't you read the Bible? Don't you know what Jesus said? That He came to seek and save the lost. How long have I been in this town?"

Candy waited. Once the group figured out she wasn't asking a hypothetical question, Florence answered, "At least two years."

"And how many of you invited me to your church or told me about Jesus? Or even said hello?"

The silence reigned for long seconds. Stewart watched several women shift uncomfortably. Not one person looked up at Candy any longer.

"I was lost and scared and I hated myself and my life. I needed seeking, like Jesus said. I needed to be saved, but He said seek first, then save, because you've got to get to them first. How can they get saved if they don't know?"

Gladys puffed her words out. "There are churches all over this town. They can come to church anytime, but they don't."

"And I don't blame them," Candy countered, "considering the way you all acted when I first walked in. Would you show up at a church if you knew everybody was going to talk about you behind your back and call you names, and look down on you because you don't have a decent outfit? The only reason I didn't run was because this man said I would be welcome." She pointed a long-nailed finger at Stewart. "I knew there was one person in this place who didn't despise me, who wasn't judging me, and that was enough for me to stay long enough to hear that Jesus didn't despise me either."

Candy held Gladys' gaze until Gladys looked away. Her voice softened as she finished. "I would never have found Jesus if someone hadn't come to me. So I want to go to them. They need to hear they are loved, that they can be forgiven and washed clean, and that their past isn't all they are. I want to tell them that."

Stewart stared in shock as his wife stood to her feet. "I'll—I'll go with you, Candy." She started to bite a fingernail but then clasped her hands together. "I may have to sit out in the car and just pray the first few times, but I'll go."

Since he was standing in front of the first pew, she was near, so he reached out and put a hand on her shoulder and squeezed. He would have to tell her later he had never been so proud to have her as his wife. He squeezed again and she smiled at him.

"I'll go, too." Florence rose and walked to stand beside Candy, whose smile went huge.

Gladys' explosion of sound was not a word, but it adequately expressed her negative feelings. "What on earth are you thinking?"

Florence's eyes filled with tears. "I'm thinking I've sat in the back all my life waiting for someone else to do the right thing. I should have stood up fifteen years ago, but I was afraid. Afraid that I needed to protect the church's reputation. Afraid of how people would talk. Candy has known Jesus less than a month and she's already braving more for God than I have my entire life.

I'm done waiting for someone else to make things change." She grabbed hold of Candy's arm. "I'll go with you, and I'll bring flowers to give to the girls. All girls like to get flowers."

"What a great idea." Candy hugged her.

"And chocolate. We can all eat it while you talk." Florence giggled.

Stewart smiled. "I think it is definitely something worth considering." Rod stood and Stewart's inner smile flattened, though he kept his outer one firmly in place. "Rod, do you have a ministry idea?"

"This is an outrage," Rod announced. "I will not have this done in the name of our church."

"It won't be," Grant put in. "It will be in the name of Jesus."

"I won't have this." Rod picked up his Bible and the suit coat draped over the pew in front of him. "Alice, let's go. We will not remain and listen any longer." He glared at Stewart. "We will be having a deacon's meeting about this."

Alice glanced around, apology on her face, before slipping from the pew to follow her husband.

"Pastor Stewart?"

Stewart closed his eyes a moment, then focused on Candy. "Yes?"

"The Bible says we're supposed to obey God over man, right?"

"It does."

She tilted her head. "Even if those men are the deacons?"

Now he was smiling inwardly while telling his face to stay neutral. "Yes, Candy."

"Well then, how about you write my ideas and Grant's idea on your list, and let's get praying!"

"In the beginning,
there was this
great feeling
of power,
of being
desirable."

Candy decided she liked living outside the town. The stars were so much brighter from here. She left her bedroom to look through the larger living room window, and saw Jean sitting on the couch.

"Couldn't sleep?"

The light from the side table lamp put a glow around Jean's profile as she gazed outside. She shook her head. "Nightmare. How about you?"

Candy shrugged. "I'm not used to sleeping at night yet." She bit her lip, telling herself for the thousandth time to think before she spoke, but Jean did not seem shocked. "Want some hot tea?"

Jean's voice was soft, like the starlight outside. "Sure. Thanks."

As usual, Candy looked through several cupboards before finding the one with the mugs. "One of these days I'm going to remember that you're organized and keep things in the same places," she called out from the kitchen. "Grant should be at Champagne's about right now." She was proud she'd said that entire sentence without a tremor. That was the real reason she'd been unable to sleep. She had been praying.

Candy took the two steaming mugs into the living room and handed one to Jean before snuggling into her favorite spot on the couch. Jean moved her feet to give her room. "Are you worried?" Jean asked.

"Yes, but I know I'm not supposed to be. I think I've written that verse about not being anxious about anything but praying about everything at least twenty times today."

Jean's nod was almost imperceptible and she looked out into the darkness again. She seemed fine with the silence, but Candy was not. It left too much room for her thoughts to get louder.

"Champagne is not much more than a kid, you know." Candy took a sip of her tea. It scalded her tongue so she set the mug down. "I was fifteen when Slash found me. He must have seen I was fresh. And scared. I'd only been on the streets for a couple of weeks. I was sick of the guys finding me in the middle of the night wherever I'd try to sleep. Sometimes I got away from them. Sometimes…" Candy shifted. "Do you want me to go away?"

Jean did not turn her head. "No, I don't mind."

"You're not crying. I hadn't told Brenda half of this the other day and she was dripping all over herself." Candy followed Jean's example and turned to look out into the black night, choosing not to add how much it had meant to her to see Brenda's tears.

"I don't cry in front of people."

Candy nodded. "Before that Sunday when I found Jesus—or He found me—I hadn't cried in ten years." She leaned farther over the back of the couch to see more stars through the window. "Anyway, Slash found me in the park one night. He talked nice to me. Didn't try to touch me at first. Gave me pretty jewelry and said I deserved better. Like the guy in the movie."

Candy felt Jean's gaze on her. "What movie?"

"*Pretty Woman.* You've probably never seen it."

"No."

"Well, I watched it when I was young and stupid. It's about a prostitute and this rich, great-looking guy who comes along, who isn't into prostitutes in general but he hires her for a week, and falls in love with her and they live happily ever after. I thought maybe if I became a prostitute, that might happen for me. I've met other girls who came from bad homes or were abused as kids and saw that movie and thought the same thing. One girl told me she'd been used since she was a kid, and at least as a prostitute she'd get paid for it."

Jean got up from the couch.

"Sure you don't want me to shut up and go away?"

"I'm going to put some honey in my tea. Want some?"

"Yeah." Candy handed over her steaming mug. Jean hadn't answered, so she kept talking while Jean went into the kitchen. "The money's great, you know, but it never lasts. It was always gone. And after the first few months, Slash never let me keep the money anyway."

She climbed up on her knees and leaned over to open the window and hear the crickets. "It's strange. In the beginning, there was this great feeling of power, of being desirable. When you spend your whole life being told you're worthless, that's a really good feeling. But over time, I realized it was all the same. They were using my body because they thought I was worthless, too. I didn't have power after all."

Jean brought the mugs back in and Candy shut the window. "I used to think about that movie a lot. In all the years I sold myself, never once did I see some gorgeous, well-dressed guy who wasn't into prostitutes in general, showing up and taking me to his fancy penthouse and ordering me breakfast, and handing over his credit card so I could buy a whole new wardrobe. No guy ever defended me to other guys who wanted to use me. No guy treated me like I was worthwhile, or wanted to spend hours hanging out with me before he wanted any action—sorry if I'm freaking you out."

Jean sat there like a stone, her gaze outside, nothing moving except her one small hand turning the spoon in her mug in quiet

195

circles. Candy got the feeling Jean wasn't fully with her, that she was talking to herself. Maybe that was a good thing.

"One night in some guy's hotel room, I got him to get the movie on Pay Per View. He was rough, but rich, and I don't know, I guess I thought maybe if he watched it, he'd get inspired." Candy intended to chuckle. It came out bitter and forced. "He just talked about how hot Julia Roberts was compared to me, and then wanted to watch a porn movie together."

Candy saw Jean swallow, hiding her face behind her mug as she took a sip of tea. She brought the mug down. "How does the movie end?"

"That's the kicker." Candy took a sip from her own mug. It was cool enough now. "Because of the hooker, the rich guy finds meaning in his life, she gets to leave the business, and they end all romantic and happy, and you know they'll get married and he won't ever wander off looking for a different prostitute. What a joke. Why do we believe that kind of stuff? I'd wait for the amazing man and I'd end up with greasy, unclean guys who run the prostitute circuit every weekend, who throw up the beer they drink and then want to get all over you smelling like vomit and sweat." She winced when Jean winced. "Sorry. You probably didn't want to know that."

She drank the rest of her tea and sighed. "Of all the weird things, Champagne is getting that tonight. An amazing guy who doesn't want a girl just for what he can get from her, who is good and will treat her like a real person. He may not be super rich, but he's got more good stuff inside him than anyone I've ever met, which is way more important in real life. I wonder what she's going to do with that."

This time Candy did not bother asking if she'd said too much. Jean's stricken face made Candy want to ask just how much she cared about the pastor's brother. Instead, Candy stood and faked a yawn. "I think I'll go to bed now." She picked up her mug. "You know something weird? I'm not worried for Grant tonight, but I am worried for Champagne. And for me, too. Something feels strange about going to Jamaica's tomorrow. Maybe because I like it here so much. I thought about not going. But I can't have 'do not fear' verses on thirty-two post-it notes all over the house and then go and be a coward because of a bad feeling, right? So instead of being anxious, I'll just keep handing it over to God and asking Him to handle it."

She walked to the bedroom but stopped in the doorway to look back. "You should get some sleep if you can," Candy said. "Tomorrow is an important day."

Jean nodded. Candy closed the door while Jean remained on the couch, her profile facing the darkness.

Thursday Night, July 31

Champagne

Champagne took stock of the expansive lobby and the hallway leading to the outdoor pool. This was far nicer than the hotels she was usually called to, dingy little places in seedy areas, dirty rooms clouded with smoke and littered with beer cans. Maybe the guy was an upgrade, too. Might as well hope.

She sauntered across the lobby, chewing her gum to the rhythm of her swinging hips, making sure every man in the vicinity noticed when she passed by. What she wouldn't give to have guys like these as clients, the kind who could afford an extra gift or two on the side. Slash kept all the money; she needed gifts she could hide, then sell. Or keep if they were nice enough.

Room eighty-five was near the end of the hallway, left side. Champagne ran through her risk factors before knocking on the door. Creeps were everywhere, even in nice hotels. She took a chance wearing her bright orange scarf and stiletto heels. Scarves could be used to choke a girl. Heels, on the feet, would keep a getaway slow. Off the feet, they could be used as a weapon against her. Oh well, the chance at getting a higher-paying regular was worth the risk.

She knocked on the door and waited. The guy must not be impatient; she sang "Happy Birthday" in her head twice before she heard the distinct click of the hotel door. Candy had taught her long ago to have something to repeat in her head when she needed a place for her mind to go. Her birthday party had been the last happy memory she had before Slash got her.

Where was Candy now? Did she get away?

The door brushed against the carpet as it opened and Champagne openly stared. "Oh, wow, this is my lucky night," she said, not bothering to hide her admiration. Guys loved flattery. For once, she wouldn't have to fake it. "Look at the muscles on you." She walked into the room as if it were her own, another trick she learned from Candy. Fake confidence even when you don't feel it. She pulled off her scarf, letting it drift down her body onto the floor. "Where do you want me?"

The bulk of a man cleared his throat. A nervous one. Must have a wife and kids back home. He picked up her scarf and set it on the bed. Not much surprised her, but he did when he sat on the edge of the bed and directed her to sit in the chair near a small writing desk. "I'd like to talk."

"Sure, gorgeous, whatever you want. Just remember, I get picked up in an hour." She crossed her legs and let her heels fall from her feet. "Wouldn't want you to waste your time."

He cleared his throat again and Champagne swung her leg, hiding her confusion with a glance around the room. "Your closet door is open."

"My name is Grant. I've come to talk with you about getting free from all of this."

Her laugh was high-pitched. Oh, brother, not a guilty one, pretending he only wanted to help her escape. She'd rather have a plain-out bad guy than a hypocrite. "My name's Champagne. Light, bubbly, and unforgettable." She slipped from her chair and took two slow steps to stand in front of him, her best feature level with his eyes. "And I don't think you're here to talk at all."

He put his hands on her waist and she felt a sense of satisfaction that she'd won so quickly. When the hands gently set her back so he could stand, she placed her hands on his shoulders and let them slide down his hard chest as he rose.

"Champagne, I really am here to talk." After he stood, he removed her hands and walked to the other side of the room near the window. "Candy sent me."

"Did the closet door move?" Champagne's gaze shot around the room. Had Slash sent this man to test her? "What is going on here?"

"You can come out," the man who called himself Grant said. Another man, who looked slightly similar but with glasses and a smaller build came out of the closet, followed by a woman with short curly hair who was holding his hand.

"What is this? What kind of game are you playing?" Champagne backed away.

"It's okay, Champagne," the woman said. "We're here to help you."

"Help me? What a rip."

"Please sit down and let us explain." The big guy, Grant, seemed happy to let the woman take over the conversation. He stayed by the window and the guy with glasses went to stand by him, while the woman took his original place on the bed near where Champagne stood, feet planted apart, shoeless, ready to run if need be.

"I'm sure you're confused, so I'll say this as concisely as I can," the woman said. "Candy is very concerned about you. She wants to get you out of this life and to someplace safe. We know you were brought into this against your will and want you to have the chance for freedom."

A line of sweat ran down Champagne's back. How could they know so much? "Why didn't Candy come herself?"

"It wasn't safe," the big guy said.

Champagne looked from the one man to the other. "Wait, I remember you." She pointed at the man with glasses. "Aren't you the preacher guy who invited us to church?"

He smiled and nodded.

"No way. I got called to a hotel room by a preacher man? Wouldn't the newspapers love to get a hold of this."

"Champagne, please, we don't have much time." The woman rose and stood in front of her. "Come with us. We have a safe place for you, where you can start all over again. We want you to be free, to know that you are loved."

She snorted, not bothering to try to act attractive anymore. "Nobody in the whole world loves me."

"Jesus does. He wants—"

"Look, don't preach at me, okay? I get it that Candy was worried and wanted me out. That was nice of her. Tell her it was a good try." She picked up her scarf and focused on it, fingering the soft material. "But there is no life for me outside of this. Not anymore."

The tall man, Grant, whispered something to the preacher. He came over and took the woman's hand and both of them walked to the door. The woman took one look back. "Please come with us, Champagne. I'm afraid for you if you don't."

Champagne shuddered. She didn't like thinking about any of this. It was easier to go numb, do what she had to do, survive. Grant came to stand in front of her, and she wasn't comfortable with how his eyes burned into hers. She usually got in and out without the man ever looking into her eyes at all. "Champagne, come with us. Please."

Was this guy for real? She paused and her hand reached to touch the developing scar on the back of her neck.

"Tomorrow." She shuddered again and wished her scarf was thicker. She was cold. "Come back here, same room, same time, tomorrow night. I'll come then."

"Come with us now."

"No." She backed away. "I need to get my stuff. Will you come tomorrow?"

Grant peered over her head to the preacher man behind her. His eyebrows went up in question, then he dropped his gaze to her and nodded. "Tomorrow."

They left and Champagne felt guilt knife through her. She sang "Happy Birthday" in her mind until the feeling eased, then pulled out her cell phone and punched in numbers for a newspaper reporter she'd entertained once or twice.

"Hello?"

"It's Champagne. I've got a huge tip for you, if you're willing to pay."

Jamaica was
unable to
answer.
She was
already
crying.

Jamaica

Candy wandered around the apartment above the coffee shop as if the place was her own. "You have great pictures on the wall. Did you grow up in Jamaica?"

Jamaica wiped a line of moisture from her upper lip. "No, but my mother did. Her family brought her here when she was a teenager."

"She must have missed it. I bet that's why she named you Jamaica."

"Yes." Jamaica picked up a few random items she'd left on the small side room bed, smoothing out the sheet. "I don't have a bedspread for this bed, but there are some blankets in the closet if you need them." She tried to keep her voice even, free from the anxiety that had kept her up most of the previous night. *God, are You there? I need help.*

"You know, Slash would have loved your name. I can see him listing it on the internet: Jamaica—your private paradise. Fortunately, you don't need a man to provide for you or give you a name. I admire your independence. You get to be your own private paradise." Candy's smile was sincere and friendly, and it cut right through Jamaica.

"I'm not as free as it looks."

Candy sighed. "Who is?" Then she brightened. "But I am now. I thought I'd go to my death feeling worthless and alone, owned by others but never belonging to anybody. Not even myself. Then I found Jesus. Oh, Jamaica, the difference is like night and day, literally. I used to live in the darkness, always hiding, always afraid. Now it's like there's light all around and inside me. I'm not scared anymore. And I'm not alone. Do you know Jesus? Has He changed your life?"

Jamaica wanted to cry. "I used to, long ago."

"What happened?"

Jamaica hid her face by opening the closet and rummaging for a blanket. "My life fell apart. I got divorced. Lost my house. I moved away with my daughter looking for a new start. Decided I didn't need anybody. Not even God."

Candy's voice was full of understanding. "Bet that isn't working out so well, is it?"

There was no need to answer. How had her life come to this? Smiling during the day, pretending to be fine, crying alone at night.

"You said you had a daughter. Is this her?"

Jamaica turned. Candy stood in front of a framed photo of her with the person she loved most in the world. The person she would do anything for. Even betray a friend.

"Her name is Pansy. She turns sixteen this month."

"Where is she?"

"I don't—I don't know." Why not tell her the truth? "She ran away a year ago, back when we lived in Atlanta. I tried to find her. From the postcards I used to get every few weeks, I traced her to this area. That's why I moved here. I think—I think she does what—what you used to do."

Candy's voice stayed even, but Jamaica saw her clench her teeth. "At that age, you can almost guarantee she's under a pimp's control." She turned and her eyes were filled with sorrow. "I'm sorry to tell you that. Do you have a computer? Have you looked for her on the internet? I know the sites used around here. Maybe I can help."

Jamaica felt the tears flood her eyes. "Candy, you shouldn't help me. I don't deserve it."

"Nobody does." Candy went wandering around until she found Jamaica's computer. Without asking, she turned it on. "That's why God's grace is so awesome. None of us deserve it, and He gives it to us anyway."

Jamaica backed away the moment Candy pulled up a site offering young prostitutes at the click of a button, like ordering a pizza. "I—I need to go make a phone call."

"Okay." Candy did not look up from the screen. "You probably don't want to see this stuff anyway. But before you go, I need to know your daughter's full name, any nicknames she had as a kid, her height, weight, and bust size."

Twenty minutes later, face washed to remove all traces of tears, Jamaica found Candy still sitting at the computer, completely absorbed. "Find anything...useful?"

Candy's head turned slowly. Her eyes lifted to Jamaica's, and what was in them had Jamaica at her side in an instant. "You found something. What did you find?"

"I've got four girls I want you to look at. Slash has connections in Charlotte and Edison, the town across from it. That's why we're all working together tonight to shut down as many of them as possible. It's killing me to not be part of it. I'd stand out there in the middle of the road if it would get Slash in the path of the sheriff."

She clicked the first window and it brought up a face. Jamaica shook her head no, her hand against her heart, trying to contain its wild beating.

"We girls get posted on four different main sites, including Craigslist and Backpage. Girls like your daughter, or Champagne, don't know much about this side of things; they just go where they're told when they're told. I was with Slash for so many years, after awhile he trusted me to do the computer work the nights he wanted to get high. Sometimes when there was no work, I'd snoop around the sites just to see who else was stuck like me." She clicked the second window. Jamaica looked closer, then shook her head again.

The third window popped up and Jamaica was unable to answer. She was already crying. Candy clicked to make the photo larger. She looked up at the photo on the wall. "That's your girl, isn't it?"

"My—my baby."

Candy read aloud. "'Hot Chocolate. Warm and smooth. Marshmallows not included.' Slash is such a jerk."

"You found my baby. I've been here for months and couldn't find any more clues. Where is she?"

"The sites never give locations. Slash and his guys don't want people like you finding their girls. But, if she's in this area—oh, I've got an idea!" Candy jumped up and shocked Jamaica by giving her a hug. She lifted her face and started talking to the ceiling. "God, You know this woman needs Your help. I think You sent me to her tonight. Of all nights. You're amazing. I'm going to go call Ian, but it's getting late already and I know they've got all their men assigned. We need a couple of them to get unassigned so they can go find her daughter. Could You do that please, for Jamaica and...Pansy? They both need to know that You love them."

Candy picked up Jamaica's hands and bounced up and down. "I am so excited. Do you have a phone? I've got to call Jean, then Ian, then...well, whoever!"

She rushed away, laughing, down the stairs looking for a phone. Jamaica sat in front of the computer and stared at her daughter's face, tears running unnoticed down her cheeks.

Grant

"I do not want to be here. This whole thing has a bad taste to it."

Five till eleven. Grant listened for a knock on the hotel room door while he stood at the window and forced himself not to pace. Stewart sat in the room's one chair and Brenda sat on the bed. "It's a big night." Stewart's words cut through the tension-filled air. "Why don't we pray for all the different men and women who will be fighting evil these next few hours?"

Grant heard the roar of motorcycle motors from the road below them. They'd driven in under Oakview's *Annual Biker Weekend* banner that afternoon, a swarm of black leather, loud mufflers, and reflective metal on wheels. Dozens of motorcycles had filled the downtown streets all evening, a party currently migrating across the road in front of the hotel. Grant knew his beat-up Chachie, parked near the hotel, fit in the mass of Harleys as well as a rookie joining a seasoned football team. He glanced out at the bikers cruising Main Street, wondering how many of them were Ian's deputies and volunteers in disguise, before letting the curtain drop and joining Stewart and Brenda.

Stewart prayed, "Lord, we need your help tonight. I—"

The sharp rap on the door caused Brenda to smile. "Well, that statement summed it up anyway." She walked to the door and opened it. "Hello, Champagne. We're ready if you are, but we were just praying about tonight when you knocked. Would you like to pray with us?"

"No." Champagne remained rooted to her spot outside the door. "Can we just go?"

"Certainly." Brenda waved Stewart and Grant toward her. "Let's go guys."

Grant closed the hotel door and pocketed the key. He looked over Champagne with a wary eye. She was dressed more provocatively than she'd been the night before, her shorts shorter, her top more revealing. "Where are your things?" he asked.

"What things?"

He frowned. "You said you had to get your things. That's why you couldn't come with us last night."

"Oh, right." Champagne looked behind her and then glanced at her watch. Grant took a look at his. Two minutes till eleven. "I left my bags in the lobby. There was no sense carrying them to the room and back. They were heavy."

They reached the empty lobby. Champagne stopped several feet from the door and addressed Brenda. "Could you go get the car and come pick us up? I don't feel safe walking out there tonight."

"I'll go with you, Brenda," Stewart offered.

"No." Champagne held up a hand. "Could you men wait here with me? If Slash got wind of the idea that I might run, he might have somebody waiting. I'd feel so much better with both of you here. Nobody would try to attack me if I had two men with me." She looked at Brenda. "You don't mind, do you?"

"Um, okay." Brenda sent a look toward Stewart, but went ahead and left the hotel.

Grant approached the hotel desk. No one was in sight, so he found the box for keys and deposited his there. Outside, Brenda walked across the street toward the parked car, weaving through motorcyclists. Stewart stood at the window watching her. Grant wondered if Stewart was guessing which of the men outside were with Ian, as he was.

"Grant, could you and the preacher help me?" Champagne stood near the hotel's window front, one suitcase and one large, filled trash bag at her feet. She did a fairly effective imitation of a helpless girl, shrugging and smiling. "These bags are so heavy."

Stewart, always helpful, headed toward Champagne right away. Grant held back. There was something in her face he didn't trust. "I got the suitcase, Grant," his brother said. "Can you get the bag?"

Grant saw Brenda pull up to the curb outside. He walked to where Champagne stood and hefted the bag over his shoulder. "Brenda's here. Let's go."

Champagne led the way. At the car, she bent down to look into the open passenger window. Grant turned his eyes away. "Could you pop the trunk for me?" Champagne asked Brenda.

The trunk lid released and Stewart opened it wide. He lifted the suitcase to put it in when Champagne placed a sharp-nailed hand on the trunk lid and slammed it shut. "Wait a second." Her face had gone hard, though the smile was still in place. She wiggled her way between where Grant stood next to Stewart behind the car. Reaching up, she placed both hands on Stewart's upper body and kissed his cheek. "Thanks for all your help."

Grant looked at his brother, so stunned he had not moved. Not even when the flash of a light had Grant searching for its source. Another flash. He squinted. There. Around the corner of the hotel. A man leaned out into view, a camera raised to his eye. Another flash.

"What—who—"

Grant looked down to see Champagne smiling toward the camera. Too late, he realized she had a possessive hand on each of them. Stewart backed away, but not in time. "Who is he, Champagne?" The demand came from Grant. Stewart was already in the car.

Giving up on Stewart, she focused her attention on him. Facing him, her hands coming toward him, he had a hard time walking backwards quickly enough to evade her touch. The camera continued to flash. He grabbed her by the wrists. "Who is he?"

"A guy who works at the town newspaper," Champagne purred. Seeing the anger in his eyes, she shrugged. "Look, I'm sorry, but there's no way I could escape, and I need the money. You should have known better than to trust me."

Grant let go of her before he did something he'd regret. "He should have named you Vodka." He looked over to see the newspaper man lower his camera, his eyes wide on Grant. He turned and ran. Grant channeled all of his anger and stress into energy as he took off at a run after him. Grant was faster and stronger, but the other guy had preparation on his side. He dashed into a waiting vehicle and the driver sped away. Grant did not slow his stride as he u-turned and sprinted back to where he'd parked his motorcycle. He kept his eyes trained on the man's car until he pulled onto the road, where he maneuvered between bikers and tourists. Quick, short glances had the newspaper man back in his sights. Grant was gaining on him.

His cell phone vibrated in his pocket. Grant ignored it and pressed harder on the gas. It was probably Stewart.

Frustration bordering on rage kept him focused until the third call. Jerking the phone from his jacket pocket, he opened it and yelled, "What?"

The voice was impossible to hear through the wind. Grant caught jumbled portions of words. He slowed enough to hear. "What?" he asked again.

The sheriff's normally staid voice was frantic. "He's early! Get over here now!"

*Slash knew how
to turn anything
—noises, sights,
memories—
into a weapon.*

"You had to know I would find you."

Candy stood behind Jamaica's coffee counter, her fingers still curled around the phone receiver. As if she had reached for a mug, filled it with terror, and drank it in one long gulp, fear flooded her body and left her weak.

Do not fear. She ordered her legs not to run. It would do no good. *God has not given us the spirit of fear, but of power...of love...of a sound mind.* If only she hadn't already hung up the phone. With deceptively casual motions, she chose two large coffee mugs and filled one with coffee, sliding it toward Slash. The second mug she carried to the far side of the counter and filled with whipped cream. "I never did like coffee," she stated, her words echoing unnecessary sound around the empty room.

She searched drawers until she found a pile of plastic spoons. Choosing one, she dipped it in her mug for a generous blob of whipped cream. What didn't make it into her mouth rested above her lips, a moustache made of clouds.

Fear not, for I am with you. Be not dismayed, for I am your God. I will strengthen you. I will help you...

"I feel sorry for you, Slash." He had taught her the art of pretending confidence. She might as well utilize the skill now. "Such a big, fun weekend event out there, and here you stand in a closed coffee shop. How boring for you."

Slash took firm steps toward the counter. Candy gripped her mug with both hands, but refused to back away. He picked up his mug of coffee, held it just past the counter, and dropped it. The sound of ceramic breaking on the tile floor was sharp, painful. Slash knew how to turn anything—noises, sights, memories—into a weapon.

"That was Jamaica's mug." Candy inserted an authority into her words she was far from feeling. "You should pay her to replace it."

"She'll get paid," he said, stepping around the broken shards and spilled coffee.

"I see you still can't bear to get your shoes dirty," she remarked. It was taking all the self-control she could excavate from shivering muscles to keep standing still as he continued to approach. She curved up one corner of her mouth, ate one more spoonful of whipped cream, then held her own mug out in front of her. "Since you have all my money, you can pay for mine, too." She let it fall.

"Candy, what are you doing down there?" Jamaica's voice preceded the sound of footsteps coming down the stairs. "Are you trying to break down the whole place? I thought you were calling..." Her teasing smile died fast when her eyes found Slash. "Oh no."

The man stopped at the broken mug shards, layered with whipped cream, that made a small fortress in front of Candy's feet. "You knew I would come tonight."

"You're early." Jamaica had stopped at the bottom step. Her hands clenched the railing.

Candy's confidence dissolved completely. "Oh, Jamaica." It was too much to bear. She took her eyes from her betrayer and watched Slash bend and sort through the broken mug pieces, stretching out his movements to inspire the most fear.

Candy had no verse for this. "God, I need Your help," she prayed aloud, earning an irritated glance from Slash as he stood. She knew he expected her to be quivering. Pleading for mercy from him. "Jesus, I know You are more powerful than this man. I need You to rescue me from him."

The more her volume increased, the more Slash's frustration revealed itself. He never could bear not being the most powerful presence in the room. "Stop that," he ordered, standing and holding a large broken shard in front of him.

For the first time, Candy saw Slash as he really was. "You have no power over me anymore," she said. The hand holding the shard wavered. "You can slice that across my skin. Kill me if you need to. But you will not control me any longer. I belong to Jesus and I will never belong to you again."

It was a new experience, seeing the flicker of fear that crossed Slash's face. He did not know what to do with a woman who wasn't cowered at his feet, terrified. Candy forgot Jamaica was there. She stepped over her broken mug and the whipped cream sliding into the rivets between floor tiles. She moved forward until she stood face to face with the man who once owned her body and her soul. The broken shard in his hand filled the small gap between them. Candy ignored it. She looked into Slash's eyes and whispered, "I am free."

Maybe an army of angels appeared behind her. Or maybe Slash just couldn't handle a woman on her feet. He dropped the shard. It hit the floor and crashed into smaller pieces. He stared at her as if he'd never seen her before. In a way, he never had.

Several motorcycles passed the coffee shop. Candy heard one motor curve around the building and cut off behind it. The sharp change in sound jerked Slash out of whatever spell he had been under. He grabbed her by the throat, hate shooting sparks from his eyes, and shoved her back against the counter. She tripped over her broken mug and felt the edges cut into her bare feet.

Jamaica disappeared to the back, screaming, the moment Slash's hands circled Candy's neck. He did not even acknowledge the screams, his every muscle intent on strangling her.

Candy saw the movement before Slash did. By the time realization dawned in his eyes, a gun barrel pressed against his temple.

"Let her go."

"Oh, Sheriff Craig." Jamaica appeared again and leaned against the counter. "Thank God you made it in time."

Candy fought the black spots invading her eyesight, the weakness that wanted to pull her into unconsciousness. She heard Sheriff Craig warn, "I *will* shoot you." Slash's hands eased and she dropped to her knees, gasping for breath.

A banging on glass had Jamaica running for the front door. Hand at her throat, Candy leaned around the counter to see Jamaica turn the lock and Grant Henderson bolt into the room. A biker ran in behind him. Was he with the sheriff, or with Slash?

Weak to the point of uselessness, Candy slid to sit with her back against the counter. "Be careful," she rasped toward Ian. "He always has a weapon hidden."

Slash cried out with animal rage. He ducked Ian's gun and slammed his shoulder into Ian's mid-section. A shot rang out. Glass shattered and the room filled with a shout of pain. Jamaica screamed. She dove behind the counter and crawled toward Candy on her hands and knees, soon bloodied from the scattered mug shards.

Ian and Slash were on the ground in a pile of indiscernible punches and kicks. Candy saw no blood on either of them. Who had been shot? Ian drew his knee up and used it with his hands to shove Slash off him. Slash landed on his back near Candy. She would have given anything to have had a frying pan in her hand to slam against his face. He reached out and she and Jamaica backed away. His hand landed on the broken pieces of ceramic. He tightened his fingers around a piece. It cut into his hand but he did not let go, pulling it up and holding it toward Ian like a knife as he stood. Ian stood. His eyes shifted from something to his left, then back to Slash.

"Grant, you okay?"

"You shot him." The answering voice was not Grant's. "He was running right towards you when your gun went off."

Late Friday Night, August 1

Jamaica

Lord, help! Jamaica had to follow when Candy grabbed the counter edge and pulled herself up. Slash swung his weapon toward Ian, who jumped to the side and dodged it. Candy walked on rubbery legs around the counter and past two overturned tables. Grant lay in the walkway. The man who had followed him in was pulling up the left side of Grant's shirt where a large round blood stain formed.

"I think the bullet went through," Grant said through his teeth.

"Go help the sheriff," Candy ordered the other man. Slash still swung the mug shard, but had switched it to his left hand,

and was pulling his knife from behind him with his right. "Ian's a dead man if you don't do something now. Where's his gun?"

The man, clad in black leather from his jacket to his boots, started tossing chairs and shoving aside tables in search of the gun. Candy ran to the counter and grabbed a hot pad. She rushed back to Grant, knelt, and pressed it to his side where it looked like the most blood gushed out. He winced but kept his eyes on the fight. One of his large hands covered hers on the pad. "Thanks." He held it to his side while she removed her hand and helped him stand. He swayed a little and his face paled. "I've got to get that knife."

Jamaica turned. Slash thrust the knife and Ian barely dodged it. Ian backed away, grabbing items from the counter and throwing them at Slash, who moved steadily forward, arms swinging in a wide arc. Ian backed right past Jamaica and Slash came after him. Jamaica crouched low against the counter. The knife swished over her head and she felt the movement of air on her hair. He could have stabbed her with little effort, but his focus was entirely on Ian.

God, it's been a long time since we really talked, but I'm needing some courage and some help here. And I need it quick!

Slash was only a few feet past her. Jamaica jumped up from her crouch and ran to the opposite side of the counter. She grabbed her heaviest coffee pot and ran back. Using the forward momentum, she lifted the coffee pot high and swung with all her might. It hit with a loud *thunk* against Slash's skull, the impact not enough to knock him out, but enough to knock him sideways. He had passed the end of the counter or it would have broken his fall. Instead, it was broken by Grant crashing into him. They both ended up on the floor, Grant groaning in pain and Slash moaning under his weight.

Ian ran to stomp his right boot on Slash's arm until he released the knife, while Grant extracted the shard from his other hand. Candy rushed to pick up the discarded hot pad and put it to Grant's side again. "You should have been a linebacker, not a quarterback," she said.

"Hey, I got the gun!" The man in black stood and waved the gun proudly. When he saw the heaped humanity on the floor, he ran forward to give the gun to Ian. "What now, Sheriff?"

"Here." Ian held out a pair of handcuffs. "Cuff him and let's get him locked up fast so we can get Grant to the hospital."

"I don't need a hospital," Grant said, his words slurring into each other.

"Yeah, which is why you're still lying on top of my criminal and dripping blood everywhere." Ian pushed a button on the radio attached to his shoulder and started talking into it. In less than three minutes, a squad car pulled up, lights flashing, in front of the shop. That's when Jamaica noticed her front door was gone. The frame was still there, but the glass had shattered.

The policeman walked right in through the frame, his shoes crunching on the broken glass all over the floor. "Nice welcome mat," he joked.

Jamaica and Candy helped Grant up. Ian and the man in leather dragged a cuffed Slash toward the car.

"I guess that's where the phrase about dragging somebody kicking and screaming came from," Candy commented. Slash was doing both, effectively enough that the policeman ran outside to help Ian prod him into the backseat of the car. Under the loud, belligerent yelling from Slash, Jamaica could hear Ian telling him he had the right to remain silent.

"I wish he'd use it," she said.

Jamaica looked up at Grant. "Don't you pass out on me," she told him sternly. He looked unnaturally white, even for a white guy. She let out a relieved, "Thank the Lord" when an ambulance wail came from around the corner and the red and white vehicle appeared seconds later. EMTs sprinted toward the shop. The first one opened the door, then stopped and stared at the empty frame. The others ran past him into the room. Jamaica's concern for Grant kept her from laughing when the EMT closed the door behind them, as if it mattered.

"It's going to take some serious bleach to get those blood stains out of the grout between your floor tiles. Sorry." Grant was still losing blood as the EMTs surrounded him and immediately put pressure on his side.

"Don't you even think about it, young man." Jamaica followed the EMTs as they helped Grant toward the ambulance. "I'll get Candy to clean it up." She winked at him before they put him on a stretcher and lifted it into the back.

"Thank you." Candy stood behind the ambulance as they shut the doors. Her voice was a croak and her hand still circled her throat where Slash had tried to kill her.

Jamaica wanted to put her head on one of her tables and bawl. The police car and ambulance sped away, and the man in black, apparently just a biker who had seen the commotion and come in to help, rode off on his motorcycle. She and Candy were left alone. Jamaica followed Candy back inside, careful to avoid the glass on the floor. "This is some mess." She inspected the cuts on her hands and knees. "And what was with you breaking my coffee mugs? Those were two of my favorites."

"I'll help you clean to pay for them." Candy looked at Jamaica. "You didn't betray me."

Jamaica's eyes nearly overflowed. "I was going to. I was so desperate to find my little girl, and felt I had no other choice. I'm so sorry." She opened the storage closet near the counter to grab a broom and start sweeping. "Then you came over and offered me grace, and I couldn't go through with it. I called the sheriff while you were on the computer. He and Grant planned to be hiding in here, ready when Slash came at midnight."

"But he came early." Candy wrapped Jamaica and her broom into a hug. "God rescued us both tonight." She pulled back and Jamaica saw her eyes flash. She pulled the broom from Jamaica's hands. "We can clean tomorrow. Right now we need to get over to Brenda's house. The night has just begun!"

*Something
must have
gone terribly
wrong.*

Jean

Jean felt her heart tighten, her insides coil, and all breath leave her when Candy called. Candy had not softened the news at all, talking the moment Jean said hello.

"Grant's been shot. They took him to the hospital. Ian and some other guy got Slash and Ian's taking him to jail. Jamaica and I are on our way to your house. We've got a lot of work to do."

Jean had not been able to respond. She mutely handed the phone to Brenda and listened with everything in her as Brenda asked questions and got more details. *Will he die? Ask them if he will die.*

Nothing would come out of her mouth and she was not sure what was coming out of her heart. All she knew was that she had to get to the hospital. Now.

Brenda had arrived less than an hour ago. She told Jean what happened at the hotel with Champagne and how Grant had gone chasing after the man with the camera. He and Ian were supposed to be at Jamaica's at midnight to arrest Slash. It was nearing one a.m. Something must have gone terribly wrong.

"Jean, are you listening?"

Jean moved her mouth and it finally produced words. "Will he be okay?"

"It sounds like it wasn't a serious wound, but I know Stewart will want to go to the hospital right away. I'd like to go with him. Can you manage covering the internet sites while I'm gone? Candy and Jamaica should be here soon to help."

No. I have to go, too. I need to see if he's okay.

"Yes, I can manage. Go ahead."

Brenda hugged her. "Thanks. I'll try to find out as much as I can and bring back word."

Jean nodded, mute once again. Brenda left the room to find Stewart while Jean told herself not to cry. Crying was a waste of energy. Didn't she know that by now?

The sound of their departing car faded. Jean returned to Stewart's study, dark thoughts tormenting her in the silence. She had to get a hold of herself. *Get busy, Jean. Do something. Get your mind off it. Off him.*

She sat at the desk and picked up the phone. Ian had men who had gone undercover into the drug trade weeks ago to learn more about the chain of command. They had set up most of the exchanges planned for the night, staggering the scheduled purchases to avoid suspicion. Several of the meetings had already taken place and four drug pushers had been arrested. For the rest of the night, Jean's job was to monitor text messages and e-mails about places to meet and information about the contacts, then once a final schedule was arranged, to relay the information to Ian so he could get it to the people set up in that particular area for the night.

Jean checked her phone, then Brenda's phone, then the e-mail account Ian had set up especially for this case. Two texts and one e-mail later, there was nothing else to do. She checked the clock. Seven minutes had passed since Stewart and Brenda left.

Grant, be okay. I need you to be okay.

Jean prayed. She looked at her hands and considered biting her nails like Brenda used to, wondering if it would help. No, she was trying to break fearful habits, not start new ones. *Keep busy.*

Think about something else. She clicked on a new page on the internet and went to her own e-mail account. She would reply to her mother's message about coming for a visit; that would fill up a few minutes. Jean was thankful her mother had not asked to come that weekend. At least she was not out posing as a prostitute, like Susan and one female officer were, providing bait to lure in men who ordered underage girls online.

Jean typed a message telling her mother a visit next week would be fine. She wrote about Candy, to some extent. Her mother would need to be prepared for the Bible verses hanging all over the house. Jean had to smile as she explained that Candy decided to write the verses on papers and nail the papers to the walls because she didn't want to mess up the walls by writing directly on them.

She started to write about Grant but stopped herself. Jean had never mentioned a man in her e-mails, ever, and knew the moment she did her mother would jump on the possibilities like a kitten with a new ball of yarn. Jean had no answers for the questions her mother would ask, so she sent the e-mail as it was.

No new texts. No new e-mails. Jean battled fear until she heard the sound of a car pulling into the driveway. Was Brenda back with news? Was Grant's injury slight enough that he could come back with them?

Jean pushed away from the desk and rushed to the window to look out the front. Of course it wasn't them. They probably had not even arrived at the hospital yet.

She opened the door to welcome Candy and Jamaica, Candy already talking about how earlier that evening Jamaica was going to hand her over to Slash, but God stopped her and then stopped Slash and now she had this wonderful idea that was going to keep them up the rest of the night.

"I hope you weren't planning on sleeping," Candy said, leaving no room for Jean to respond before continuing. "We are all going to be very busy for the next several hours." She looked around. "Where's the computer in this house?"

Jamaica entered behind Candy. She looked at Jean's face and Jean wondered if her heart was on display there, for Jamaica's eyes filled with understanding and she pulled Jean into a hug. "He's going to be okay," she whispered.

Jean nodded. She could have produced words at this point, but did not trust her voice to say them without revealing a depth of feeling she was not prepared to admit existed.

"I found the computer," Candy yelled from the study. "Let's get to work!"

Jamaica followed Jean to Stewart's study. Candy was at the desk, pulling up sites that made Jean turn away. Such young faces. Painted up and touted as older, put into suggestive poses near bold words promising things Jean did not want to read.

Candy was obviously less affected by the sites than she or Jamaica. "North Carolina passed this great law not too long ago, that any girl under eighteen is a victim, no matter what she says. Before that, a lot of times the girls would get arrested, and they'd be treated like criminals, even if they were just kids who'd been forced into it. I remember when the law changed, because Slash made me go through all the sites and change the age of all the younger girls. I had to list them all as eighteen years old, but put code phrases in the rest of the profile that let buyers know they were actually younger."

Jean put a hand to her mouth, fighting nausea. The study suddenly felt too dark. The whole house was too dark. She walked to the door and flipped on the light switch to the study and to the hallway outside it.

"Slash never guessed telling me those code phrases would end up in me helping get girls out." She laughed with joy. "This is going to be the best night of my life!"

226

The desk chair swiveled around. "Hey, this chair turns circles." Candy did a few rotations, happy as a child, before jumping up and grabbing Jamaica's arm with one hand and Jean's arm with the other. "I called Ian earlier and we got it all planned out. Arresting the drug pushers and johns and traffickers is great, but what about all the kids already trafficked? Charlotte is the worst city in North Carolina for human trafficking, you know."

"I only know my baby's out there somewhere," Jamaica said. "And I'll do anything to get her back."

"You have a child?" Jean didn't try to hide her surprise. Jamaica told her about Pansy while Candy made a phone call. When she hung up the phone, Candy's fingers flew on the computer keyboard. She grabbed the mouse, moved it, and clicked it with a gesture of determination. "It's all set! We're going to have guys ordering different girls, ones I know are below the age limit, to hotels all over the city, where Ian's guys will be waiting to take them into custody, and from there, to a safe house where they can get help." She danced around the desk chair, using it as a partner. "Want to know the best part?"

"Y-yes."

Candy looked at Jean. "You don't sound all that sure."

"I'm not."

Her eyes gleamed. "Well, you will be when I tell you." She maneuvered Jean across the office to the desk chair. "Sit," she ordered. Once Jean sat facing the computer screen, she clicked and pulled up a string of e-mail messages. "Scroll down to the third one from the bottom and read it."

Jean obeyed and read aloud. "Great to know you've got what I'm looking for. I've decided to trust you. What I really need is a whole batch of girls, as young as you've got. One of the guys in our group is turning twenty-one this weekend, so we're all celebrating. If you can supply up to twenty girls, let me know and we can talk prices and where to meet. I'd like you to bring them in person."

"Isn't this exciting?" Candy leaned over Jean's shoulder and scrolled upward. "The guy said he could bring twenty. That's twenty girls we'll rescue tonight, and get the guy who is selling them, too. I told Ian I have to be there. He'll need somebody those girls can trust. They've been taught to fear and avoid policemen, never to believe anything they say. Naturally, nobody has told them about the new law."

"Don't you need to stay somewhere safe?" Jean looked back at Candy and Jamaica and noticed the bandages on Jamaica's hands. What all had happened at the coffee shop at midnight?

"No way am I hiding out at this point." She chuckled and nudged Jamaica. "Not to mention Jamaica's place is wide open to the public right now anyway. Slash is in jail, and I think God did that whole thing so I could get out there and help rescue girls. Speaking of, what time is it?"

Jean checked the clock on the computer screen. "Almost one."

"I'd better get going. It's all going down in an hour. After Slash showing up early tonight, I'm not taking any chances. Jamaica, can I take your car?"

"Sure, but why don't I go with you?"

"Thanks, but you'll want to stay here with Jean. Your daughter is scheduled to meet a guy at a hotel in Charlotte soon. I told Ian to call Jean when they got her. Jean can tell him to bring her here. It would be good for her to see you as soon as possible. She'll probably be pretty scared."

Jamaica started crying. Jean put an arm around her.

"Jean, can you walk with me to the door?"

Jean patted Jamaica's shoulder, then followed Candy without question. At the door, Candy turned and said quietly, "I thought about asking if Jamaica could be at the hotel, but I decided it would be better for her to wait here, in case the girl is...needs some cleaning up, or some counseling or a doctor's visit first. You know what I mean?"

"Not fully," Jean admitted, trying to keep her imagination from filling in the blanks. "But enough."

Candy nodded. She put a hand on Jean's arm. "I'm glad you're here with her. You're a calming influence on everybody. It helps." She opened the door and on her way down the porch steps said, "I may be calling you later to come help me deal with twenty freaked-out girls. Be ready!"

The car drove off and Jean leaned her head against the closed door. Be ready? How? How could she be a calming influence on others when she couldn't even calm herself?

"God, help us all this night," she whispered against the door. "Susan, Ian, Candy, Jamaica, and all the men and women part of this important work. And God, please help Grant." Her voice dropped to barely audible. "And me."

*"I'd rather
not get shot
again."*

Grant

"This is pointless. I should be out there right now." Grant's jaw clenched, partly from the pain, mostly from the frustration. "I want to go and help. I can recover tomorrow."

Stewart stood with his hands on the back of the chair where Brenda sat. "It won't do anybody any good if that wound starts bleeding again and you drop unconscious somewhere."

"I won't. They bandaged it up so tight I can hardly breathe."

"What about the pain?"

A nurse entered the room and used two fingers to check Grant's pulse. "We gave him some powerful painkillers. They should be taking effect soon." Stewart's cell phone rang and the nurse frowned. "You aren't supposed to have cell phones in here."

With an apology, Stewart said, "It's Ian," and left the room. Grant shared the situation with the nurse, who promised to discuss it with the ER doctor. The doctor came into the room and Stewart entered behind him, a frown on his face.

"What is it?" Grant asked. He sat up, making sure the pain did not show. He had to get back in the game. No, back in the fight—this was no game.

"There's a problem. I'm supposed to go pick up two girls on a street in Edison, and the others are meeting Candy at the hotel in thirty minutes. Ian needs one more man. Pansy, Jamaica's daughter, was called in to meet a guy about ten minutes ago. She came, but when he explained who he was, she panicked and ran.

He chased her to a construction site where she darted into some little shed they'd left unlocked. She's got the door barred somehow and won't let him in. He can't wait her out because he has another girl coming soon, but he doesn't want to kick the door down since she's already scared and would probably run again." Stewart paused to turn toward the doctor. "He said if it's at all possible, he needs Grant to come right away, if nothing else to just sit and wait and make sure she doesn't leave before Ian and more guys can come deal with the situation."

The doctor looked over several papers on a clipboard. Brenda stood and approached the side of the bed. "Would you promise to come back to the hospital tomorrow?"

Grant attempted a grin. "Tomorrow would be Sunday, since it's Saturday already."

"Don't be a teenager. Later today then."

"Yes. As soon as this is over, I'll come back here."

The doctor signed a paper and handed his clipboard to the nurse. "I'm letting you go, but strongly recommend you keep that promise and come back here as soon as you are no longer needed. You lost a lot of blood and that bullet damaged an area several inches deep through your left side. You shouldn't be running around any more than absolutely necessary. Literally speaking, you shouldn't be running at all until this wound heals."

Grant swung his legs off the bed and sat up. He had to grip the handrail until the room stopped spinning.

"Try not to make sudden moves like that if you can," the nurse warned, a little too late in Grant's opinion. "Those painkillers are pretty potent and you might find yourself a little dizzy or sleepy or feeling kind of out of it. You are definitely not allowed to do any driving."

"Then how am I supposed to get there to help this girl?"

Stewart went to his right side to help him stand. "Ian called Candy first when Pansy ran. Candy's already called Jean and she's waiting for you at our house. She'll drive you there."

Grant felt his head spinning. Was that the pain meds? "Why Jean?"

"I don't know. But I'm glad somebody's taking you. You're swaying like a drunk man. Will this medicine knock him out?"

The nurse took off her latex gloves and washed her hands. "Different people are affected differently by medication, but he's a big guy. I would expect any side effects to wear off within an hour or so."

Grant felt his brother at his side, holding some of his weight. They moved toward the door. "Don't forget Brenda."

Stewart smiled. "I haven't forgotten her. She's right behind us."

He heard Brenda's voice from behind. "We'll be praying for all of you. Great things have already happened tonight, and more are to come."

"I hope you're not referring to me getting shot, because I'd rather not get shot again."

Stewart looked sideways at him. "You're starting to sound a little drunk, too."

Grant chuckled. "How many drunk guys have you been around, Stewart? You've probably never even seen a drunk guy except in movies."

"You're way off," Stewart said, helping Grant into the car. "I've seen them on regular TV, too."

Grant wanted to laugh but his whole body felt too heavy. He tried to remember why he felt so strange. Some part of him recognized the pain was gone, a major relief. He looked across the front seat of the car at his big brother. There was something he wanted to tell him. What was it?

"I always felt like I never measured up to you." Grant wasn't sure if he had gotten the words out until Stewart glanced over at him with surprise all over his face.

"What?"

Grant shook his head. "You were the smart one. You learned Greek. You liked studying. The favorite son who would go into the ministry like Dad. I could never measure up. Made me feel..." He held up a finger and thumb about an inch apart. "...this big."

They rode in silence for what seemed a long time, but Grant was not sure. Stewart finally spoke. "I had no idea. I felt like I couldn't measure up to you. The guy so great at sports. So great at making friends. A natural leader. I wanted to be more like you."

"Really?"

"Really."

Grant rubbed his head with a heavy hand. "Seems we were both kind of mixed up."

"Yeah..." Stewart pulled into the driveway. "So what should we do now?"

"Go rescue girls."

"I mean about you and me needing to appreciate and utilize our differences rather than being put off by them."

"Um." Grant opened the car door and told his body to get out. He was not quite sure, but it felt like he was moving very slowly. "How about...we appreciate and utilize our differences rather than being put off by them?"

Stewart laughed out loud. "Good idea."

Brenda came around the car and held his arm on his bad side while Stewart supported his good side. "I'm not so sure about this," she said. "I think this medicine is hitting you harder than they expected. I think we should reconsider having you go anywhere."

"I would agree with you," Grant said. He raised his eyes and saw Jean standing in the open doorway, the light behind her making her kind of glow. Or was that the medicine, too? "But there's nobody else. Hopefully it will wear off in a...while."

Brenda glanced toward the house. They were still far enough away that Jean would not be able to hear them, but she still whispered. "You'll take care of Jean, won't you? She's not trained for any of this."

Grant nodded. "Of course I'll take care of her. I love her. I don't want anything bad to happen to her."

His brother grinned at him. "Tomorrow I'm going to tell you what you just said."

"What'd I say?" Grant tripped. Now even his legs weren't working right.

"We'll talk about it tomorrow." Stewart stopped. "You know what? Let's take you straight to Jean's car and skip going inside." He called to Jean and she was soon beside Brenda, asking questions, looking at Grant like a worried wife. Maybe. He'd never had a wife, so he wouldn't actually know.

"Hiya, Jean," he said. "Jean Louise. Pretty Jean Louise." Stewart opened the passenger side door of the car and Grant sat. Jean slipped into the driver's side and started the car. "You're wearing blue jeans." He rested his head back on the headrest, but to the side so he could watch her. "They look good, but don't be Blue Jean tonight. Be Jean Louise."

She stared at him as if he was talking crazy. Was he? "They gave me pills. I feel really weird."

"Oh."

Stewart had gone to her side and was talking to her through the open window. Grant let his body sink into the seat. It was comfortable. He should rest on the drive there. Maybe that would help. Yes, a little rest would help his body not feel so heavy. He would just...

"I don't
like
closed
places."

He was asleep. Jean had no idea what she was supposed to do. Twice on the drive he had woken up. The first time, he just looked at her and smiled. The second, he told her he had heard her crying in the church one Sunday night, and he didn't want her to be sad anymore. Her heart had stopped. She had wanted to pull over and find out what he knew, but a quick glance told her he had already fallen back asleep.

Her thoughts flooded with questions until she forced herself to focus. The city roadways in Charlotte were confusing and it would not do for her to get lost because she was worrying about herself instead of Pansy. She followed the directions Ian had given, and though a few street signs were difficult to find in the dark, she finally ended up at a large construction site between two finished buildings. She pulled off the road onto a patch of packed dirt that looked like it might become a parking lot. Nearing the partially completed building, she saw the small shed, not much bigger than a phone booth, next to a port-a-potty. Thank goodness Pansy had not chosen to hide there.

Jean turned the car so the headlights did not hit the shed, and left them on until the man who emerged from behind the shed showed his badge. He approached the car and she looked over at Grant one more time before lowering her window a crack. "I'm Jean."

"I'm glad you're here," the man said. "I'm Davis. Ian's got me assigned back at the hotel in ten minutes, so I have to go right away. My car is down the street." He motioned toward the shed. "She's in there. I've asked questions, but she won't answer. In the hotel as soon as I said I was a policeman and was here to take her away, she ran like I was some kind of murderer. I hope you can help."

"I'll try."

The man nodded. He shone his flashlight into the car and onto Grant, slumped against the door and sleeping soundly. Jean watched his mouth open, as if he wanted to ask a question, but then he shrugged. "I've got to go. You're okay here?"

She didn't feel okay, but she nodded. Brenda had said the nurse expected Grant's meds to wear off by the time they ended the drive. She nudged him. He did not even twitch.

"Lord," she prayed, turning off the car and locking it after she got out. "I wasn't wanting to do this alone. I thought I'd be able to lean on someone big and strong and not scared. But he's sleeping." She took careful steps toward the shed, using the small amount of light from a street lamp thirty or forty yards away. "I don't want to do this. I don't want to be here." She took in a deep breath. Just a few more steps. Why hadn't she thought to bring her can of mace? "This girl needs help, and though I can think of several people who would do a much better job at this, I'm the one who's here. So I need Your help, please. I can't do this without You."

She stood at the door to the shed, took one more deep breath, then spoke. "Pansy? Are you in there?" She rapped a slight knock on the door. "Pansy?"

"How do you know my name?"

The voice was young and frightened. Jean's heart clenched. "My name is Jean. I'm a friend of your mother's."

"I don't believe you."

"Her name is Jamaica. She lives in Oakview now. She came there looking for you. She's been searching for you ever since you ran away."

Jean heard movement inside. When Pansy spoke again, her voice was closer. "I didn't run away. He tricked me. I mean—Wait. No. I did run away. I didn't want to be at home anymore. I want to be where I am."

"Pansy, I'm here to help."

"No." The voice became panicked. "Go away! I want to be here. I want to do what I do. I like it. It's my choice."

"Pansy, would you let me come in and sit with you for awhile? It's creepy out here."

"It's creepier in here."

Jean gulped. "Probably. But at least I would not be by myself."

"Are you alone?"

She looked back at the car. No sign of life. She felt much more alone than she wanted to be. "Yes."

Jean heard shuffling inside, then the creak of the door. Pansy opened it just enough for her to squeeze in, and Jean barely got a glimpse of the girl's face before she shut the door and pulled something heavy up against it.

"You're alone, aren't you?" Jean looked around but could see nothing. She feared moving. Sheds were full of tools and sometimes tools were sharp or jagged or other kinds of dangerous. She hadn't gone inside the shed at her own home in months, not since a large mouse or small rat had run across her foot early in the summer.

Something brushed Jean's arm and she jerked away. Pansy made a sound like a whispered laugh. "You seem more scared than I am."

"I might be," Jean admitted. "I don't like closed places."

"For real?" Pansy sounded skeptical until she touched Jean's arm and Jean felt herself react again. "I thought you cops were all cool with whatever."

"I'm not a cop. I'm just a friend of your mom's who cares about you."

"Then the cops must be all around us, waiting for me to come out."

Jean shivered, though she was not cold. "I wish they were. They're all busy getting other girls right now. And my supposed-to-be partner in this is conked out in the car because of all the pain medicine they gave him at the hospital after he got shot."

"He got shot? What's he doing here?"

Some kind of web, soft and scary, drifted onto Jean's hair. She flapped her hands around her to get it off, telling Pansy the entire story to fight the panic rising in her.

"I was supposed to just do text messages and e-mails, and now I'm here in a tiny dark box and I'm trying not to be scared out of my mind because you're more important than anything I'm afraid of, and I shouldn't be afraid anyway because God is with me. So I'm going against everything in my head, because doing right is not about how I feel but about what I choose."

"Wow, cool speech."

"Thanks. Listen, I'm not trying to pressure you, but could we please talk just outside the shed, or even with the door open to let a little light in?"

"You really don't like it in here, do you?"

"I really, really don't like it."

"I do. It feels safe. Like I could hide forever and none of those awful guys would ever find me. You promise there's nobody out there waiting to grab me?"

"I promise. I'm here to take you to your mom, if you want."

"Not to jail?"

"No."

"Not back to the terrible guy with the scar around his neck?"

"Slash is in prison. That's how the guy in my car got shot. They were at your mom's place."

"You said my mom runs a coffee shop?"

Jean had to smile. "Yes, and she keeps us all up on the latest news of everybody in town."

"Okay, now I believe you know my mom. I'll go with you."

It was hard not to verbally sigh in relief the moment the shed door opened. Jean deliberately slowed her steps to match Pansy's hesitant ones toward the car. Jean opened the car door and Pansy stepped back when she saw Grant.

"He's big. Hey, this isn't some sick-o plan and he bribed you to get me into his car, is it?"

Forcing a lightness into her voice, Jean answered, "No. Go ahead and poke him. He's out."

Pansy reached across and, with a flash of movement, jabbed Grant's arm, then backed several feet away from the car. Grant did not move. Jean waited as Pansy waited.

"Okay," she finally said. "I believe you. I think." She climbed into the back of the car. "Can you tell me more about my mom? Is she mad at me?"

Jean answered questions and kept talking as they drove from Charlotte back into Oakview. They were almost to the house when Grant woke up. Pansy shrieked and dived down behind his seat. Jean jerked the steering wheel in reaction and had to right the car before she drove them into a ditch. "It's okay," she said, keeping her voice calm despite the adrenaline shooting through her. What had this girl been forced to endure?

The car pulled into the driveway. Jean saw Jamaica rise from a rocking chair on the lit porch.

"Pansy, look. Your mom is here."

Pansy's small head poked up to look out the window. She screamed again, but this time it held emotions other than fear.

She flung the door open and left it there as she ran into her mother's arms. They clung to each other, laughing and weeping at the same time.

Grant looked over at Jean in sleepy confusion. "What happened?"

Jean smiled at the man, his hair all tousled and his eyes droopy. "You slept through the whole thing."

Early Saturday Morning, August 2

Candy

"It's ten minutes till two. Does everybody remember what to do?"

Heads around the table nodded. Candy had to say that asking real bikers to join their group was a stroke of genius. Most of the undercover bikers didn't have beards, or the right jackets, and the bandanas they wrapped around their heads looked ridiculous. They would only look the part to people who didn't know much about bikers, or were drunk.

One of the new recruits held up his beer bottle and saluted Candy. She looked him over. "I'm not sure you're sober enough to be useful," she said. The cops looked at each other, uncertain at her bluntness. They'd done that at least three times already. The bikers didn't flinch. Some of them guffawed and one slapped the beer bottle guy on the back. "What's the plan?" She pointed to him. "Run it by me."

"Okay, Candy." He set his bottle down and sent her a rakish once-over. "I like you. You're a tough one, like hard candy. I like hard candy. Say, I think I remember you. From last year. Weren't you—wait—were you—?"

"I was, but I'm not anymore. Jesus totally changed my life and now I'm free from all that. Tonight I'm helping other girls get free, too."

"I always figured girls like that wanted to be there. They act all happy like they're having fun. I mean, some of them are begging you to take them to your room."

Candy nodded. She held out her hand and the man looked at it for a moment before placing his bottle into it. Candy talked as she walked to the trash can in the hotel's conference room and poured the last bit of it out. "Sure they do. They know there's a pimp waiting for them later, and if they don't meet their quota, they're going to pay for it."

"You mean, have to give him their money?"

"No." Candy put the empty bottle back in front of the man. "He already gets the money. They'll pay with a beating, or a threat against the girl's family, or maybe a sister getting taken and forced into prostitution, too."

"So you're saying prostitutes don't really want to be prostitutes?"

Candy noticed the cops were listening with as much interest as all the bikers. "Some do. Others think they do until they get in and find out how degrading it really is. But a lot of girls, a lot more than you'd ever guess, are forced into it. They hate it. They hate you for using them and not ever really seeing them."

She felt a surge of energy run through her body as she stood and leaned her hands on the table, looking each man in the eye, including the cops. "Listen to me, all of you. I've been reading the Bible, and I think God made every man to be a protector, to be strong, to fight for something that matters. Here's your chance. Stop paying for a quick rush with a girl that never lasts and just leaves you with a guilt hangover worse than—" She picked up the empty bottle and shook it. "—you'll have tomorrow from all that beer."

The men laughed, but quickly focused again when she continued. "I know you're lonely. I know getting a girl to come spend time with you fills that up for a little while. But we all know it only makes you feel worse later on. Like drugs."

"Yeah." A man with a tattoo of a naked woman on his arm nodded. "You're right."

"So listen up. God made you for more than this. You have the chance to change everything. When you go into a town, call for a girl, order one online. Pick the youngest one you can find. But when she comes, ask her about herself. Ask her if she's doing this against her will. Think about what you'd do if that girl were your daughter, and someone had kidnapped her and forced her into all of this."

"I'd smash the guy who did it."

"He'd be too good for smashing. I'd kill him, after I tortured him."

Candy waved her hands until she had their attention again. "Better than that, you can call the human trafficking hotline and get that girl rescued. You guys have cell phones, right?" They nodded. "Punch in this number: 1-888-373-7888. You can call anonymously. These people have access to law enforcement all over the country. They know how to help." She leaned forward over the table to get closer to them. "Guys like you are rescuing girls all over the country. You can be part of it. Take that passion that you feel and use it to rescue girls instead of use them. I promise you it will feel better."

"Better than sex?"

"Better than that kind of sex." She crossed her arms. "I hope you can't ever look at a prostitute or stripper again without wondering whose daughter she is and if she's desperate to get home."

"Come on," the drunk man whined. "You're ruining it for me."

"Good." Candy pointed at the clock hung high on the wall. "It's two minutes till two. Anybody have any questions?" She faced the drunk man again. "You still haven't run the plan by me."

"Right." He took a swig from the bottle, forgetting it was empty. "We wait in here and act excited when the girls come. The pimp is bringing them all to this conference room supposedly so we can choose which one we want and take them back to our rooms. So a couple of the cops are going to take the pimp out to pay him, but they'll pay him with handcuffs and a free ride to the clinker." Candy laughed with the men. "And then we help the girls call their families or go free or whatever you're going to do with them."

"Great." Candy looked around the room. "Everybody got it?" At their nods, she looked at the clock one more time. "He'll be here any minute now. Let's pray before this happens. It's a great plan, but we need God's help." She ignored the surprised glances and shrugs and started praying out loud. When she lifted her head a minute later, she saw one man wipe his eyes. Another kept his head bowed.

"Any last questions?"

The man with the bottle stood. "I have a question."

"Okay."

"When this is over, will you come back with us to tell us and the rest of the guys what happened to you? You aren't at all like I remember from last year."

A guy in the back said, "Yeah, last year she was all over you. Maybe she sobered up and realized you were ugly!"

Candy joined the laughter, but then leaned toward the man, looking him in the eye. "You're not ugly, and you're worth more than one-night stands with strangers you have to pay for. I'm worth more than a line of men who don't even know my real name, and don't care. And these girls coming in are worth more than whatever price is being asked."

One of the policemen, who had been watching through a crack in the door, said quietly, "They're coming in the front door. Arrival in one minute."

That rush of energy was back. She looked over the group. "Help me rescue these girls, then I will come with you and talk to anybody you can get to listen. I have some really good news for you all." She headed for the conference room bathroom to hide until the pimp was gone. At the door, she looked back. "By the way, I think you all are fantastic. Now prove me right."

*She told
herself
she had
no choice.*

Champagne

These were the jobs Champagne hated most. Two of the girls clung to her, and more would if she had extra arms. She dreaded what was coming. Slash had disappeared somewhere. He hadn't told anyone where he was going, so when the call came for twenty girls, one of his cronies, a guy they called Whip, who did Slash's dirty work in Charlotte and the town across the way, called her to be in charge of the girls. Some party of bikers, in Oakview for the weekend, had ordered a whole group. They wanted them young, which made Champagne's stomach churn. She'd been one of the young ones once, scared and ashamed.

At eighteen, she was years ahead of all the other girls. She had worked her makeup and clothes to make herself appear younger, but Champagne knew her eyes were ages older. Maybe that was part of the appeal of the younger girls; they were not yet the walking dead.

"Make sure every girl gets her money, and is back here in the lobby by four."

Champagne sighed. "I know."

"Get them to stop whining." Whip headed for the first floor conference room, his massive shoulders shifting side to side as he walked. Champagne had never seen him with his fists unclenched.

For a moment, she wished she had gone with the preacher man and his brother. A pang of regret seared through her at what would be in the papers later that morning. She reached down and pinched the flesh of her right thigh until the pain pushed the thoughts away. "Listen up," she announced. The group of girls huddling in the small space where the lobby became a hallway looked at her with such horror in their eyes. She hardened herself against any emotional response to their fear. "You will walk into that conference room and you will smile. You will flirt. You will seduce these men out of as much money as they have. Any special requests, you charge extra. You will do anything and everything they ask you to do, and you will pretend to like it. They bought you for two hours. Make sure they're happy they did."

She frowned as several of the youngest girls started crying. "Don't cry. It will mess up your makeup." What an awful way to experience their first night. Then again, what way was good? "No matter what they say or request, you must be back in this lobby in two hours. If you are late, it will cost you." Whip was at the door of the room now, talking with someone inside. She lowered her voice. "And whatever you do, do not try to escape. Whip has no mercy. Please..." Her voice caught at the memory of her own first night. The girls stared at her with wide, frightened eyes. "Just don't, okay?"

Whip walked back toward them, two men with him, and the group of girls maneuvered behind Champagne. As if she could protect them. "They're ready for you."

Champagne gave a slight nod. Whip led the men outside to discuss payment. He had informed Champagne that the tourists offered double the going rate. It was her job to make sure they had a good enough time to want to repeat the offer. She was to oversee the men choosing the girls, then she would target one of the two men who paid. She had a small packet of heroin in her purse. If possible, she was to get whichever man she chose high, keep him happy, and if possible convince him to hire the group again the following night before they all left town after the weekend.

She knew it was useless to resist being put in charge, but the desire to refuse felt overwhelming. She wanted to sing "Happy Birthday" in her head and shut her mind off to what was happening. The last thing she desired was being fully focused on what she was doing, to herself and others. Whip led the men out the front door. He looked back and saw her hesitation. His eyebrows lowered over his eyes and Champagne felt the threat in that one look. "Let's go," she told the girls. "Get it over with."

None of them moved. Clenching her jaw, curling her hands into fists at her sides, like Whip's still were, she compelled her body forward. One step at a time, she counted to keep her mind dwelling on her feet instead of rushing away from what was waiting in that room. The girls followed, but not one moved forward enough to walk by her side. Champagne looked sideways to a mirror hung on the far wall of the lobby. It was clear, painfully so, that she was leading these girls to that room. She was the one in front.

She told herself she had no choice. When the memory of the preacher's offer of escape resurfaced, she pinched herself again, this time on her left thigh so she would not make a bruise, or damage the property, as Slash would say.

A man with a long beard and a bottle of beer in his hand held the door open and welcomed them into the conference room. Champagne assessed the situation as the girls silently filed into the room. From left to right, she surveyed. A long table, big enough for at least fifteen people, stretched to fill most of the room. On the left wall was a door with a restroom sign on it. At the left side of the table, several men in biker jackets played poker. Next to them, two men were drinking and joking. In the middle, a portable CD player perched on a wheeled cart played, "I've got friends in low places," and several men were singing along. Nearly every man in the room looked drunk. If the girls were smart, they would work to get picked by the most drunk among them. If they were lucky, the guy would pass out before anything happened, and he wouldn't remember either way once he woke up. He'd pretend whatever he wanted to pretend to his buddies, and the girl would get to own her body for two full hours, maybe even get some sleep.

The men whistled and cheered at their entrance. "Dance for us!" one said. She sent a warning glance at the line of girls and saw the trembling smiles and their young, inexperienced attempts at provocative poses.

A man looked over the group and focused on Champagne. "Do we get to pick yet?"

"Not yet." Champagne motioned the girls out of reach. "Wait until the men come back so I know they paid."

"We're here." The two men entered the room. One crossed over to stand near the bathroom door. The other closed the door to the conference room and locked it. Champagne felt her senses go on alert.

"Is it done?" the man who had originally welcomed them in asked. He lifted his bottle and Champagne noticed it was empty.

"It's done." The man looked over the girls. She must look her part of being in charge, for he, too, focused his gaze on her. "The man who brought you tonight has just been arrested."

The girls began to cluster together in panic, fearing arrest even more than the unknown expectations of the men in the room. Champagne held a hand up to silence their cries and faced the man. "Who are you? What do you want?"

"We want to help," the man said. "I'm a policeman."

"You're not here to help us!" one girl wailed. "You're here to take us to prison!"

"Sit down, please." Men all over the room stood to free up chairs for the girls to sit. Champagne remained standing, her hand reaching into her pocket for her cell phone. She had to call Slash somehow without them realizing it. She inched toward the bathroom door while the man spoke to the girls. "North Carolina law states that if you are under eighteen, we recognize you are a victim. You will not be prosecuted as a criminal. We will take you to the police station, but only to get your information and help you either contact your family, or find a safe place to stay."

"You want to help us go home?"

"He really does." An older biker stepped in and put a hand on the man's shoulder. He pointed out several men around the room. "These guys are all cops, and they asked us if we'd help them get you here so they could arrest your pimp and get you girls out. We're all here because we want to help."

Someone had turned the music off. All the beer bottles were now on the table. No man looked drunk now, except the one passed out and snoring loudly, his head face down on the table. Champagne was close to the bathroom door. If she could get inside without raising suspicion, she could call Slash. Wherever he was, he would answer a call from her. She never called unless it was an emergency.

A man punched his large fist into his palm. "Nobody should make you little girls do this. You should be home watching cartoons or playing with dolls."

"I'm too old for dolls," one girl said.

"Well, you're too young for this," the man countered. The girl started to cry and he walked over to give her shoulder an awkward pat.

"What are you doing?"

Champagne froze. The man near the door to the bathroom blocked her way. Even if this whole thing was legit, she was eighteen, and carried heroin in her purse. The law wouldn't help her. She had rejected her offer of escape when it came and now would be headed for prison. She had to get in that bathroom to flush the drugs and make a phone call.

"I—I need to use the bathroom."

"It's occupied."

Champagne reached around for the handle. "I doubt it."

The knob turned and Champagne stepped back, gasping when the door opened and Candy stood in front of her.

"Hello, Champagne," she said softly. "I was hoping I wouldn't see you tonight."

Saturday Morning, August 2

Grant

Grant rubbed his head and tried to regroup his short-term memories. Stewart had brought him, Jamaica, and Pansy all to the hospital after they'd eaten a two a.m. snack and he had convinced Jean to get some sleep. His brother had organized getting Pansy to a doctor and Grant back to his nurse from late the night before, then sat at Grant's bedside for at least ten minutes. Grant was not sure how much longer he stayed. The nurse gave him another dose of those painkillers and he was out.

When his eyelids opened, light was shining in through the hospital room window. He had that heavy feeling again, but it was much less than…than something. Not much from the night before came to mind. He had gone in a car with Jean somewhere, but he couldn't remember where.

"Good morning."

Grant shifted to see it was Jean, rather than Stewart, now sitting beside his bed. "Hey," he said, hearing the word echo in his head. "I feel weird."

"You said that last night." She smiled but looked withdrawn. He must have triggered one of the trip-wires that seemed to be rigged up all around her. What else had he said last night?

In a flash, he had a memory of Stewart leaning over his bed earlier that morning. "I can't wait to find out what you told Jean last night," he had said, grinning like his team had won the Super Bowl. "When Brenda and I dragged you to her car, you told us you loved her."

His face flushed with heat. Surely he hadn't actually said that. Had to be a dream. Grant hadn't fully decided how he felt about Jean just yet.

He needed to get off these pain pills as soon as possible.

Jean stood and came close, her face covered in concern. "Are you okay?" She put a hand to his forehead. "You're clammy. What does that mean?"

He shrugged. "I don't know. I've never been hooked up to this many tubes and machines in my life. I feel like a video game console." His brow furrowed. "But you have. Jean, you shouldn't be here. I don't want you to catch something and get sick again."

His hand was hovering beside him. He had intended for it to go toward Jean's hand, but it missed. He rested his head back against the pillow, dizzy. She grasped the lost hand and wrapped her fingers around his. It felt better than the pain meds. "Would you stop already about that?" He heard the exasperation in her sigh. "I'm not going to get sick."

"You're mad. Are you mad?" Man, he hated the way his brain felt like mush. Why was he in the hospital anyway? He tried to sit up and pain shooting across his side reminded him. "I got shot."

"Yes." Jean pulled her chair next to the bed and sat while still holding his hand over the handrail.

"Um, is that a 'yes' that you're mad or a 'yes' that I got shot?"

"Yes, you got shot, and you should be resting."

"This stuff they gave me makes me feel all fuzzy. I don't like it. I can't remember anything about last night. Did I say or do something I shouldn't?"

She squeezed his hand and her sigh this time seemed relieved. "No, you didn't say something you shouldn't, and on the contrary, you did something very good. You helped rescue Candy from Slash at Jamaica's."

He was getting snatches of memories back. Pictures. Words. "Ian shot me."

"Not on purpose."

"And then they needed me to help Jamaica's daughter because she was hiding in a port-a-potty."

"In the shed near the port-a-potty."

"Did I help her?" She was biting her lips closed and he wondered if something bad had happened. "You came with me, didn't you? Did she run away? Did someone get hurt?"

"Yes, no, and no."

"Start over; that was too fast." He shifted and moaned. His muscles felt like jello. He decided he'd rather deal with the pain than this mental marshland. "I'm feeling slow. And heavy. And stupid."

She rubbed a finger across his hand and the gesture was comforting. "It's okay. It's just the medicine and it will wear off after awhile. I'll start over."

She told him about going to get Pansy, about standing with her inside the dark shed, about Pansy coming out and then Jean driving her to Stewart's house where Jamaica was waiting.

"Where was I?" he wanted to know.

"In the car." Jean bit her lip again. This time he was sure she was trying to bite away a smile. "Pansy screamed when you woke up."

"Woke up? I was sleeping?" He sat up, ignoring the pain. "You went out there into a dangerous situation and I was sleeping in the car? What kind of jerk would do something like that?"

"The kind of jerk on pain meds that knocked him out." The smile burst through. "Only you're not a jerk."

"I don't believe this. I missed half the night."

"For a good reason. I really think the whole thing was of God. Pansy would never have gotten in the car if you'd been awake and with it. She even poked you to make sure you were asleep before she would trust me and get in."

"I can't believe I slept through everything. What if some guy had been hiding out, waiting for you?" His frown deepened. "I only agreed to have you come with me because I was sure I could protect you."

"That's not your job, Grant." Her answer was soft. "I'll admit, I was scared. Then I had to remember that safety is of the Lord." She smiled wider. "I figured if God wanted you to get involved, He could wake you up in time."

"Jean," he whispered, lowering himself back against the mattress. "I'm glad God kept you safe."

She stopped rubbing his hand. Her grip tightened. "I'm glad God kept *you* safe. When we heard you were shot, I was so afraid that—that—"

Finally. The edge of the heaviness was wearing off. Grant focused all his mental energy on Jean. "Afraid that what?"

The nurse knocked and entered the room. Jean pulled her hand away from his, stood, and was over by the window before he could process that she'd moved. His hand missing her touch was his only concrete thought.

While the nurse checked seemingly random parts of his body, Jean headed toward the door. He braved transparency and told her he wished she would stay.

"I'm sorry." She really did look sorry. "I can't watch her change your bandages. I'm terribly squeamish." She picked up a purse Grant hadn't noticed was hanging on the doorknob. "I'll go get some breakfast at the cafeteria, and call to see how Pansy and Jamaica are doing." She paused. "Something you should know before I go. Pansy was released from the hospital, but she has an STD they'll need to treat. And…she's pregnant."

Another knock intercepted whatever Grant would have said. Stewart's head poked in. "You're awake. Good. We need to talk."

"Well, hello to you, too," Grant said. "What happened to your usual morning cheerfulness?"

"It lasted until I got this morning's paper." Stewart nodded at Jean, then tossed a copy of the *Oakview Journal* on Grant's lap. He flipped it to see the front page. Jean looked over Stewart's shoulder and gasped. Even the nurse's eyes widened at the photo front and center, spread over half the page.

Champagne stood up on tiptoe, her lips pursed to kiss Stewart's cheek, one hand over on Grant's chest. Both Grant and Stewart were staring toward the camera, looking for all purposes like they'd been caught red-handed.

"New Pastor and Brother Caught with Local Prostitute," Jean read the headline aloud. "Oh no."

Grant started to ask what they should do. How they should react. Instead, he watched, feeling heavier than he had from the medicine, as Jean dropped the paper and left the room without a word.

"God can use
the worst of
who you were
to shine light
on the best of
Who He is."

Candy

The chink of glass on glass sounded like an echo, but was in reality the sound of shattered pieces being swept up from several different sections of Jamaica's coffee shop floor. Candy looked around with pride. Jamaica and Pansy worked together. Jamaica had not let Pansy out of her sight all day, and stopped working regularly to cry, give her daughter a hug, or praise Jesus aloud for bringing her back. Near the counter, Brenda and Susan chatted while they mopped up the whipped cream and blood stains from the night before. Here and there around the shop, like angels disguised in black leather, bikers had given up their afternoon to come help sweep, clean, and repair.

"You must be tired out after last night," the white-haired man next to her said. He pulled a long strip of duct tape from the roll in his hand, while she waited with a large sheet of plastic. "I hope this makeshift door will hold until she can get new glass installed."

"I am tired," Candy admitted. "But the best kind of tired. Except I'm sad that I had to help arrest someone I really care about. Other than that, though, we got the rescued girls to safe houses in Charlotte, great places, and several of them have family on the way to get them. We did something good last night, and that's much better than being up all night for...other reasons."

"Yes." The man did not look her way, keeping his attention on the door. "I thanked God when I heard what you told the biker group early this morning. I was sorry I missed it. My wife and I had gone to bed around midnight and didn't know about any of this until breakfast, or we'd have wanted to help."

"You're a Christian?"

"Yes, ma'am." He smiled. "And I've been praying for you for a year."

Candy heard her jaw pop as it dropped open. "For me?"

He yanked a crooked line of duct tape off the frame and repositioned it straighter. "My wife and I traveled with this same group last summer. We made a list of people we saw or met all along the way who needed to know Jesus, and we've prayed for them all year. And look at you now. What an answer. You make me think of the woman at the well."

Candy smiled wide. "I read about her! She's the one who had all the guys, but after she met Jesus, she ran back into town and told everybody about Him."

He nodded, his eyes bright, the skin bunched up around them. "And the people were so surprised that she was saying such things, they came out in bulk to meet Jesus and hear His message for themselves. She changed a whole town." He chuckled. "I heard you invited the group to church tomorrow. I have a feeling a lot of them are so surprised that you're the one saying these things, they'll come just to find out for themselves if it's for real."

"Oh, it's real. I'm living proof."

He nodded. "You are indeed. Don't ever stop telling people your story, Candy. Don't ever get to the point where you want to hide the dark parts. God can use the worst of who you were to shine light on the best of Who He is."

She helped him pull the sheet of plastic across the frame and held it tight while he taped it on. "You talk like a preacher."

"I should. I'm an evangelist."

He was taping down near her feet. She scooted away, leaning over while still holding the top portion of plastic. "What's an evangelist?"

"Hey, Candy," Brenda called from across the room. The floor was clean and she stood near Jamaica and Pansy, an arm around each. "Help me convince Jamaica to come to church tomorrow. She says she doesn't want to be the only black woman there."

"I'm black, and I'll be there," the evangelist said. He laughed. "But I'm not a woman, so you're still out of luck."

"I don't want to make a big stir," Jamaica said across the room.

This time Candy laughed. "I don't think anybody can make more of a stir than I did a few weeks ago. But you could try. Then again, if the bikers do show up—and I invited a whole bunch of them—everybody will be so busy watching Gladys faint over them, nobody will notice you anyway."

The evangelist followed Candy toward the group. "The Bible says with Jesus there is no race. God's family is built from higher and stronger bonds than any surface things. God's people, those who truly love as God loves, will welcome you with open arms."

Pansy spoke, young and soft words, tinged with sadness. "Even if they find out I'm pregnant?"

The man answered with an action rather than words. He pulled Pansy into a grandfatherly hug and prayed for her right there in the shop.

"Whatever an evangelist is, I like it," Candy said.

He turned to regard her. "An evangelist travels around telling people about Jesus and how they can be saved." He smiled. "And from what I heard about last night and this morning, I think you are one already."

Candy felt herself beaming at him. "Not yet. I don't travel. But I will. I'm going to start a strip-club ministry."

The man turned to grin at Jamaica. "And you think *you're* going to cause a stir?"

Sunday Morning, August 3

Florence

Florence had thought nothing could top Candy coming to church for undiluted surprise, but fifteen big men and two women wearing Harley jackets and carrying motorcycle helmets walking into church might do it. They came down the aisle, passed where she and Gladys sat, and settled along the front three pews.

Gladys started hyperventilating and Florence decided to take a trip to the restroom downstairs. There she could giggle without reproach, and it would leave Gladys alone. If no one was sitting next to her, for once she might not speak her mind.

Florence was trying to hold in her laughter until she reached the restroom, but Grant entered the church through the downstairs door and seeing him made it burst right through.

"Morning, Miss Florence," he greeted her. She noticed his walk was stiff and he held a careful hand over his side. "What's the joke?"

She veered from her path to the restroom and walked with Grant toward the room for children's church. "A motorcycle gang showed up at church this morning! Do you think the pastor invited them?"

They had arrived at the children's church door and Jean stopped setting out snacks to smile and approach them. Grant

264

smiled at Jean but then frowned at Florence. "I doubt it. After what was in the newspaper yesterday, I think he was concerned no one would show up for church at all."

Florence sobered. "Oh yes. I read that. And Gladys told me Rod called another emergency meeting and said you all had to go, right away, before you damaged the church's testimony irrevocably. Those were his exact words, Gladys said."

Grant leaned against the wall outside the children's church room. "None of that article was true."

"I believe you." She patted his arm, but noticed he pulled back, his hand still on his side. "But you have to admit that photo is real, and it looks pretty bad. It looks really bad." She reached out but this time patted his other arm. "Gladys came today to support Rod, but I came today to support you and the pastor. I'm sure it will all work out." She smiled up at him, hoping it would help. "But I do need to warn you that they plan to have a vote this Wednesday about kicking you out."

Florence heard music from upstairs. That was Susan on the piano, which meant church would start in five minutes. Jean stood near Grant now, her eyes warm and concerned. Another woman came into view from inside the room and Florence rushed inside to hug her. "Grace! I didn't know you were coming!"

Jean's mother, always friendly, enveloped her in a return hug. "It's so nice to be back, Flo. Can you pass the word to all the ladies that I want to have our summer ladies' tea on Thursday? It will be at my house, just like every summer." She glanced at Jean. "I mean, Jean's house. Don't forget to dress up and wear a hat!"

"Oh, I will. What fun." Florence clapped her hands. "You'll have an extra lady this year. Well, I guess she's a lady now. Hmm, I don't know."

"If you mean Candy, I've met her. She's staying in Jean's guest room, while I'm sharing Jean's room with her." Grace leaned in to whisper, "She's nailed Bible verses all over the house."

Florence gasped. "Truly? Oh my. What will you do about decorating for the tea?"

Grace laughed. "It seems this year I won't have to!"

"Grace, you're a wonder. I wish you had stayed."

"I'm sorry I couldn't. I've missed you." Grace settled a few arriving children with their snacks, then walked to where Jean talked with Grant at the door. Florence followed.

"Have you met our pastor's brother yet?"

Jean turned and gestured from her mother to Grant. "Mother, this is Grant Henderson."

"Grant." Grace held out a hand and Grant shook it. "I'm so glad to meet you in person. Jean told me you're the one who got shot in this weekend's raid. I hope you are recovered enough to be out of danger."

"You got shot?" Florence put a hand to her heart. "Land sakes! What on earth happened?"

"He was rescuing Candy and Jamaica from Slash, Candy's—um—her boss," Jean answered.

Grant looked at Grace. "I'm happy to meet you, Mrs. Jameson, and I never was in any danger after the shot." He sent Jean a wry grin. "Except maybe from the pills they gave me."

"You're off those already?"

He shrugged, then winced. "I'm only taking over-the-counter stuff now. I'd rather hurt than be wandering around saying things I don't remember." He cleared his throat. "Or sleeping when I shouldn't be."

He and Jean shared a secret smile and Florence stared. Oh, this was good. She didn't want to interrupt the moment, but her curiosity came out of her mouth anyway. "Why was Candy's boss trying to shoot her?"

"He wasn't. It was Ian, the sheriff."

"The sheriff was trying to shoot Candy?"

Jean shook her head. "No, the sheriff shot Grant."

"Heavens! What on earth for?"

"He didn't mean to. His gun went off when Slash charged into him."

Florence would not be satisfied until she had heard the whole story. The congregation above started singing, but still she stayed. Grace had the children organized and doing their craft while Jean and Grant filled in the details. Oh, she'd be the one running the lunch conversation today. Gladys would want to talk about the motorcycle gang, but Florence would have actual news to share.

"Why isn't this whole thing in the newspaper instead of some nasty article about you and—and—bad women?" she asked.

"We got set up." Grant's brow furrowed. He looked to be in pain. Florence felt the urge to make him some chicken noodle soup. "I guess the pastor doing the wrong thing is bigger news than the pastor doing the right thing."

"Not for long."

Grant looked at Jean. "What do you mean?"

She smiled and Florence noticed it made her look pretty, like a sunbeam had hit her just right. "I went to that newspaper office yesterday after I left the hospital, and I stayed until they let me talk to the head editor. We agreed I would give him an exclusive interview about the weekend raid, with the possibility of Candy giving an exclusive interview about Slash, in exchange for him printing an entire article revealing the truth about what happened with you and Champagne that night."

"Jean," Grant breathed out. "They agreed?"

"Agreeing to trade the interview for the article wasn't difficult, but it was a battle getting them to agree to my condition—the article absolving you and Pastor Stewart had to be on the front page, in exactly the same spot as the original article, with as big a headline."

Grant put a hand behind Jean's neck and pulled her toward him. He kissed her forehead, almost reverently. "Thank you," he whispered.

Florence sighed. This was better than a movie. Jean looked up and Florence wondered if her eyes were shining with happy tears or sad ones. "You're welcome," she said, and Florence was disappointed when she pulled away. From the look on Grant's face, he felt the same way. "I need to get back to the kids, now that the service has started."

"Oh, yes." Florence could hear Pastor Henderson's voice upstairs. He must be giving announcements already. "I haven't been late to church in twenty years. What will Gladys say?"

She put her arm through Grant's, the side that wasn't shot, and waved back at Jean before having him escort her toward the stairs. "You know, Gladys may still be gaping at those motorcycle men, and not even notice yet that I'm not there!"

*She was
so small
and she
looked
terrified.*

Grant

"Come outside and play."

Jean sat curled up on her living room couch. She looked up from her book. "You're kidding, right?"

Candy, who had let Grant in the house, nudged Jean on the shoulder. "You've learned to smile. You even start conversations. Learning to play would be a great next step."

Her book closed, but Jean did not move to get up. Grant waited as she crossed her arms and scowled at Candy. "You sound like you're trying to be my therapist."

"Girl," Candy threw back as she headed for the guest room, "I can think of people who would pay for a session of therapy with that man next to you. Your mother is out buying groceries for the party she's planning, and you know that book is boring. Go have some fun for once in your life!"

The door slammed behind Candy and Jean looked over at Grant. She was blushing, but her voice remained casual as she rose from the couch. "At first I thought she was angry all the time, but now I know she just doesn't know how to shut a door without slamming it."

He tried to keep his voice equally casual, covering over the unexpected feeling of nervousness that washed over him when she came to stand a few feet away. "Maybe once she's finished teaching you all her lessons, it can be your turn."

"Oh, not slamming doors wouldn't be the first lesson." Jean led the way out to the yard in front of the house. "The first lesson would be asking before pounding nails into the wall."

"She's been hanging up stuff in your house?" He reached for the football he'd left on the front lawn, then tossed it from hand to hand.

"Bible verses. She finds one she likes and writes it in big letters, using colored markers, on a piece of paper, then nails it to the wall."

"That's got to be frustrating, having her putting holes all over your place."

Jean looked warily at his football, but then smiled at him. "I don't mind that, but I do mind the fact that she nails them up without warning. She'll be studying at any hour of the day or night, and then suddenly I'm flying out of bed because she just starts hammering. I've considered taking the hammer away, so at least I'll get warned when she comes to borrow it."

He chuckled, and the chuckle turned to a full laugh when the sound of hammering came from inside the house. Seeing Jean laugh along made something good happen all around his heart. Right there, Grant decided, by the end of that afternoon, he was going to ask her on a date. "I read the paper this morning. The article was great. I wanted to thank you, and—"

"So are you going to do anything with that ball, or do we just stand here for this first therapy session?" She had her hands on her hips, a playful smile on her face.

He chuckled again and tossed the ball to her. She caught it. "That's a good start. Now throw it back to me."

Her brows were up and her smile turned skeptical. "This counts as playing?"

"If you were three years old, I suppose it would. However..." He bent over and fake hiked the ball, then ran past her toward the log near the brook. "Since you're not, I just got a touchdown on you." Even that short run felt good, except for the pull in his side. He checked the bandage beneath his shirt. No blood; he was good. "It's been too long since I've played."

"You shouldn't be doing this, Grant."

"I can handle it." Okay, so it hurt, but he wasn't about to miss this opportunity with Jean. "I'll hold the ball on my good side."

She stood still while he jogged in place. Her arms were crossed, but she unfolded them and held her hands out for the ball. He tossed it her way, and before he had the chance to compute the information, she had charged around him and stood on the fallen log. "I do believe that makes us tied, Mr. Henderson."

"I wasn't expecting that." He heard the admiration in his tone and didn't bother to mask it. "But I won't be so slow next time."

"Slow? You didn't move from your spot at all. I thought you said you were off those pain meds."

"Ouch. That's a challenge if I've ever heard one."

She laughed and tried to run past him again. This time he was ready. He reached out and caught her around the waist, pulling her off her feet and against his right side. He spun her in a circle, laughing, until his foot caught the edge of the log and he tripped. The ball felt like the only solid matter amidst arms and legs as they fell. He tightened his grip around her waist, swiveling to keep her from hitting the log. They landed next to it.

"Oh, man, that hurt." Grant grasped his side. He started to apologize until he looked at Jean's face. "Are you all right?"

Her eyes were more than closed. They were clamped shut. Her head turned away from him. Her hands released the football and pushed weakly against his chest. "Please..." she whispered.

"Jean, are you okay?"

He felt her body shaking against his. Scared now, he pulled up onto his knees, his hands running down her arms, feeling for broken bones. "I'm sorry. I forgot the log was there. Jean..."

"Please stop. Please."

Grant didn't know what to do. She was so small and she looked terrified. "Are you hurt?"

Her hands, still shaking, went over her face. She shook her head no. "Please could you...please move."

He realized his kneeling position had her body trapped between his legs. "Oh, sorry." He pulled away and the moment her legs were free she clamored to a sitting position, then stood, backing away as if he were a threat to her.

"Jean, I don't understand..."

"I'm sorry." Her hands were out. Her voice breathless. She took more steps back. "I'm sorry." She turned and ran to the house, leaving him mute and dumbfounded in the middle of the yard.

Grant stood and stumbled a few steps back until his leg bumped against the log. He sat, hard. What had just happened? He hadn't meant to fall. She knew he wasn't the kind of guy who would plan something like that as a ploy to get her into his arms. Didn't she?

The front door of the house opened and Grant looked up with hope, but then dropped his gaze to his feet again. Candy crossed the yard and stood several feet away. "I guess playing wasn't such a good idea," she said. "I apologize for suggesting it." She shrugged. "And while I'm at it, I should probably apologize for watching you from the window. I don't often see guys who are kind, and fun, so I...well...I was spying."

"She acted like I attacked her." He stared down at his hands, still shell-shocked.

"Yeah."

Something in Candy's tone pulled his face up to look at her. "Do you know why?"

For the first time, her direct gaze faltered. "I think so. I've been wondering for awhile now, but wasn't sure."

He stood. "Wondering what?"

She looked out at the brook, over to the honeysuckle vine running up a tree, then shifted and looked back at the house. "I hope I'm wrong. I really do." She turned and faced him. "But from my experience, when something…real bad…happens to a kid." She chewed on her lip. "They tend to sometimes turn out like me…" She nodded up toward the house. "Or they sometimes turn out like her."

Like Jean had, Candy started backing away. "Wait," he called out. "I still don't understand."

Candy shrugged again. "I know. But it's not something I should be the one to tell you. Sorry."

Grant dropped down on the log again and stared at nothing. He was not aware when Candy opened and closed the front door of the house. What did she mean? Something real bad. What…

His mind saw the words carved into the school desk. A picture in the desk he had wanted to forget. He imagined a young Jean sitting there, afraid, and pain overtook his heart. Had Jean's father hurt her? Beat her? Worse? Is that why her parents separated? Florence had said Jean was sad when her father left, but could it have been sadness over what he had done to her instead?

Facts came together. Her sickness. How she was never the same afterward. How she avoided being touched. How she feared…him.

Grant put his head in his hands and prayed. When he lifted his eyes, he thought he saw Jean behind the curtain of the upstairs window. As soon as he glimpsed her, she moved back, out of his vision.

God, please. He stood and made his way across the yard toward his motorcycle. Today marked the shortest football game he had ever played, and his worst defeat. *Please let Candy be wrong.*

Tuesday Afternoon, August 5

Flowers were waiting on the dining room table when Jean arrived home from work on Tuesday. Lilies. In glorious colors and large blooms.

"I may not know a lot of guys in the amazing category," Candy remarked from her position on the stairs, where she stood nailing another verse written in bright pink marker to the wall. "But I'm pretty sure that, even for amazing guys, he's pretty amazing."

"I know." Jean took slow steps toward the flowers, dreading reading the card yet wanting to at the same time. She reached for it and silently read the words: *Can we talk?* Her heart tightened at the memory of how she had left him out in the yard the day before. She should apologize.

A knock sounded at the door and her heart pounded in response. She stood still for so long, Candy went around her and opened it. "Hi, Grant. Come on in. I'm going to go write some more verses in my room, so the living room is all yours." She turned, but Jean heard her whisper, "Nice flowers."

"Thanks."

Jean rotated, scanning the newest verses in large print along the wall. "Love never fails" was the last one she saw before Grant's face came into view. He stood still, waiting. She still held his card in her hand, and set it down so he would not see her hand shaking. "Thank you," she said, her voice quiet. "And I'm sorry. I shouldn't have run away."

He shifted his feet and took in a breath, then pulled out one of the dining room chairs and sat. "Jean, I'm no good at coming up with the right words even if I do understand the situation, and honestly, I don't understand this one. As much as I'd like to have the perfect thing to say, I don't. I feel like I get somewhere with you, then something happens and I'm back down at the bottom of the hill."

She winced. He looked so confused, and perhaps hurt, too. Guilt knifed through her. The tension between them was thick, but she knew what he did not, that anything she could say would only make it worse, not better.

He stood and came to stand near. She noticed he made a point of not touching her and felt her heart clench again.

"Jean, I'm not sure how, but you have worked your way into my heart." He grinned. "Maybe it was the lollipop."

She wanted to smile. She wanted to cry.

"Maybe it was the way you opened your home to someone in need, or how your face lights up when a child talks to you. I want—I want to pursue the possibility that you might be my best friend." He looked into her eyes and she saw nothing but sincerity and goodness in them. He reached into the bouquet of lilies and chose a butter yellow one with burgundy edges. He held it out to her. "Will you go on a date with me?"

How could she tell him? He didn't understand. Couldn't understand. She lived in a cave of secrecy, dark and cold and frighteningly small. She would never invite him into it; he should walk free in the light. But she could not leave it. There was no place for them to be together.

She could not love. He had to know that. She had to tell him.

Jean did not realize she was standing in silence, her eyes closed against the pain, until his soft voice, so close, brought her back to the dining room table where he waited for an answer. "Jean Louise, I think I'm starting to love you."

Such pain. It cut through her, the possibilities, the hope he held out to her in that one exquisite flower. "You shouldn't love me." Her voice came out broken, hoarse with grief. "I'm not...I can't..." For one brief moment, she allowed her eyes to meet his, then had to look away. "Grant." In his name, she tasted the bittersweet mixture of her own regret and desire. "I'm so sorry." Her voice broke. "I can't..."

She forced herself to turn, to start up the stairs, to keep from looking back at him. She made each step upward, her legs feeling as leaden as her heart. She heard the front door open, then close. Jean pressed a fist against her aching heart and looked down to see the vase of flowers still on the table, the bouquet's most beautiful bloom lying alone and abandoned where it had dropped on the floor.

No tears. Jean closed the door to her room, made her way to the bedside table, and pulled out a small pad of paper and a pen. She sat down on her bed and wrote in small, tight letters.

Dear Grant,

I can never tell you this, but you are dear to me. There are so many reasons why I want to love you, but they get devoured by all reasons why I can't. You are a good and wonderful man, and deserve someone like those lilies you gave me. Someone beautiful and colorful, and willing to bloom. I'm all shut up tight, and I would never burden you with all that is trapped inside. Please forgive me for running away, but I think someday you will be glad I did. Even so, my heart is breaking, because if I could bloom for anyone, I would want to bloom for you.

Jean read the note. She pressed it to her heart. Then, like the flower, she let it fall. It drifted to the floor. Jean stared at it for several seconds before climbing into her bed, curling her knees up, and pulling the covers tight over her head.

The anger
rose, fast
and familiar,
a dark and
dangerous friend.

Rod

"He has to go. Since the day he came, our church has been out of control. First prostitutes, then a bunch of wild bikers. And now we find he's been out late at night with a prostitute himself. He and his brother." Rod stopped trying to maintain calm and slammed his fist onto the table. Deacons all around the room looked at each other, gauging each other's response. He hated their cowardliness. Could no one make a decision in this church besides him? Was everyone so passive and incapable he had to lead them by the hand to the obvious conclusion?

"This has gone on long enough. I have waited for you to figure it out on your own, to realize that any man we bring in is going to be wrong for this church." He looked around the room. The time had come. "I am the leader of this church. I have been since Jim Chase left. I have brought men in and I have sent them out. And I say Stewart Henderson is done here. He and his wife and his brother need to leave. Now."

As the silence lengthened, Rod heard himself complain, "I suppose a loyal response would be too much to ask."

John Standard stood to his feet and Rod felt his teeth grind together. "Rod," he said, in that grave tone of voice Rod had always found irritating. "We have followed you for fifteen years. We chose your side when Pastor Chase accused you of misconduct because we believed in your integrity and character." John looked around the room as Rod had done, and Rod felt his

281

blood pressure spike at the heads nodding to John's words that had remained still to his.

Another deacon stood. Then a third. "Is this a mutiny?" Rod asked, knowing they all could recognize that his joke was no joke at all. No one stood in the deacon's meetings except him—and Stewart Henderson since he had arrived, the arrogant boy.

Henry Redding, who had never said a word in a deacon's meeting before, was the last to stand. "We have opened our minds to the possibility that we might have been wrong. Pastor Stewart is a good man who wants to serve the Lord and let Jesus be in charge of his ministry. He does not seem to long for power as you do."

"What are you saying?" Rod was breathing heavily. The anger rose, fast and familiar, a dark and dangerous friend.

John picked up his Bible and looked at it. Then he looked Rod in the eye. "We choose Pastor Henderson. You know he was not doing wrong with that prostitute. The paper printed an entire article clearing his name. He was part of a great ministry that happened over the weekend, a ministry we all missed because you would not even consider the idea."

"You think meeting filthy women in hotels and pretending to buy drugs is God's work? Have you already been brought down to their level of degradation?" Rod searched for a way to gain the upper hand. He had always stood over them, using his voice and his gestures and his position to keep them in line. Now that they, too, were standing, facing him, he felt his position, the position he had given twenty years of his life for, begin to crumble.

Henry picked up his Bible and answered. "We decided we want to follow God's Word, not yours. Stewart Henderson is already our pastor. He has been since the day the church voted to invite him to come and stay. To force him to leave would require a vote from all of us." He looked straight into Rod's eyes. "We just wanted you to know you can stop trying to convince us, because we will not be voting him out."

Rod felt his authority being ripped from his hands. One by one, the men, his men, walked from the room. This could not be happening. Not after all he had worked for. All he had given up. He had stayed despite Jim Chase's accusation, months of whispered suspicions, the school shutting down, Jean taking the children. None of them had been able to get him to leave. This church belonged to him by right.

The last deacon left the room and Rod stood alone, his fist still pressed against the table, his mind refusing to acknowledge that he had just lost it all.

Thursday Afternoon, August 7

"Whoa." Candy looked across the dining room table in amazement. "I didn't know people like you actually existed."

Jean's mother was decked out in white lace from the band around the white hat on her head down to the lace-edged skirt that draped over her white-slippered feet. She wore a turquoise and orange necklace, turquoise set of earrings, and one turquoise and one orange bracelet. A large orange flower perched under her hat behind her ear.

Grace Jameson's glory was nearly surpassed by her transformation of Jean's serviceable dining room table into a lavish piece of furniture that seemed to be blooming. A white lace tablecloth draped over the table and the four corners nearly touched the floor. Flowers in bold colors graced each expensive-looking teacup and saucer, and the table was centered with more tea bag options than the entire church congregation could drink in one setting.

"Would you help me move these chairs into the living room, Candy?" Grace asked. "I'd ask Jean, but I think she is still dressing."

Candy helped move the dining room chairs, plus several more Grace must have borrowed from somewhere, to round out a circle that included the couch and recliner.

"There." She looked over her work with a satisfied sigh. "When I lived here, my tea was the highlight of the summer. All the church ladies came." She sighed again. "Of course, back then, there were many more people at the church than there are now."

Candy thought of the bikers in church and almost laughed. "There have been a lot of visitors lately."

"Thanks to you, from what I hear." Grace's smile was knowing and Candy decided she liked Grace, even if she did turn Jean's house into one big flower arrangement. It wasn't like Candy could judge; her verses were in every color of the rainbow on walls all over the house. Jesus said the flowers showed about God, so maybe, in a way, she and Grace were doing the same thing.

Descending creaks on the stairway caught Grace's attention. "Jean must be ready." Candy followed her gaze toward the stairs leading from the living room up to Jean's room. "Oh Jean, honey, don't you have anything else to wear?"

Jean looked like she was going to the guillotine rather than a party. Her entire outfit was one bland shade of grey. Her shirt was long and bulky, her skirt unflattering in nearly every way possible. Even her face seemed grey and lifeless.

"Jean, I spent all morning making the table look beautiful. I told you all the colors I would use so you could coordinate." Grace glanced at her flowery concoction and looked back at Jean. "Couldn't you change before everyone comes? There's nothing wrong with colors, you know. God created them. He loves bright colors." Grace crossed to the coffee table in the living room where she'd set the vase of lilies Grant had sent. Candy noted Jean's face went from placid to pained. "Look at these gorgeous flowers. How can you be ensconced in so many incredible colors and choose to wear something that makes you look like you work in a morgue?"

Something was wrong. Candy had lived with Jean's quietness long enough to know that this silence was different. Jean touched one of the verses nailed in a nearly aligned pattern down the stairway. "I'm here, Mother," she finally said. "Please don't ask for more today."

Grace's face turned from disappointment to concern. Candy could see questions working their way from her mind to her mouth, and hoped she was doing the right thing by intervening. "Jean, here." She swiped one of the flowers from the immaculate table and tucked it into the waist of Jean's skirt. "Let's get you upstairs and I'll do your makeup till it's time for this party to start."

It was clear Jean was grateful as she nodded and trudged back upstairs. What wasn't clear was why. Candy had locked herself into her room and plugged her ears to keep herself from eavesdropping when Grant had come over after sending the flowers. She was trying to break the habit, but now wished she had listened. What had happened to make Jean look so—Candy tried to think of the right word—so lost? Alone? Withdrawn? She remembered the night before, at church, when Grant had confided to her about Jean and the shredder and the church bulletins on Sunday night. He had asked her advice and she had none to give.

Shredded. That was the word. Jean looked as if her world had shredded.

"You want to talk about it?" Candy sat Jean down at the small vanity in her bedroom and began brushing her hair. Jean shook her head, and Candy respected her answer by keeping silent as she pinned the sides of her hair back, then added a slight amount of color to her face. She smoothed a layer of sparkly eye shadow across Jean's eyelids, but the missing sparkle in her eyes would make Candy's efforts worthless. The wasted effort did not matter though. She was merely killing time to keep Jean from having to small talk with arriving guests, or answer questions from a worried mother.

"Jean? Candy?" Grace's cultured voice drifted up the stairs. "We're ready to get started."

Standing behind Jean to give her hair one more comforting brush, Candy put a hand on each of Jean's shoulders and prayed. After Jean's whispered thanks, she said, "You can make it through this party, and I'll pray things will look better in the morning."

She felt a sob
come from deep
within, from
a place that
had been
locked away
for fifteen years.

Jean

Jean took a bite from one of the cookies on her plate, but tasted nothing. She nodded to the ladies' comments about how her mother's chocolate truffles were as good as ever, and how her decadent éclairs were full of too many delicious calories to be decent. She smiled at Florence's journey into memories past, when Grace used to live there and how her voice blessed everyone in the church. All the while, her eyes saw Grant's face, the hurt there when she turned him away. The quiet sound of his footsteps as he walked out the door. Her door. A door she would have to keep closed to him forever.

She wanted to leave the desserts and the teacups and colorful flowers to the women who gushed over them with such sincere delight. She wanted to run upstairs, find someplace as grey as her outfit where she did not have to hide how miserable she felt.

"Jean, do you remember when your mother used to sing in the choir?" Florence had her pinkie out as she lifted a china teacup covered in hummingbirds, a nostalgic smile on her face.

Alice Carson, the surprise guest of the evening, for she had never come to a ladies tea before, set down her teacup with a slight nod. "I remember. That was back when Rod organized the children's Christmas pageant." Jean pulled her lips back to imitate a smile, even as her body froze and her heart rate increased. "He was so happy working on those sets and planning those events. It's such a shame we don't do them anymore."

Jean swallowed and put her shaking plate on the coffee table. Gladys, next to Florence and wearing a large floppy hat with one feather sticking out from it, puckered her lips before she spoke in Jean's direction. "I think we still would, if Jean hadn't taken over and decided no one but her could do anything with the children." She sat straighter in her chair and Jean saw Florence flash her a worried glance. "And after all Deacon Carson had done for her and her mother. You'd think she would have felt gratitude, wanted to work together. But no, she had to—"

"Gladys, have you tried one of these truffles?" Florence interrupted. "They're to die for. I can feel my waistline bulging but they're too good to resist."

"Your waistline could use a little resistance," Gladys snapped. "And I, for one, am getting tired of how everyone seems to think Rod Carson is the enemy these days. Have you all forgotten he was principal of our school? He's been here longer than anyone except me. I think—"

"And me," Florence added meekly.

Gladys ignored the comment. "He has stayed with this church when every other pastor has left. I think it's terrible what happened at the deacon's meeting last night."

"What happened?"

Jean looked around the circle of women. The question came from Susan. Next to her, Brenda had her hands clasped so tightly her knuckles were white. On Susan's other side, Jean's mother rubbed her bracelets around and around her delicate wrists. She had done that ever since Jean was a child, whenever things went wrong and she could not figure out how to fix them.

There had been so much she could not fix.

Everyone seemed surprised when Alice answered, her voice so soft all other conversations quieted to hear, her eyes down on the hands in her lap. "He called the meeting because of the newspaper article about the pastor and his brother with…with…"

"With a prostitute." Jean heard a hardness in Candy's voice for the first time. "We're all girls here. You can say the word."

Alice glanced up, but only for a moment, before her eyes dropped again. "He planned to tell the men they had to vote Pastor Henderson out of the church, immediately, and vote Rod in as leader instead."

Teacups clattered and women shifted as they tried to glance at Brenda without being obvious. Jean waited for Brenda to look up, but she kept her head down. Was she praying, or was she sad? Had Rod succeeded and she would be moving away? Would Grant move away?

The sharp ache gripping her heart told Jean what she already knew. She loved him. She wanted him to stay, to teach her how to be loved without fear. She put her head in her hands, oblivious to any stares or whispers in her direction. If he left, how would she bear it? Yet, if he stayed, would that not be worse? To see him every week, know he was near, see him come to care for someone else, would be unendurable.

She pressed her fingers against her eyelids. Gladys was talking. "I don't know what you all look so shocked about. Isn't he the rightful leader of this church? Isn't he the one who stayed all those years ago when Jim Chase left? If Pastor Chase had been in the right, why was he the one to leave, I ask you?"

"Gladys…" Florence said.

"I will not be silenced this time, Florence." Jean looked through her fingers and saw Gladys shove her hat away from her face. She shifted to sit imperiously, spine straight. "I thought Brenda would not be here tonight, but that can't be helped at this point. I came here to have my say and I will have it. Stewart and Grant Henderson have brought scandal and—and scandal upon our church since that first Sunday. I never know what to expect from one Sunday to the next. The pastor is bringing in people right off the streets, as if we were some kind of homeless shelter or—or juvenile detention center. And his brother wants to start playing sports and call it a ministry. Will we be forced to pay for that nonsense? I don't like what they are doing and I don't like them. Rod should be our pastor. He knows us and our ways, and respects how we think things should be done. He deserves our loyalty, our admiration, our—"

"Stop it! Just stop it!"

Jean still had her hands against her eyes. "He's not a good man. He shouldn't be in charge."

Gladys clutched her shawl around her. "Jean! What right do you have to—"

"Every Sunday, he took me downstairs and locked me in that room. He—he touched me, and—and hurt me."

She felt a sob come from deep within, from a place that had been locked away for fifteen years. She looked up at the shocked faces, at her mother, who sank to her knees on the floor. "No," Grace whispered.

"You were so sad already," Jean told her mother. "And so happy that he was helping us. He said—he said it was my fault. That I made him do it, that I was bad. By the time I was old enough to understand it wasn't true, I just couldn't tell you."

For long minutes, the whiffs of air entering and leaving open mouths were the only sounds in the room. Jean wrapped her arms around herself.

Gladys spoke, her voice much less certain than it had been. "That's a lie."

Jean looked at her and Gladys leaned back, away from the fire in her gaze. "Why did I stay, Gladys? I hated it here, everyone knew that. I was miserable, and no one got close enough to me to ask why. I made myself sick so I could stay home on Sunday nights. I started carrying mace at age eleven.

When I was fifteen I took over everything in the church that had to do with the children. Why do you think I did that, Gladys? Did you think I was power hungry like he was?" She stood. "I stayed here because I could not bear the thought of him choosing another child to be his 'special helper.' To know that a child wept every Sunday night, while the choir sang above her and praised the man who hurt her."

All Jean's energy drained out with her words. "After Mother moved away, I convinced Alice to give me the second church key, and I stayed after church every Sunday night."

"To collect the bulletins," Florence gasped out. Her teacup rattled in its saucer. "You said it was too small a job for two people, that you didn't want any help."

"I didn't." Jean fell back into her seat, body numb, her eyes on the floor but seeing a darkened office and locked door. "I had to be alone so I could take the bulletins downstairs to his office and write on them, every Sunday, exactly what he did to me. The words I said to beg him to let me go. The words he used to keep me. The way his hands—"

"Why didn't you tell me? Oh Jean, why didn't you tell me?" Grace Jameson wept openly, but Jean knew her own eyes would remain dry. Even now, she would not cry in front of anyone.

"I'm sorry, Mother. You wanted everything to be all right so badly. And I believed him, that it was my fault. I couldn't tell you."

Jean stood, uncertain of who she was or what to do. The party was over. She looked at Gladys and said, "Grant and Stewart Henderson are two of the most godly men I have ever known. They do not ignore the lost and hurting world around them. They care more about reaching others than maintaining your high opinion, and you should not—"

With sudden clarity, Jean looked around at the shocked faces and realized she had just said everything. She had told them. The secret that had defined her life for fifteen years was out, never to be retrieved and protected again.

Jean's chest heaved. Her own horror matched that of the faces she saw. Shaking her head, backing away, she turned, ran up the stairs to her room, and locked the door.

Thursday Evening, August 7

Florence

God, please make it not be true. Florence sat in a stupor as the room erupted into chaos. Women hovered over Grace, who kept repeating that she didn't know, she hadn't known. Gladys stopped fanning herself and sat silent and still, as if willing away everything she had not wanted to hear. Susan was calling someone on her cell phone, someone named Ian, telling him everything and asking what legally should be done and could he arrange it? Candy gathered teacups and plates and took them to the kitchen, somehow separate from it all, as if she understood in a way none of them could. She probably did.

Brenda was on her knees in front of her chair, praying. Florence wanted to pray, she wanted to beg for forgiveness. When Pastor Jim Chase had called them all to a meeting and told them his suspicions, Florence had thought he was trying to get rid of Rod because he felt him a threat. How could she have been so blind? And how much of her blindness had been by choice?

Florence looked over at Alice, still, quiet Alice, who never had an opinion of her own. Had she known? Surely she had suspected. Florence felt her eyes fill when Alice looked across the circle of sound and panic, just looked at her, and Florence knew they saw farther into each other's souls at that moment than either had ever seen themselves. Each had chosen to see what she had wanted to see. Florence dropped her head, unable to bear the shame she saw reflected in Alice's sad eyes.

When she looked up again, wiping away tears, Alice was gone. What on earth would Alice say to her husband when she got home?

Sliding from her chair, Florence bent until she faced where Grace still sat on the floor. Grace had not even tried to get up, her words bewildered and frightened and lost. "How could this have happened?" she asked. Her eyes found Florence. Her hand reached out and grasped Florence's arm. "How could we not have known?"

Florence allowed her tears to flow. "I beg your forgiveness," she said. "In school, some of the girls were struggling. Their grades dropped and they stopped caring about being involved or making friends. When any of them came to me to talk, I—I—" She shut her eyes, seeing their faces. "I sent them to the principal to be counseled. I'm the one who sent them to his office. God, forgive me."

She covered her face with her hands but Grace pulled her hands away. "You're saying Jean wasn't the only one?"

Sobs interrupted her words as she spoke. "I don't think so. I can think of four, maybe five girls, about the same age as Jean, who all struggled at different times. I would send them to him, and over time they stopped telling me they were struggling. I thought that was because they were doing better. I didn't know they stopped confiding in me because I was sending them to—" She put her hands over her face again but this time Grace did not stop her.

Once the words had started, the rest came flowing out. "Pastor Chase accused him of acting inappropriately with students, but we teachers and the church members couldn't imagine him doing anything wrong. The people of the church started taking sides and fighting, and finally Pastor Chase left the church. He said he couldn't prove what Rod had done, but he could no longer stay in a church that supported him." Florence grabbed a napkin folded into an origami swan, and wiped her nose. "It was after he left that Rod took over the Christmas pageant, and started spending time with Jean. And we all talked about that as proof that he was a good man. Oh, Grace, I'm so sorry."

"It wasn't your fault," Grace said, her reaction wooden, her gaze up on the door at the top of the staircase.

"It was! Not fully, but partly. It was all our faults for worrying about the church's reputation and not digging until we knew the truth. I didn't want it to be true so I told myself it wasn't. We were trying to protect the ministry and Jean suffered for it. All these years. All those times I offered to watch the children and she said no. All those times I knew she carried something dark and sad deep in her soul, and I was so afraid of what it was I let her continue to suffer so I could be comfortable."

The room had nearly emptied. Most of the women were congregated on the front lawn, or had gone home in shock. Brenda rose from her position of prayer and opened her cell phone. Florence listened, too drained to care that she was being rude, as Brenda talked to Stewart. She told him about the deacon's meeting, and Florence wondered if he had not been informed about it. Then she asked to speak with Grant. Her voice broke as she told him he needed to come to Jean's house right away. After a pause, she looked at Grace. "May I tell him why?"

She nodded and Brenda walked outside, talking through tears.

Gladys finally rose from her seat. More sober than Florence had ever seen her, she talked with no one but Florence, stating only, "We should go home now," then mutely making her way toward the front door. Florence grasped Grace's hand one more time, in sorrow, in shame, then rose and followed.

What was she to do now, knowing that who she had thought herself to be, what she always considered the best part of her life and the best part of herself, was a failure and a lie?

He infused
all his anger
into the force
and broke
the door
in one kick.

Grant

When Grant's motorcycle swerved into the drive, only three cars remained: Jean's, her mother's, and Brenda's. The house was quiet. A bright blue streamer had been torn from one side of the doorway and now drifted, its edge jagged, as if trying to reach the floor so it, too, could get away. He parked near the porch and Brenda opened the door and came out.

"How is she?" It was an inept question, but he had no other. All the way there, and now here, only two thoughts had made it through his rage and pain. Concern for Jean, and an overwhelming desire to tear Rod into pieces.

Brenda shook her head. "She ran upstairs and hasn't come down. I want to help her, but Candy said she probably needs to be alone for awhile. Candy knows about...things like this, so I trust her judgment." She wiped her cheeks. "I feel so helpless." She put a hand on Grant's arm, as if she needed to touch someone. "Candy is sitting out on the log near the brook, praying, so I guess I'll just go home and pray, too."

Grant nodded. If Brenda didn't know how Jean was, there was only one other thing to ask. "And Rod?" He hated even saying his name, wanting to use a pile of other words he'd heard at college but never said. *God help me. You said it's wrong to hate, but I want to find that little desk and pummel him to a pulp with it. I want him to suffer as much as he made her suffer, and then I want him to die.*

The hand on his arm gripped tighter. "Susan called Ian. Ian contacted someone local and, thanks to Florence, they're getting a warrant to take Rod into custody until they can do an investigation. Florence actually went in, right after she took Gladys home, and gave a statement that will be enough to hold him for now. She also gave them the former pastor's number, the one who accused him, so the police could call him for questioning, too."

Grant's jaw clenched so tight it hurt. "I hope they get him in prison soon."

"To protect Jean?"

"No. To protect him from me." *God, You'll have to take the hate I feel away, because I admit I want it there. I want to find him and make him pay. You said vengeance is Yours, but I want it to be mine.*

Brenda looked up at a light coming from behind the upstairs curtains of Jean's room. "You got closer to her than anyone, Grant. That's why I called you. I think she needs a friend, and her mother is too devastated to help. But, please." The hand on his arm gripped hard. "Not like this. Your anger won't help her right now."

"I know." His voice was hoarse. He knew the rage burning like lava through him needed to go, but where, and how? How could love get through what was volatile and frightening?

Brenda sniffed, removed her hand, and after one more look toward Jean's room, turned and slowly walked to her car.

He stared at the upstairs window, his heart praying. Then he pulled in a deep breath and walked inside without knocking. A look around found Jean's mother in the dining room gathering flowers off a table covered in desserts, teacups, and small, crumb-covered plates. She looked up when he entered, but did not seem to see him. "I didn't know," she said. Her voice and her face were haunted. "I didn't know."

He looked around the dining room, pictured the kitchen, the living room. He almost went outside until he remembered Candy was praying out there. "Mrs. Jameson." His words sounded like they'd come through rocks. "Is there someplace with a solid wall I can hit without busting a hole in it?" The energy it was taking to control his muscles had them shaking. He needed an outlet for his emotions. "I need to hit something, hard, before I go talk to Jean."

She motioned to a door positioned at the bottom of the stairs. "My husband kept a punching bag in the basement. It might still be there."

He didn't respond, only went toward the door. "It's locked."

"I locked it years ago. Everything down there was his and I couldn't bear going through it. I'm afraid I got rid of the key." She seemed to finally focus on him, on the fury barely contained. She closed her eyes, bunched the flowers together, and said, "I should stop trying to hide away everything I don't want to deal with. Would you do me a favor and kick the door open? I'd like to replace the door anyway, and if I had your strength, I'd want to kick something right now until it broke."

He did not need to be asked twice. Lifting the leg on his good side, he infused all his anger into the force and broke the door in one kick. It swung open and he took large strides down into a dark, musty cellar. The light from the open door at the top of the stairs was enough to see several support beams, a few weights leaning against a concrete-block wall, one dirty towel covered in mold, and, hanging from the ceiling in the center of the area, a punching bag.

Grant ran toward it and threw a fist against the bulk. Pain tore through his side and soaked up some of the pain ripping through places that could not be bandaged. Thrust after thrust, he punched the bag until his knuckles cracked and bled. It was not enough. With a shout of rage, he threw his fists harder, pounded more, not stopping even when he heard the cry of alarm and heard her say his name.

Jean

The sound, sharp and hard, like a gunshot, was terrifying enough to get Jean out of bed and running down the stairs. "Mother? Mother!" Had Rod come and shot her?

She looked around frantically, steeling herself to find a bloodied body, when her mother emerged from the living room, Grant's vase of flowers in her hands.

"Mother, what happened?" Jean put a hand to her throat where her pulse beat wildly. "Are you all right?"

"He's here." The answer was strange and Jean looked around, seeing no one. Then she noticed her mother's eyes were on Jean's lilies. "I told him to knock the door down. We need to talk, Jean, but first he…"

By then Jean's searching gaze had found the splintered basement door. Behind it, down the stairs, she heard pounding, fast pops of sound. When he yelled, the agony in his voice was more than she could bear. She forgot everything—her fear of darkness and closed spaces, her fear of him and all the feelings he provoked in her—and pushed the door aside to run down the stairs.

"Grant!" She called his name, but he did not hear. Her eyes took in the sweat stain down the back of his light blue shirt, and the red stain across his left side. His wound had opened. "Stop! Grant! Stop it!"

His arm was pulled back, ready to strike again. She rushed to put her body in front of him, blocking the punching bag. The path of his fist halted as his eyes registered her presence. "Jean?"

The fist in front of her ran with blood. She reached up and wrapped her fingers around it, around his pain, her other hand up against his chest to bring his attention to her, away from whatever caused such torment in his heart that it showed so fully on his face.

"Grant, please. Please stop. You're breaking my heart."

His fist dropped to his side as if the anger drained out of him and left him without any strength. She put her hand that had covered his fist up to his face, ignoring the blood on her hand and the sweat running down his skin. Her palm rested against his cheek; she hoped it was soft, gentle, comforting enough to help. "Grant."

His eyes found hers and looked deep. She did not look away. "Jean," he whispered and his face filled with the same agony that had brought her to him. "Jean."

Without warning, his arms moved, circled around her and crushed her to him. She stood stunned until the panic hit. Fear filled her. She could taste it. The arm she had reached up to touch him was pinned against his side, her other held tight between them against his chest. She tried to move, to push him away. Terror brought memories, awareness of the darkness behind him, pictures, scenes, words. Rod Carson. He always appeared whenever she was touched. Whenever it was dark. Whenever she was powerless and afraid.

Her breathing grew rapid, shallow, and her body trembled with violent force. Her face, the only part she could move, shifted to pull back and beg him to let her go.

At that moment, she felt a drop of moisture hit her hair, run down, and fall away. Another found the skin of her face. It was cool. She stilled, stopped fighting, and remembered this was Grant. Rod was gone. Grant was here.

And he was crying.

He was crying for her.

Something deep within Jean shattered. The pieces flew throughout her body, and like a dam, the flood behind crashed to freedom. Tears built up. Burst from her eyes. Pain washed out. Jean felt her hands stop resisting and begin to cling. Instead of pushing away, she smashed her face into his chest and wept. She sobbed for the child she had been. For the woman she had wanted to be. For all that was taken.

Hopes. Goals. Dreams. Promises. She had kept them all locked tight in the shell she'd thought was her heart, hidden away to remain protected and untouched. Jean felt that shell splinter open like the basement door. Grant had broken through both.

They stood for an hour, arms around each other, their tears creating tiny rivers that dropped and joined together between them, and flowed from there as one.

The group
went silent
and an instant,
heavy grief
filled the air.

Brenda

"I'm so glad you all came today." Brenda felt like a mother hen gathering her chicks as the women ordered specialty coffees from Jamaica and Pansy, then wandered back to the cluster of tables Brenda and Candy had set up for their first ladies Bible study at the coffee shop. The women had all been whispering about Jean and the ladies' tea, as was only natural, but Brenda wanted to curb that topic in case Jean came. "Thanks, Jamaica, for letting us use the shop for our meetings on Saturdays."

"You can thank Candy. She'll be the one in charge after this weekend." Jamaica wiped the counter, then she and Pansy came to join them.

"Really?"

"I'm moving in here," Candy said, a cup of whipped cream in her hand. "I'll live above the shop, where Jamaica lives now, and she'll pay me for running things."

Brenda looked back at Jamaica. "You're moving?"

Jamaica put an arm around her daughter. "I'm taking my girl back home. We need to start over, and I think this is a great place to do it, but first we've got to go back and get our things and say our goodbyes. And I want everybody back home who has been praying all this time to see Pansy and know what God did for me."

Pansy put a hand to her barely rounded belly and Jamaica pulled her into a side hug. "But we're coming back here in time to have a baby shower, right here in this shop! I've always wanted to be a grandmother. I'll provide free coffee, and you can bring the presents!"

"Well," Candy said after the laughter had died down, "I want to thank God for providing me a job—though I'm going to be calling you, Jamaica, every day to ask how to work all this stuff—and I'm excited about so many of us doing a Bible study together. But I think we should get started. If you all have lists half as long as mine, we'll be here till midnight."

"Is that your list of questions?" Jamaica pointed to a folded paper Candy pulled from her Bible.

Candy flung the paper out of its folds. "Yep. These are just for today. I only brought five. The rest are in my notebook back at Jean's house."

"How many do you have total?" Brenda waved a welcome to a newcomer then focused back on Candy.

"Um…" Candy cocked her head. "Forty-seven so far. But I'm only done with the book of Matthew, so I'll have more later."

Florence put a hand to her forehead. "How could you possibly come up with forty-seven questions just from one book?"

Candy shrugged. "Oh, I had more. Those are only the ones I wrote down. For starters…" She propped her elbows on the table and rested her chin on her hands. "I need to know where the list of cuss words is in the Bible."

"What?"

"I stopped saying all the words I know are bad, but at the ladies' tea, before everything fell apart, I said a couple that I didn't think were cuss words, but Gladys' mouth dropped open so wide, a full-grown bullfrog could have jumped right in. So where in the Bible is the list of cuss words so I know what I shouldn't say?"

Brenda coughed to mask her smile. "Can I see your list of questions?" Candy passed the paper and Brenda skimmed over it. "How about you mark that question for you and I to talk about after the study, and for now we'll focus on your question number four: Why, when Jesus healed people, did He tell some to tell everybody about it, but others He told to not tell anyone?"

The women were turning to the book of Matthew when the bell on the coffee shop's new door rang and Jean stepped in. The group went silent and an instant, heavy grief filled the air. Brenda watched the women's faces crease with worry, especially Florence's. "I don't know what to do," she whispered.

"Should we just avoid talking about it? I don't know what to say," another woman added as Jean took time to shut the door carefully. The bell stopped.

Brenda wanted to wait for someone else to move, to say something. She wanted to bite her nails. She cared about Jean, but pastor's wife or not, she had no more idea what to do than the rest of them.

God has not given us the spirit of fear, but of power, and of love...

The verse she, Candy, and Jean had quoted so many times came back to help. If her love for Jean was greater than her fear of doing the wrong thing, what would she do?

Brenda prayed silently for courage and stood to her feet. "Jean."

Jean had been looking down at her purse, standing near the door, cloaked with uncertainty. She glanced up at Brenda and her smile was hesitant. "I hope it was okay that I came."

Brenda swallowed the emotion that wanted to overtake her and gave Jean a hug, surprised when Jean, after a moment's pause, hugged her back. Brenda led her to the empty chair she'd saved beside her in case there was a late arrival. They both sat, and Brenda tried to speak for them all. "You've been through something horrible." She told herself not to cry. "We all care about you, and we hate what has happened to you, but to be honest, we don't know if you want to talk about it or want us to avoid talking about it. We don't know what would be good, or what would make it worse." She gestured around the table and the women nodded their support. "Please tell us what you need. How can we help you get through this?"

Jean's eyes filled with tears. Brenda was not sure why, but the sight seemed to shock the ladies around the table. Florence rose and approached to hug Jean from the side. She whispered something to her, and Jean actually pulled her into a hug in response, something Brenda never expected to see. Candy went to the counter and returned with a cup and spoon.

"It's whipped cream," she said, smiling at Jean. "I didn't know if you liked coffee or not."

"Thanks."

Candy repeated Brenda's question. "So how can we help?"

Jean dipped her spoon into the whipped cream. "This is a good start."

Brenda put her hand over the free hand Jean had rested on the table. One by one the others, every woman within reach, added their hands until Jean's was covered in layers of love.

"Will you please pray for my mother?" Jean asked. "She feels so guilty, but I wish she didn't. I need to know how to talk with her about it." She stirred the whipped cream absently. "And will you pray for me? It's hard having everyone know…and the police want to know if I'm willing to testify in court, which means even more people will know…And they'll ask for details..."

Jean's voice drifted into silence. Heads nodded. One woman said, "We will."

Candy shook her head. "So what are you waiting for? She asked us to pray for her. So let's pray."

Brenda rose and stood behind Jean's chair, her hands on Jean's shoulders. The other ladies followed her example and came close, and by the time Brenda finished, most of them were using napkins to wipe away tears.

"What else can we do?" Brenda asked as they returned to their seats.

Jean wiped her cheeks and smiled. "I want to start over, be the person I was always meant to be."

"*Old things are passed away. All things become new*," Florence quoted, her eyes shining.

"Exactly. So..." She looked around the table. "I was wondering, if after the Bible study, would some of you—would you come shopping with me? I'd like to buy some clothes that are pretty, and colorful, like flowers."

Candy threw her hands up and shouted, "Hallelujah!"

Saturday Morning, August 9

Stewart

Stewart was winded and they hadn't even jogged the subdivision once. If Grant did not have a stiff and aching side, Stewart knew his brother would be a mile ahead of him by now.

"I had a talk with Jean's mom this morning while Jean went to the store," Grant said as they rounded a cul-de-sac.

"She's leaving this afternoon to go back to Virginia, right?"

"Yes, that's why I needed to talk to her today. But she told me not only did she and Jean finally talk about what happened, which is good, she also told me she's planning to come back much more often, like when Jean has to testify. I was glad to hear it, for Jean's sake and mine. It's a little too soon to ask her blessing, but that's not the kind of thing you want to do over the phone."

Stewart stopped in his tracks. "Did you just tell me you're going to ask Jean to marry you?"

"Not right away." Grant jogged in place while Stewart stood as if bricks fell on his feet. "But I will. I want her to know someone will love her through all of this and beyond it."

"Is she—does she—?"

"I'm not sure how she feels about me, if that's what you're asking. Come on, run with me." He started off again. "It's easier to talk about this stuff while I'm moving."

Stewart pulled his legs upward and told them to move again. "To be honest," Grant added, "the idea of getting rejected again is about as fun as facing three huge linebackers with no one on my own team open for the ball. You have that scary feeling in your gut that you're either going to get sacked, or duck through them and make the best play of your life."

"I'll pray for the second." Stewart was dripping. The humidity had to be a hundred percent. At least. "So does all this mean you're thinking of sticking around here?"

Grant paused and Stewart added, "We'd love to have you stay, if I've never said so before."

"Would you?"

He felt a pang to remember how that had not been true when they first arrived. "Yes. This church is being set free from the past, and you've been a big part of that. I'm grateful. Now that drugs aren't available in town like they were before, those teens you were concerned about need something to keep them busy and keep the trade from starting up again. Your idea for a sports ministry would be a real asset to the work here." They turned the corner near the house and passed it to do another lap of the neighborhood. "And Jean could do a Bible club with the kids while you're working with the teens."

"It's a thought." Grant's answer was noncommittal. "I'll pray about it."

"Good enough." Stewart slowed to catch his breath. "I'm more out of shape than I thought." Even with his wound, Grant could run circles around him, and at the moment was doing so, literally. "You don't have to rub it in."

Grant laughed. "It's from all that studying. You need to get outside more."

"Maybe you should study more."

Stewart stood upright and stretched, surprised when Grant stopped and stood still. "You're right." He faced him. "In fact, I wanted to ask you about that."

"About what?"

Grant looked off into a half acre of trees filling an un-cleared lot. "About forgiveness." His face was grim. "I know I have to forgive him. I've even chosen to. But choosing once doesn't make all the junk go away—the anger and the temptation to hate or want revenge. I need to know how to forgive the everyday, lifetime kind of way, not just the moment."

Stewart pulled his t-shirt from his body to let the air cool his skin. "You're not the only one in the church with that struggle right now."

"I know. Every one of them was swindled or hurt or deceived in some way. And anyone who still had doubts about Rod being guilty won't anymore."

"What do you mean?"

Grant rubbed his sleeve across his sweating forehead. "The police searched his house and found enough on his computer to put him away for years even if no one testified."

"Found what on his—" Stewart shook his head. "Never mind. I don't want to know. So he's in jail now?"

Grant frowned. "He's gone missing. There's a warrant out for him, but I have a feeling he heard about what happened when his wife got home from the tea, and he skipped town." He motioned and they started jogging again. "That's why I wanted to ask if you'd pray about maybe preaching a series about forgiveness. If he stays on the run and isn't brought to justice, it's going to be even harder to forgive. I was going to ask about just the two of us studying it together, but, thinking about Jean and Florence and so many others…"

With a nod, Stewart picked up the pace. He could see the house and headed for it. "It would make a good Wednesday night study. We could move it to the fellowship hall, where we could sit around the table and people could talk and ask questions."

"And if Candy comes, she can give us all assignments on how to apply the verses we learn."

Stewart chuckled. "That wouldn't be such a bad thing." They ran in companionable silence over the lawn and into the open garage. Stewart grabbed a towel from the dryer and tossed it to Grant, pulling another out to wipe his own face and neck. "You know, if you marry Jean, you'd get a major upgrade in accommodations. Are you sure you're not wanting to marry her just to get out of that tiny room in the church?"

Grant laughed again. "She does have a nice house, but it'd be no picnic to move into. I've already noticed at least five major projects I'd have to work on, not to mention cleaning out that basement."

He felt an eyebrow go up. "Noticed all that already, huh?"

He enjoyed seeing his brother redden. "Well, I might get an upgrade in accommodations, as you say, but you've got to admit…" He gestured toward the motorcycle parked out front. "She'd get an upgrade in transportation."

Stewart laughed. "Ask her if that would feel like an upgrade."

"Maybe I'll wait on that till after I see if she wants to marry me." Grant tossed the dirty towel into the washing machine. "You heading over to the church?"

"After a shower."

"Good. I'll meet you there. I need your help on something."

Thirty minutes later, Stewart found Grant moving a pile of items near the downstairs exit door of the church. "You always did take showers faster than me," Stewart commented.

Hair still wet, Grant motioned for him to follow through the propped-open exit door. "The little shower in the bathroom down here isn't a luxury place you want to take your time in. I'm thankful for it though. They must have put it in because of the school."

Stewart shrugged. "Beats me. We could ask Florence why it's there."

"Or Gladys."

"No thanks." He grinned. "So what am I helping you with?"

Grant led him down the hallway to the room he had renovated into his own. Stewart entered behind him and turned sideways to look over shelves filled with crocheted plant holders and yellow-paged hymnals.

He sneezed. "I thought you cleared all the old stuff out. Or are you still looking for clues?"

"No clues left in here." Grant opened the room's one window, which he had finally managed to conquer after hours of coaxing with that crowbar borrowed from Stewart's shed. "Unless you're looking to discover that the decorations they used twenty years ago were kind of tacky. These shelves are what I need your help with. The deacons gave me permission to clean out this room entirely and make it into a ministry room, and if that's okay with you, then I want everything from the past gone from here. I could use your help getting rid of the shelves, and then with painting. I called Brenda awhile ago and she said she'd find an opportunity to tell the ladies at the Bible study about my plan before Jean arrived."

"Aren't you going to keep living here?"

"No, I've got a better use for this room—the room that used to be Principle Rod Carson's office."

She had rejected it, and him. Had that changed?

Grant

She appeared at the door in the early morning light, the yellow material of her flowing dress soft and appealing, her feet wrapped in heeled sandals, her hair loose and silky around her shoulders. Grant's heart swelled. Her dress was the same color of that lily he had chosen and offered to her. "You look beautiful, Jean." She smiled but he did not, suddenly remembering he had left that lily behind on the floor. She had rejected it, and him. Had that changed? "You ready?"

"Yes, and curious, too. On the phone, you wouldn't tell me where we were going or what you had to show me." She looked at his motorcycle. "I guessed you were taking me to breakfast before church, but I don't have a helmet, and I'm afraid I didn't dress for a motorcycle ride."

He recalled how she'd hung on to him the one time he had convinced her to ride with him, and his smile was back. "I'll buy you a helmet someday. Today, though, we'll be walking. What I want to show you is at the church."

The breeze captured the edge of her dress and caressed her legs with it as she moved toward him down the porch steps. "You still haven't told me what you want to show me."

"I know."

They walked in friendly silence until Jean passed the fallen log and neared the brook. Slowing to a stop, she stood looking across to the church for a time. Finally she said, "I'm done hiding, Grant."

He stood at her side. "I know, and I'm glad." He didn't want to say too much, so he waited while she dropped her gaze and watched the water slide over the jutting rocks.

"Before we go, I—I wanted to ask your help with something," she said abruptly, her hands clasped in front of her and her eyes still on the water.

"Anything."

She turned to face him, but her gaze only lifted to his jaw and settled there. Her nervousness was making him nervous. He spread his legs to stand comfortably and crossed his arms, but winced and uncrossed them when his side complained. He had run through the pain when he and Stewart jogged the day before, and that earned him a lecture at his doctor's appointment that afternoon. He was told in no uncertain terms to take it easy. "Stop being such a jock," were the doctor's precise words, right before the doctor warned him if he opened the wound again, he'd have to get stitches.

"I was wondering...um..." His thoughts left his side and were back on Jean, who had her hands twisting around each other. She looked down at her feet, then over at the brook again. "I was wondering...if..."

The sadness or nervousness, whatever it was, spread through the space between them and touched him with concern. He stepped toward her and lifted a hand to touch her hair, stopping himself at the memory of her face when he'd fallen against her there near the log. He pulled his hand back away. She looked at it with something like sorrow.

"What is it, Jean? You're killing me with suspense." He added a shrug to pretend he was joking and tried to make his words as soft as he had wanted his touch to be. "Go ahead and say what's on your heart."

"*You* are on my heart." Her face flamed and he had no desire to stop his mouth from spreading across his face into a grin. "Oh, I didn't mean to say that. I—I mean—"

"You mean you didn't mean it?"

"No, I meant it, I just didn't mean to say it." The flame spread across her cheeks and down her neck. He was grinning so wide it hurt his jaw.

"What I was going to say." She put her palms to her cheeks and closed her eyes and turned a hundred-and-eighty degrees until her back was to him.

The unpleasant suspense was gone. In its place came a heady anticipation. Grant decided he could soak in that all day long.

Jean's shoulders lifted as she breathed deeply. She dropped her hands to her sides and looked upward. After a moment, she turned and came close. "I would like to ask you...would you...would you please help me learn to enjoy being touched?"

Wow. He could not decipher what the feeling was, but it was filling him so fast and so full he was afraid something would bust. "Jean."

"I know it's a strange request. I debated for hours even asking, but—"

"No," he interrupted. "No, I'm glad. I'm honored that you asked me." He grinned at her. "And I would have hated it if you'd asked anybody else."

She smiled in a way he had never seen, more gentle and at peace. Oh, he loved this woman. He was aching to touch her, for all the right reasons, plus a few extra that would be right once he convinced her to marry him.

"I hoped you would understand."

"I think I do. It's like smiling and starting conversations. New thoughts and new habits need practice."

She nodded, her smile lighting up her eyes. "Exactly."

"Well, I doubt it would surprise you to learn that I'm all sorts of ready to help you practice, but this needs to be done at your speed. I don't want you to get uncomfortable or scared." He walked over to sit on the fallen log and invited her to join him. "How should we start?"

Her manner was shy, more than shy, as she sat on the log as close to the edge as she could, leaving two solid feet between them. He chuckled. This was going to take awhile, which was fine with him. He had all morning to offer. A lifetime if she wanted it.

"I hadn't thought that far. I was too anxious about asking to think about what to do if you said yes."

He looked down at her hands resting on her lap. "How about we start with your hand? I'll put mine here..." He set his hand on the log, but kept it near his leg. "You can put your hand down next to you."

She did, with a smile. "I knew you were the right man to choose." She blushed scarlet again, but lowered her hand.

He moved his an inch or two toward hers, leaving at least a foot still between them. She mirrored the action. He felt his heart thundering. He could not think of anything any woman had ever done, no matter how blatant, that made him feel more pure desire than this woman's gentle, hesitant reach toward his hand. He looked at her. That was the difference; it was pure desire, not the kind that flared and faded. This kind would last till the day he died.

When he sat there, staring, she scooted slightly in his direction. "It's your turn."

The grin was back, on him anyway. Her face still held that soft smile. He moved his hand, this time to the spot exactly in the middle between them. She lifted her hand, paused, then so lightly he barely felt it, set hers on top of his.

Her touch, and the fact that it was intentional, surged through him with a power that was far from reasonable. He turned his hand palm upward and enfolded her small fingers in his. She sucked in a breath, then sighed. "That's nice," she said, her lips tremulous.

"Should I let go?"

"No." She stared at their entwined hands. "I don't want you to let me go."

Someday, he was going to ask her to marry him. For now, what she had just said, and the slightest squeeze he felt from her hand as she said it, was more than enough.

Sunday Morning, August 10

Jean

They crossed the creek, Grant leading the way, Jean behind him. On the other side, he held out his hand. An invitation. Jean bit her lip, looked up at the kindness in his eyes, then reached for him. They walked together, hand in hand, to the church, where he unlocked the main entrance door. He'd had another key made when he moved into that room, the room which held such horror for her and was now his home. She still had not found the courage to tell him so.

He ushered her inside, releasing her hand to prop open the double doors to the auditorium. He walked on ahead as she hesitated in the foyer.

"Jean Louise, you coming?"

She looked up. Grant was at the end of the aisle, waiting. She started toward him, for the first time in her life wondering if one day she would walk down this middle aisle in a long white dress. He would be standing at the end with that same smile on his face. Their friends and family would stare, and she would not even notice, or care. Let them look. Let them see that she was free, was loved, walking toward the future God had always intended.

"You look someplace far away," Grant said when she arrived at his side.

"No." She smiled. "No, I'm right here."

He grasped her hand in his own again and they traveled down the stairs and into the hallway. "Smells like fresh paint." He was walking toward his room. Jean felt her heart quicken, more than it had upstairs, and not for any reason that was good. "So let me guess." She put a light tone to her words and hoped her teeth would not chatter. "You painted that last wall of the nursery that I hadn't gotten to yet."

He squeezed her hand. "No, I don't know how to paint ladybugs and butterflies. I'll leave that to you."

"Grant." She slowed and their hands stretched out between them. "I need to tell you…"

He turned and came back to stand close. "I know, Jean Louise." He reached up and touched her cheek and she shivered. "I know it was his office. I know what happened there."

She trembled and felt tears rising. She shook her head. "I'm sorry I keep crying."

"You've had a lot of tears stored up. I don't mind them coming out." He hesitated, then stepped closer and used one finger to lift her chin until her eyes also lifted to his. "I didn't know if you would want to leave this place and never come back, never be reminded. But in case you wanted to stay, I decided we should replace what was bad with what was good. Make everything new."

The tears overflowed. "I don't—I don't understand."

He put his hand behind her neck and she forced herself not to pull away in fear. His lips, so soft, brushed against her forehead. "Come with me, Jean Louise. I will show you."

Her body wanted to run; her heart told her to stay. Grant stood, silent and patient, waiting for her to decide. She gripped the hand around hers. "Okay."

The last few steps to the room were slow and took all her strength. She had not neared that room for fifteen years, not since a younger Florence had asked for her company as she had stacked the desks someone had lined up for her in the hallway. Jean had suffered quietly as Florence talked about how she would miss the students, how it was so sad that the school had closed, before locking the room and asking Jean to put the key on the pastor's desk. Jean had run from the building, not listening to Florence's questioning call, not stopping until she reached her safe place. The waters of the brook had been cheerful that day, gurgling and dancing high after a week of rain. She had thrown the key into the brook so the water could carry it far away, but it sank to the bottom. It was still there.

"Grant, I can't do this. I can't."

"I love you, Jean." His eyes spoke strength to her. "And you can."

His words were hope and pain. She wished for the courage to ask him to hold her. That is what should happen at this moment, not what he was asking. He gently wiped the tears from her face and opened the door. "I won't leave you. I promise. But please trust me."

Again, he waited while she cried, struggled, wanted to tell him it was too soon and too much. Finally, carried forward by her own prayer for help in time of need, she stepped toward him and looked into the room.

She gasped. "Oh, Grant."

"No more Blue Jean," he said softly.

"You did this for me?" She did not need an answer. She stepped inside and let all she saw fill her heart.

The room had been emptied of the desks, shelves, pictures on the wall, everything. The walls were a bright, inviting shade of green. Two chairs, comfortable and waiting for guests, sat close together near one wall. In front of her against the opposite wall sat a simple round table covered with a white tablecloth. On it lay a stack of paper, and near the stack, a Bible and one of Jamaica's large mugs full of markers.

The nails and hammer next to the mug were her undoing. Tears blinded her as she turned and reached out. Grant found her hands and held them, but Jean pulled them free and put herself between his outstretched hands to push her face into his shoulder and cling to his shirt near his heart. Grant wrapped gentle arms around her and stood, quiet, the only movement the beating of his heart against her hands.

She wanted to say thank you. To say that she loved him. Instead she sobbed, once again, in the shelter of his arms with the feel of his cheek resting down against her hair. A few days ago, he had broken through her shell of silence. Today, his embrace, the safety and love in it, swept the pieces away and she, like the room, felt brand new.

Gladys might
just try to
hit her
with that cane,
and it looked
heavy.

Candy

Candy was the first to walk in. "Warning, a bunch of ladies are coming," she said, giving Jean time to pull from Grant's arms. "Here." Candy held out the box of tissues she'd brought until Jean took two, then set the box on the last available spot on the table. "I have a feeling you won't be the only one needing these, so I borrowed the box from the ladies' bathroom."

She was right. Florence entered, gasped, and right away started crying. Susan did not cry, just walked to the table and started asking questions about what the papers were for.

Brenda was next, her face filled with joy as she hugged Jean and smiled at Grant. "We're supposed to write verses on them, like at Jean's house, right?"

He nodded, but then took the top sheet of paper and handed it to Jean. "I think Jean should go first."

More women filled the room to capacity and watched as Jean chose a royal blue marker and wrote words on her paper. Candy leaned toward Grant. "You should have told me. I could have had these walls filled."

He smiled but shook his head. "You've got plenty of wall space at Jean's. This room is for everyone else, to practice letting God's words set them free."

"Hmm, you're even smarter than I thought." Candy reached for the hammer and pounded in the nail Jean held to her paper, then read the verse aloud. "*If the Son makes you free, you shall be free indeed.* John 8:36. Great verse. Who's next?"

"We can't have a wall full of verses without putting up ours." Brenda used a red marker to write II Timothy 1:7. She nailed it to the wall. "Florence, you take a turn."

Florence, still somewhat in a daze, pulled a black marker from the mug and started writing. She nailed her paper up and Candy read it aloud. "*Forgetting those things which are behind and reaching forward to those things which are ahead...*"

Florence edged around several ladies to stand in front of Jean. "I will help in any way I can. I will testify with you, go with you to court sessions once he's found and put in jail, anything I can do. I'm already collecting information to try to contact the others I fear also might...have reason to testify. Jean, I'm so sorry I didn't try to find out what was really wrong. I'm so sorry I didn't—"

Candy felt her own eyes prick with tears when Jean hugged her and whispered, "I forgive you. Now go read your verse again, as many times as it takes."

One after another, women wrote verses and Candy helped nail them all over the wall. Several pulled tissues from the box before leaving the room.

"This is a wonderful place, Grant," Brenda said from the chair where she sat. "I love these chairs. But what about you? Will you be staying with us again?"

"No, now that I've got a steady job with Doug, I started renting a place in town. I want this room to stay open so people can come before or after church and study or pray together."

"Or hammer if they need to," Candy added. "It's good stress relief."

Brenda checked her watch and rose. "I need to go. Sunday school will be starting in a few minutes." On her way to the door she motioned toward the wall. "Why don't you take a turn, Candy?"

"I have enough room at Jean's house." Candy smiled over at Grant. "But I would like to put one up as a prayer request?"

"Please do," Grant said. Candy noticed he was next to Jean again as she pulled another tissue from the box. Candy wrote, then chuckled at the paper she held against the wall. "I wrote the verse, '*Pray without ceasing*,' and then wrote 'for Champagne' under it, before I realized how funny that would sound to a visitor."

Florence, writing on another piece of paper, giggled. "Just think what Gladys would—"

Candy put a quick hand on her arm and quirked her head toward the door where Gladys had just walked in. "What is all this hammering?" She marched around the room, looking at the papers, stopping in front of Candy's. "Pray without ceasing for Champagne," she read aloud.

Florence giggled again and Gladys sent her a glare that could have fried an egg. "That is not funny, Florence." She turned to Candy. "Would you like us to start asking God to rain cigarettes down from the sky, too?"

"Gladys, really," Florence said.

"Really what?" She yanked the paper from the nail, crumpled it up, and held it out. "I've been at this church for—"

"Gladys, I'm thinking of moving out and getting my own place."

Only five people remained in the room, but it felt like a whole group had quieted. Grant and Jean exited, but Candy remained as Florence calmly wrote, "Pray without ceasing for Candy's friend named Champagne" on a new paper and nailed it to the wall.

Her sister was huffing and attempting to fan herself with the useless wad of crumpled paper. "What you said....What on earth do you mean by it?"

"Gladys, I have listened to you gripe and complain for as long as I can remember. All these years, I thought it was being loving to stay and give you someone to boss around, but I think I might have been wrong. I'm giving you two weeks, Gladys. If you become a person enjoyable to live with, I will stay. If not, I will move out and you can wallow in your misery by yourself."

"How can you say such things to me?" Gladys stomped her cane on the floor. "I gave up years of my life to take care of you as a child. I raised you, and—"

"I was fourteen, and did need you at first, that's true." Florence had settled into one of the chairs, but she stood. Candy tried to fade into the corner. She'd leave, but Florence might need some moral support. And who knew? Gladys might just try to hit her with that cane, and it looked heavy.

Florence stood face to face with her sister. "I haven't been fourteen for a long, long time, Gladys, and you can't use that excuse anymore. For the last forty years, I'm the one who chose to stay with you, not the other way around."

Gladys' eyes narrowed. "You stayed because there was nothing better offered to you."

Florence shook her head. "No, I stayed because you needed me. Doug Jennings asked me to marry him on my twentieth birthday. I told him no, that you wouldn't have been able to stand being alone."

Gladys stood paralyzed, her hand gripping her cane. "You've been living with me our whole lives out of pity?"

"Not pity. Love." Florence put a hand over Gladys' on the cane. "But I won't live in your bitterness any more. I only have so many years left, and I want to live them with joy."

A sniff, and Gladys choked out, "I never realized…"

"We can start over if you want." Florence smiled. "All sorts of things are being made new these days, Gladys. I know your heart hurts. Jesus could make it new, too."

Gladys almost fell into a chair and stared at her sister, who sat next to her and took her hand before she started praying aloud. Candy decided it was time for her to leave. As unobtrusively as possible, she looked up a passage Brenda had shared at the Bible study, then went to the stack of paper and wrote a verse on the top sheet. If Florence saw it, she could nail it up later.

Candy left the paper face up, showing bright pink words that said, "*He has made everything beautiful in its time.*"

Monday Morning, August 11

Jamaica

The morning started like a cup of black coffee, dark and bitter to the taste, but then the shop door opened and Pastor Henderson and Brenda, Grant and Jean, and Ian and Susan entered. The food, baby gifts, and genuine care they brought with them was scoop after scoop of sugar and cream added to her cup.

"We'll miss you, Jamaica," Brenda said. "I heard you singing behind me in church this past Sunday. If you come back, I think we should start up a choir again."

Jamaica sent a cheeky grin back toward the stairs where Candy helped Pansy bring their suitcases down. "Oh, I'll be back. And I'll have to make it soon, before Candy slurps up my entire stock of whipped cream."

"It's cheaper than the decaf coffee that Pansy's been drinking all morning," Candy retorted.

"It helps with my nausea," Pansy argued, smiling and releasing her suitcase when Grant offered to carry it to the truck for her. "Thanks."

Jamaica wanted to stay in the safe circle of love she'd found here in this little town. She prayed God would let them return, that she and Pansy would become a family again, that God would show them how to create a happy home for the baby to grow up in. Her friends were packing up food for them to take on their drive, and Candy filled two Styrofoam cups with their favorite coffees to go. She looked around for some excuse to hold the goodbyes away and her eyes landed on Jean. "Jean, girl, you are a totally different person these days. That emerald green outfit makes your eyes bright green, and I'm loving those sandals." She pointed toward Jean's reflection in the window. "I think you have arrived."

Jean laughed. "I've arrived, but to where?"

"Someplace very good." Grant's voice was full of love and Jamaica wasn't the only woman in the room who sighed.

"Momma, you ready?" Pansy held the baby gifts to the barely noticeable bulge around her middle. She had thanked everyone, had her decaf cup of coffee in hand, and was standing near the door.

"Almost." Friends hugged, said goodbye, promised to stay in touch. Jamaica tapped Jean on the arm. "I need to talk to you for a minute."

The others left and Jean sat across from Jamaica at one of the tables. "I hope you come back soon, Jamaica," she said. "We will all miss you."

Jamaica waved her hand. "You can skip all that. I don't have much time, since everybody's waiting outside near the truck, but I had to get this out. Ever since I gave my life back to God, He's been whispering to me to talk to you, and I didn't want to get all the way to Atlanta and have to come back because He wouldn't give me peace until I said what He told me to say."

Jean looked concerned. "Of course, Jamaica. What is it?"

"It's about you and that hunk of a man God sent your way."

The smile on Jean's face turned soft. "I'm so thankful for him."

"I am too, but listen up." She scooted her chair forward. "I know right now it feels like he's the whole world, along with the sun and the stars. But don't you go thinking that he's going to fill up everything you need. I look at you and that boy and I know that if you can let out all that stuff you've been hiding away those years, your marriage is going to sizzle. But—"

"Jamaica!" Jean whispered, her eyes darting to look around the shop. "He hasn't asked me to marry him. We haven't even gone on a real date yet."

"Well, that's just a matter of time." Jamaica saw Pansy waving to her from outside. She held up a hand, then focused back on Jean, hurrying her words. "Listen, when I got married, I expected my man to fix all the broken pieces of my past and be everything I needed, and he just couldn't do it. I realize now that one of the reasons my divorce happened was because he got tired of trying to carry the weight of all my expectations. For a long time I resented him, hated him even. I blamed him, out loud in front of Pansy and anybody else, for all my heartache. That's why I have to go back to Atlanta. To make it right."

Jean reached out to put a hand on hers. Jamaica took the hand and held it tight. "You have something beautiful, but don't put on Grant Henderson what only belongs to God. It ends up all wrong. I asked my husband to provide all my needs instead of asking God. Think of Alice. She stopped following God to follow Rod's selfish version of what the Bible says about submission. Florence said she visited her twice this week and she just sits there, alone and confused."

Jamaica stood and Jean walked with her to the door. Before she opened it, Jamaica stopped, nodding her head to where Grant waited with Pansy and the others. "As wonderful as that man is—and he's really something—don't ever put him, or your love for him, above God. God is the only One who can provide your deepest needs. He'll provide a lot of them through the man He asks to love you, but always keep straight where it ultimately comes from."

Jean surprised Jamaica by wrapping her in a tight hug. "Thank you, Jamaica," she said. "I know God wanted you to say that to me. I needed it." She actually grinned and Jamaica found her own smile widening in response. "I think I should go home, find some verses about that, and nail them to my bedroom wall."

"So there's a spot in your house Candy didn't take over?" Jamaica felt the laughter deep inside. "She's not moving in here till tonight, but I've already got verses all over the place from that one weekend she stayed. I told her I was repainting when we came back, so she decided she could skip the nails and write straight on the walls here."

Jean laughed and opened the shop door. The bell jingled, as if rejoicing with her.

Jamaica had Jean hold her cup while she got into the vehicle. She couldn't resist one last bit of rumored news. "Oh hey, I heard that Florence Simmons almost got married to your uncle, Doug somebody, over forty years ago. I asked Susan and she told me he's been single for the past ten years since his wife died. You got any plans for that?"

Jean closed the door and handed Jamaica her cup, a gleam in her eyes. "Grant's taking me to Uncle Doug's for a little visit this afternoon."

*She looked
up at him
and could find
no words
beautiful enough
to respond.*

Chapter Thirty-Three
Sunday Morning, September 7

Jean

The mirror reflected Jean's powder blue silk dress and white sandals. She had no discernible reason, but today felt important and she wanted to look her best. Or perhaps there was no reason other than the delight she felt whenever Grant's eyes lit up at the sight of her.

She brushed her hair until it shone, smiling at herself in the mirror. The past four weeks had flown by, weeks of joy and love. Grant came over nearly every night after work to invite her to dinner, try to convince her to ride on his motorcycle again, or just sit on the porch and talk. They had studied the Bible together, shared their childhood stories, argued a time or two. Even the times they sat in silence, watching the sunset, were precious. He had become her best friend, and so much more.

Small rocks clanked off her upstairs window. A month ago, she would have startled, frightened and wary. Today, she smiled and went to open the window. "I'm not riding that motorcycle, not even if you serenade me."

Grant stood below, arms out, grinning. "It's a good thing, since I can't sing. What if I quote poetry? You know, roses are red, violets are blue...etcetera, etcetera ending with something that rhymes with blue."

"That was inspiring." She leaned out until her hair fell down over her shoulders. "What are you doing here? It's too early for church and too late to ask me to breakfast."

"I have something to show you."

"What?"

"Not telling. Come with me. I know you're ready early."

She couldn't deny it. "I'll be right down."

His grin was still in place when she opened the front door, but as she walked down the porch steps toward him, it softened into that smile that made the ludicrous, irrational phrase about one's knees turning weak feel totally appropriate. Brenda told her Jamaica had called Grant's eyes "melty, like dark chocolate" once. Indeed.

"What are you thinking about with that smile on your face, Miss Jameson?" he asked.

"Dark chocolate."

He crossed his arms. "A guy can't compete with chocolate."

She glanced sideways at him. "Oh, I don't know..."

Grant reached for her hand and she loved the feel of her small palm encased in his large, warm one. "Where are we going?"

"To church."

"Did you re-paint the green room or something?"

"No, but this does have something to do with paint."

"Mysterious as well as charming. I'll have to tell Florence to add that to your list of qualities."

He put a fist to his heart. "We spent the last month together, and you only have two things on my list of qualities? You know how to beat a guy down."

She kissed him on the cheek and then pulled his hand forward when he stopped and stared at her. "I was talking about Florence's list. My list of your qualities is quite long."

"You kissed me."

"Just on the cheek." She looked away self-consciously. "You should stop looking at me like that. You make me nervous." She let go of his hand and crossed the brook first.

He caught up. "But I like looking at you."

"Now you're flattering. Why do I get the feeling we're going to church so you can ask me to do some chore you don't feel like doing?"

Grant caught her hand again. "Because you haven't gotten used to the idea of being attractive."

She had nothing to say to that. She followed him inside the church and toward the green room. A glance inside showed Brenda and Candy with their Bibles open, sitting in front of the wall nearly covered now in verses. Jean waved, but was surprised when Grant continued on past the room and to the nursery.

"What are we doing here?"

"Wait and see."

He turned the knob and pulled open both parts of the split door. She stepped inside. He couldn't want to paint more ladybugs. She had finished the final wall a week ago.

"Grant, what's this all about?" She turned and froze. He had shut the door behind him. They were alone. He turned the lock and her body instantly responded. The old fear came flooding back. She started shaking from the inside out. "Grant..."

"I didn't expect anybody to be here so early," he commented with a shrug. He glanced her way, then focused, looking her over. "Jean, what's wrong?"

She could not pull her gaze from the lock. He noticed and went back to the door. "I'm so sorry. What I had to say—I didn't want to be interrupted. I wasn't thinking." He undid the lock and started to turn the doorknob.

"No. No." She would not live like this. She would not live in fear. Jean stopped his hand. "Leave it. I trust you. And I refuse to spend the rest of my life fighting shadows. Memories." She turned the lock back into place. "Not to mention, if we ever have kids we're going to want privacy sometimes, and—" She clamped both hands over her mouth and looked at Grant, eyes wide, her words mumbled behind her hands. "Oh my goodness! Did I just say that?" His face might as well have turned into one big exclamation point. She yanked at the doorknob. "I have to get out of here. I'm so embarrassed. I've never in my life—"

His arm snaked around her waist and pulled her away from the door, against his hard chest. "Jean Louise." His voice was warm and low and curled her toes. "I want to have lots of kids with you, but don't you think that before we discuss that idea, I should at least kiss you first?"

She was trembling again. He must have felt and misread it, for he released her and stepped back. Jean longed to explain but did not dare. Not after what she'd already said.

Grant backed into the changing table. "Oh, the reason I brought you here." He turned and lifted the piece of furniture with ease, setting it down several feet away.

He pointed and Jean looked at the floor. "The paint splotch." A small circle of yellow paint dotted the carpet. "I'd forgotten it was there."

"That's what I wanted to show you."

She knelt and took a closer look. "The paint splotch?"

"It's something about the paint that I want to say to you."

"That I'm uncoordinated?"

He chuckled and pulled her to her feet. "Would you let me finish? I've been working on this speech for a week and you're messing me up."

Curiosity piqued, eyebrows up, she nodded. He took both her hands in his. "The day this happened, you had been singing while you did something good for others. Then you dropped the paint and all you could think about was the tiny bad thing that happened instead of all the good. I covered it over." He smiled.

"And I must have done a good job because you forgot it was there."

She looked at the carpet as he continued. "What happened to you when you were a child was no small thing. I will never think so. But I want to cover it over. Every bad memory, I want to replace with good ones. Every hurt, I want to cover over with so much love, that in time you might have days where you forget it's there."

Those frustrating tears were near the surface again. She looked up at him and could find no words beautiful enough to respond.

His hand caressed her cheek, her hair, and settled just under her jaw to hold her face toward his. "I wasn't going to say so yet, but since you already brought up kids..." His lips curved when her face flushed, but then his voice changed. It was at once husky and soft. "I plan to love you for the rest of my life."

She gasped. "Grant—"

Someone knocked loudly on the nursery door and Jean let out a surprised cry. "Hey." The voice was Candy's. "Brenda asked me to open all the doors. Sunday school is going to start in ten minutes."

"Okay," Grant called out. "So much for privacy," he murmured, and Jean laughed.

"Mr. Henderson, may I have a turn to say something before we go?"

He tipped an imaginary hat. "Miss Jameson, be my guest."

She pulled back a little to face him. "I'm...I would like you to kiss me, please."

He looked at her for a long time, long enough for her to feel self-conscious again. Then, with slow, careful movements, his hand found that place beneath her jaw, and lifted her chin. "I love you, Jean," he whispered. His lips brushed her forehead.

"I love you, Grant," she whispered back. "But you missed."

He smiled, kissing the tip of her nose.

"You missed again."

He kissed each cheek.

She was breathless by the time his mouth neared hers. "I love you, Jean," he breathed against her lips. She shivered and he hesitated. It was she who moved to fill the space between them. Their lips touched, very slightly. His were soft and warm and full. She sighed into him and he kissed her a second time.

A knock on the door parted them again as Candy called out, "Nursery worker headed this way."

Jean wanted to stay exactly where she was. In this moment. In his arms. Candy's wry comment, "As in soon," made her reluctantly pull away. Grant gave her one more quick kiss before releasing her.

He took her hand and they walked to the door, his eyes on her full of love. "Remind me later," he said with that amazing smile, "before we discuss how many kids to have, to ask you to marry me."

Grant
re-entered
the room,
a familiar,
large black
trash can
in hand.

Stewart

"Welcome, everyone."

Stewart adjusted his glasses to look over the congregation. His wife smiled up at him from the front row, her hands comfortably in her lap, her nails long and painted a feminine shade of pink. Grant sat behind her, his arm around Jean, who was so changed he scarcely recognized her as the scared young woman he had met that first Sunday here. Around the auditorium, he saw deacons with their families, men who not only enjoyed having a say at meetings now, but who were bringing years of withheld ministry ideas to the table. On his left, halfway back, Florence sat next to Gladys. Stewart wasn't sure what had happened with Gladys, but she hadn't fanned herself or said one caustic comment in the last three weeks. It was refreshing, but he hoped she wasn't falling ill. Next to Florence was a man Jean had introduced to him as her uncle Doug. He seemed rather besotted with Florence, and she kept borrowing Gladys' fan and using it on her red face.

Up near the front sat Candy. With a smile in her direction, Stewart led the congregation to Luke chapter 7. He read a familiar story about a woman, and Jesus, and a man named Simon, ending with Jesus' words to them both. *"Therefore I say to you, her sins, which are many, are forgiven, for she loved much. But to whom little is forgiven, the same loves little."*

Stewart left his Bible open on the podium and walked down the stairs to be level with the pews. He leaned over the first one to whisper something to his brother, who smiled and nodded. Grant then whispered something to Jean. They both rose and slipped from the pew and out the door near the choir loft that led downstairs.

"I want you to imagine if something like this story happened in our time, maybe even in our church. Imagine a woman came in, one everyone knew as a sinner..."

Candy was grinning already.

"And she approached Jesus in a way that was rather scandalous..."

Heads turned. People whispered. Gladys still had not fanned herself though, so Stewart wasn't sure if he was getting through.

"And at least one person, who felt himself religious, thought Jesus shouldn't get anywhere near her."

He looked around at the congregation he had come to love. "Jesus didn't stick up for Simon, the religious man, but nor did he lecture him. He simply told him a small story about two people who owed money. One owed much. One owed not as much. However, neither could pay, so both were doomed. When both debts were forgiven, one of them loved more."

Grant re-entered the room, a familiar, large black trash can in hand. Jean followed, carrying something wrapped in her arms. Stewart was curious, but did not want to get distracted, so he looked back toward the pews. "The thing I find so interesting is that Simon knew the right answer, but he didn't seem to understand what it meant for him. My question for us today is not whether you know the answer. My question is, if the story happened today, which person would you be?"

He welcomed Grant's approach with a smile. His brother stood beside him, the trash can set in front of him. Jean now sat near Brenda, the blue item she carried now in her lap.

"Would you be Simon, angry, certain you know what is right and others are wrong, to the point that you're telling Jesus what

He should and shouldn't allow? Are you Jesus, ready to accept anyone who comes in genuine repentance and love?" He pulled the trash can in front of him. "Or are you the woman, needing to come and be forgiven much, ready to worship, no matter what anyone says or thinks?"

He went back to the pulpit and looked at his Bible. "The story doesn't end with Simon. I don't know what happened to him, but he did not seem to be willing to change. Rather, the story ends in verse fifty, with Jesus saying to the woman, *'Your faith has saved you. Go in peace.'*"

Stewart closed his Bible and went back to stand behind the trash can. "This morning, I put a stack of papers and pens at the end of each row. I want you to pass them down, and, if you are willing, I want you to write on that paper whatever it is that keeps you from coming to Jesus as this woman did. Are you worried people might talk? Are you afraid of giving something up? Are you holding back something that keeps you captive?"

He held out the trash can, knowing a huge smile was on his face. "Weeks ago, we watched someone come to Jesus. She utilized this trash can, dumping in her old life and asking Jesus for a new one. I'd like to invite you to follow her example. Whatever you write on that paper, would you come and give it to Jesus? What should you throw away so you can 'Go in peace' as Jesus said?"

After a few minutes, one or two people rose slowly, hesitantly, papers in hand. They tossed them into the trash can, and he rejoiced to see their faces break out in smiles before they returned to their seats. One couple came, both holding one paper, then holding each other once the paper was gone. More came, until nearly everyone in the church had tossed in something. One man took the money from his billfold and threw it in. "Money has run my life," he said. "Not anymore."

Stewart wasn't the emotional kind, but he wanted to shout for joy. Then Candy stood and walked his way. She had no paper in hand. He felt his Adam's apple bob as he swallowed. She wasn't going to wipe his feet with her hair or anything, was she?

She touched the trash can almost lovingly, then spoke softly into his ear.

"Are you sure?" he asked.

She nodded and looked out at the church. "I want to get baptized to show the world I'm a follower of Jesus," she said, not waiting for Stewart to share her news. "And then I want to join this church."

Stewart was pleasantly surprised when the congregation clapped their approval. "Ladies and gentleman," he said when the noise died down. "I'd like to present to you this woman, who wants to join our church." He looked at her once more and she nodded. "Her name is Candace."

Grant put the trash can to the side a little and Stewart prayed to end the service. He had forgotten to ask the congregation to come greet…Candace…officially, but he was again pleasantly surprised to see she was already surrounded.

"I'll replace it."

Stewart turned back to Grant. "Replace what?"

Grant nodded to where Jean approached, her hands around the blue thing that, as she got closer, Stewart realized was a small desktop shredder. It must be the one Jean used on the leftover bulletins every week, though why she took the time to shred them was still a mystery to him.

She sent a smile of love toward Grant, then smiled at Stewart. Without a word, she looked at the shredder held in her hands, then dropped it into the trash can. It landed with a thump and multiple papers flew out around it.

Brenda came to look. "Don't you need that?"

Jean's eyes were still on the shredder, now just a piece of trash. She shook her head with a smile. "Not anymore."

And behold, a woman in the city who was a sinner, when she knew that Jesus sat at the table in the Pharisee's house, brought an alabaster flask of fragrant oil, and stood at His feet behind Him weeping; and she began to wash His feet with her tears, and wiped them with the hair of her head; and she kissed His feet and anointed them with the fragrant oil. Now when the Pharisee who had invited Him saw this, he spoke to himself, saying, "This Man, if He were a prophet, would know who and what manner of woman this is who is touching Him, for she is a sinner."

And Jesus answered and said to him, "Simon, I have something to say to you."

So he said, "Teacher, say it."

"There was a certain creditor who had two debtors. One owed five hundred denarii, and the other fifty. And when they had nothing with which to repay, he freely forgave them both. Tell Me, therefore, which of them will love him more?"

Simon answered and said, "I suppose the one whom he forgave more."

And He said to him, "You have rightly judged." Then He turned to the woman and said to Simon, "Do you see this woman? I entered your house; you gave Me no water for My feet, but she has washed My feet with her tears and wiped them with the hair of her head. You gave Me no kiss, but this woman has not ceased to kiss My feet since the time I came in. You did not anoint My head with oil, but this woman has anointed My feet with fragrant oil. Therefore I say to you, her sins, which are many, are forgiven, for she loved much. But to whom little is forgiven, the same loves little."

Then He said to her, "Your sins are forgiven."

And those who sat at the table with Him began to say to themselves, "Who is this who even forgives sins?"

Then He said to the woman, "Your faith has saved you. Go in peace."

-Luke 7:37-50

ACKNOWLEDGMENTS

My thanks to Shelly Lantz for sharing your story and showing in person the freedom of a changed life. It's a blessing being your friend. And to Robby Dilmore for asking me to speak on your radio program so I got to meet her!

Thanks to Pastor Todd Braswell, now at Waterlife Church, whose telling of the story of the scandalous woman got me imagining that scene of Candy walking into church with all her stuff. I had a hard time paying attention after that, but it wasn't because you weren't inspiring. Quite the opposite!

Though I doubt she'll ever see it, my thanks to Francine Rivers for writing *Redeeming Love*. A friend of mine, years ago, said, "This book changed the way I see God," and I remember thinking, *That's the kind of book I want to write*. Thank you for writing stories that matter and leading others to have the same goal.

Thank you to my agent, Diana Flegal, for believing in this book, and helping hone it to make the writing tighter.

Thank you to author Yvonne Lehman, for your excellent critique of the beginning that helped me switch things around and make the story more focused.

To the real Jamaica, thank you for letting me borrow your name. It inspired one of my most fun characters!

Thanks to Sue Huey for reading, finding typos, and encouraging every book since the very first one.

To all the readers who write and share how much you love my books, or how they've made a difference, I thank you. You keep me wanting to write more!

READER CLUB/DISCUSSION QUESTIONS
PART ONE: Chapters 1-7

1. The story begins with Jean, who carries a terrible secret. Do you think most women have secret hurt in their past somewhere? We often think we are the only ones with deep fears or dark memories or hurtful secrets. Why do you think that is?
(See Proverbs 14:10; Psalm 44:21b; Psalm 139:1-12)

2. Do you feel this is especially true in the church? Do you think people tend to act like things are fine even if they aren't? Why?
(See 1 Samuel 16:7; James 5:16)

3. Grant struggles with comparing himself to his brother and feeling his mom favored his brother. In your opinion, do you think Grant's parents were right in asking him to accompany his brother and help him for six months? Why or why not?
(See Proverbs 27:17; Galatians 6:2; Philippians 2:4)

4. Stewart stops and talks with prostitutes. Do you think that, as a pastor, this was wise or unwise for him to do? Your reasons? In your opinion, would have been better for him to ask Brenda to talk with them instead?
(See Luke 5:31-32; 1 Corinthians 10:12; Proverbs 6:25-27)

5. Candy has lived in the town for years but never attended church. Do you think we hesitate to reach out and invite the lost people in our area because we assume they'd come on their own if they were seeking? What was the reason Candy finally came?
(See Luke 19:10; 2 Corinthians 5:20)

6. How do you think your church would react if a known "sinner" showed up this Sunday? Would the person be welcomed or ostracized?
(See Matthew 7:1-2; Matthew 22:37-40; Romans 13:10)

7. How would you personally feel if someone like Candy came to Jesus in such an unconventional manner? What do you think would be the right way to respond? Would you have a battle choosing between what you think is right and how you feel, or how you worry others might perceive your actions?

(See Galatians 1:10; Colossians 3:23; John 12:42-43)

8. Brenda's fear keeps her from acting. Why does worrying what others think of us paralyze us so much? Whose approval should we be seeking?
(See Proverbs 29:25; Colossians 3:1; 1 John 4:18)

9. What might have happened to Candy that Sunday if no one had braved approaching her and sharing the Scriptures? Do you think lost people sometimes turn away from church because of the way they are treated if they do go? Do you think sometimes we expect people to act righteous before God makes them righteous? How is this different than what Jesus taught?
(See Matthew 7:12; Romans 5:8; Luke 14:23)

10. Does the Bible verse about abstaining from all appearance of evil (I Thess. 5:22) mean we should avoid doing anything anyone might misunderstand? How would living that way cripple us and our ministry? Did Jesus work hard to avoid people misunderstanding Him?
(See John 7:40-43; Luke 7:33-35; John 6:66)

11. Is Rod a good example of a judgmental person? If you've ever known someone like that, did the people who tried to make them happy ever succeed? Do you think judgmental people will find something to criticize regardless how much we try to please them? Why or why not?
(See Proverbs 19:19; Proverbs 28:23; Proverbs 22:24-25)

12. How hard would it be not to gossip about Candy? How could women of God talk about her and about helping her without gossiping? What might you say to a group that is speaking in a judgmental or non-edifying way?
(See Ephesians 4:29; 1 John 4:20; Proverbs 29:11)

READER CLUB/DISCUSSION QUESTIONS
PART TWO: Chapters 8-15

1. Stewart admits it is hard for men to avoid looking when women dress in a way that draws attention to their bodies. Do you feel women should be able to wear what they want, and guys just need to not be affected? Do you think we women have a responsibility to help our brothers in Christ by dressing modestly? What does the Bible say about how we are to dress?
   (See 1 Timothy 2:9-10; Ephesians 4:1-3; Philippians 2:2-4)

2. What do you think of Stewart's rule about not taking the second look? Can you think of a parallel for us women? Pornography is a growing addiction for women, but there are other ways we give in to temptation that may be more subtle or seem less sinful. What are some of the temptations we women are drawn to more than men?
   (See 1 John 2:15-17; Colossians 3:5; Ephesians 4:20-32)

3. Rod manipulates situations to make certain people look bad and him look good. Do you think people who desire power might be drawn to religious settings? Why or why not? How can we spot people who are not serving for God's glory but rather their own?
   (See Matthew 7:15-17, 20; Psalm 115:1; Psalm 97:10a)

4. Jamaica desperately wants to find her daughter. When that desire is offered at the expense of doing wrong, Jamaica feels she has no choice. Is there ever a time when we have no way out? Were there other options for Jamaica? How would you have advised her?
   (See 1 Corinthians 10:13; Psalm 34:4; Psalm 118:6; Psalm 37:5)

5. Candy is broken. Torn to her soul, as she puts it, and she wonders if God Himself could heal a wound that deep. What verses would you give her to heal the hurts of her past?
   (See 2 Corinthians 5:17; Psalm 34:18; Jeremiah 31:3; Hosea 2:14-16, 19-20)

6. Candy's past shows. Many women's do not. Do you think we might cover over our hurts and shame, pretending them away rather than bringing them to God for healing. Why? What are we

afraid will happen if we show who we really are or things that have happened to us?
(See Psalm 62:8; Isaiah 1:18; Isaiah 55:1-2; Matthew 11:28-30)

7. Do you think we sometimes fear Jesus judges us like people often do? When we confess our sins as He tells us to, what does the Bible say happens to them?
(See Hebrews 10:17; Hebrews 8:12; Jeremiah 31:34; Psalm 32:5; Psalm 103:12; Isaiah 38:17, 1 John 1:9)

8. Candy calls Jean "Lemon Water." What drink would best fit you? Can you think of someone who could use some sugar in theirs (but no need to share it out loud!)?
(See Proverbs 11:22; Proverbs 25:24; Proverbs 17:14)

9. Does *Shredded* seem like a unrealistic fiction story to you? Candy's experience might be out of the ordinary, but do you think the lives and fears and experiences of Florence or Brenda or Jean mirror women all around us? Even in our churches? Do you think if we asked, would we discover that every woman has a story worth hearing, and if we heard it, we would understand better how to love them like Jesus does?
(See Ephesians 4:32; 1 John 4:7-8, 11)

10. How did you feel when Candy said she knew some of the Bible verses didn't work because of how Brenda and Jean lived? Is there a truth in the Bible that you know in your head but do not live like you really believe it?
(See James 1:22; John 14:15)

11. Can you implement Candy's idea of finding verses specifically about what you struggle with, writing them down (maybe not nailing them to the wall!), and then determining to live them? How can you personalize that idea so it works for you?
(See Psalm 119:105; Psalm 119:133; Psalm 119:11)

READER CLUB/DISCUSSION QUESTIONS
PART THREE: Chapters 16-22

1. Jean keeps pushing Grant away, though she is drawn toward him. How is that similar to how so many people are with Christ? If Grant's gentle, continued pursuit of Jean is like Christ's pursuit of the lost, does that change the way we see people who might get upset or push away when we give the Good News?
(See Galatians 6:9; 2 Peter 3:9; 1 John 4:19)

2. People are getting hints that abuse happened within the church. All along the way, it is easier to ignore the hints than try to find out the truth. Why do you think people sometimes turn away from red flags or disturbing possibilities? What are some of the "reasons" you might hear within the church for not exposing sins like abuse within the church? Are they Biblical?
(See Proverbs 28:13; John 3:20-21; Ephesians 5:8-13)

3. Grant suggests a sports ministry and Rod and Gladys object. Whenever there is a new idea, what do you think should be the criteria for deciding if it is a good ministry or not?
(See 1 Corinthians 10:31; Romans 12:1-13; 1 Peter 4:10-11)

4. What do you think of Candy's strip club ministry idea? Do you think you'd be able to go with her? Why or why not?
(See John 8:7; Luke 15:1-7; Luke 14:12-14)

5. Have Candy and Champagne's stories changed your perception of prostitutes? What are some of the stereotypes we tend to think when we see women on the streets? If you knew a woman felt worthless, had been abused, and was forced into that life, would you think of her, pray for her, and approach her differently than if you assumed she wanted to be there?
(See Mark 10:43-45; Matthew 21:28-32; Jude 22)

6. If our perception of prostitutes might be wrong, is it possible that our assumptions about other groups of people could be wrong as well? Personally, is there a group or type of person you tend to think is beyond the reach of God's love, or you shouldn't bother sharing Christ with or inviting to church because they surely aren't interested?

(See 1 Timothy 1:15-16; Mark 16:15; 1 Corinthians 1:25-29)

7. Do you think it was smart for Grant to go meet Champagne in a hotel? What would you have suggested they do?
    (See John 17:15; Jeremiah 17:9; Proverbs 4:27)

8. Candy's new faith is tested when Slash finds her at Jamaica's. How did memorizing God's Word help her in time of need? How did it benefit her more than just reading the Bible every day but not memorizing specific verses?
    (See Psalm 37:31; 2 Timothy 3:16-17; Ephesians 6:10-17)

9. John 8:36 says that if Jesus makes you free, you are free indeed. Is that really true? In what areas of life, or circumstances, is it true? How would it apply to the struggle you are having, or fear you are facing, right now?
    (See John 8:36; 2 Timothy 1:7; Galatians 5:1; Philippians 4:11-13)

10. Candy is much more comfortable looking into internet sites where girls are being trafficked, while Jean cannot bear it. Do you think God wants all of us doing the same thing, or are certain people equipped for certain ministries? Should we push people into whatever work we are passionate about, or does God give us different passions to pursue for Him?
    (See 1 Corinthians 12:4-7, 17-18; 2 Corinthians 10:12)

11. What is your passion? What do you want most to do for God? Are you doing it?
    (See Luke 10:2; Isaiah 6:8; Ephesians 4:1-3; Psalm 37:3-5)

READER CLUB/DISCUSSION QUESTIONS
PART FOUR: Chapters 23-35

1. Because of circumstances (Grant being asleep and there being no one else to do it), Jean is forced into a situation that shows her she is braver than she knows. Can you think of a time God put you into an uncomfortable situation that you wished He would get you out of, but then in the end you realized it helped you grow?
(See Proverbs 3:5-6; Psalm 32:8; Deuteronomy 8:16)

2. The picture of Stewart and Grant in the paper looks very incriminating. Satan loves to use such things to undermine God's work and His people. How can we respond when people see something or hear something secondhand and assume the worst? What is the way to find out the real truth?
(See John 7:24; Exodus 23:1; Proverbs 6:16-19; Proverbs 17:15; Proverbs 19:5)

3. When Jean finally admits her secret of abuse, everyone is devastated, including Jean. Is it understandable that she would want even more to hide after revealing her secret than before? For a victim, knowing it wasn't their fault doesn't always make it feel like it wasn't their fault. How can we assure victims of past abuse in a way that helps them see the truth?
(See Psalm 9:9-10; Hebrews 12:12; Joel 2:25a; Psalm 72:4; Isaiah 58:6)

4. Does forgiveness mean ignoring the sin? How has that idea led to continued abuse within churches or other Christian settings throughout history? Do you think it was right for Rod's abuse to be reported to the police? Why or why not? Do you think churches should seek to keep such things quiet to "protect the ministry"? Why or why not?
(See Revelation 2:2; Matthew 18:15-17; 1 John 4:1; Romans 13:1-5)

5. How does God's command of submission for a wife differ from what Alice Carson was taught by her husband?
(See 1 Peter 3:7-8; Ephesians 5:21-33)

6. Do you think it was good for the ladies to address Jean's pain and ask how to help? Do we sometimes shy away from saying

something because we're afraid of saying the wrong thing? Can that make the person feel isolated, or that we do not care? What is a better option?
(See John 13:34-35; Romans 12:15; 2 Corinthians 1:3-4)

7. Victims may have a hard time seeing any kind of touch as positive. How did you feel with the way Grant responded to Jean's request that he teach her to enjoy being touched?
(Psalm 18:35; Zephaniah 3:17; Psalm 42:8)

8. Was it good for Grant to re-make Rod Carson's office, or would it have been better to board it up and leave it locked away? Explain your reasons for your answer.
(See Ecclesiastes 3:11a; Philippians 3:13; Ecclesiastes 3:1-8)

9. Florence finally stands up to Gladys. Do you think that was a godly thing, or a selfish thing? How had each of them let their false ideas keep them miserable for so long? Why do you think we avoid the one hard conversation that can heal years of hurt or misunderstanding?
(See Ephesians 4:15; James 5:19-20; Matthew 18:15; 2 Timothy 2:24-26)

10. Jamaica tells Jean not to put all her hopes and expectations on Grant, when only God can meet her deepest needs. Do you think that is true? Do we sometimes see romance as the ultimate fulfillment of our emotional needs? Do you think God wants us to think that way? Where should we go for our deepest needs?
(See Psalm 62:5; Philippians 4:19; Psalm 68:19; Psalm 16:11)

11. If your church had a room like the green room, what verse would you nail to the wall?

12. In the end, some of the people in *Shredded* choose to be free, and their lives are changed. Some choose to remain enslaved to their fear or their circumstances or their sin. Do you think they all realized that was the choice they were making? Do we realize it our own lives? What is your choice?
(See 1 Peter 5:7-9; 2 Peter 2:19-21; 2 Corinthians 10:5; 2 Corinthians 3:17; Galatians 2:20; Matthew 16:24-25)

I have loved
you
with an everlasting
love.

Jeremiah 31:3

The door slid open. Champagne cast a wary glance at the uniformed officer who motioned her out of her cell. "Your bail was set pretty high," he said. "You must be special to somebody."

Champagne did not know anyone other than Slash knew she had been arrested. Except Candy. "Who paid my bail?"

"He's waiting for you outside. You can thank him, but not till after we do your paperwork."

When the policeman ushered Champagne through the exit doors, she pulled her arm from his grasp and breathed in deep. She hadn't expected to see the outside of the prison for a long time.

"Try not to come back anytime soon, okay?"

She ignored the officer and focused on the stranger waiting near a parked truck. He was big. One of his hands could palm her entire face. A hand like that, in a fist, could do a lot of damage.

He stepped toward her with recognition. "Who are you?" Champagne asked, moving down the steps with caution born of experience. Getting bailed out of jail was not always a good thing. Sometimes it meant punishment was coming. Payment for the mistake of getting arrested.

"Slash sent me. I can't believe he thinks you're worth the amount I just paid." His eyes surveyed her, like a buyer would an appliance that was outdated and worn. It shouldn't bother her. She should rejoice anytime a man didn't think she was attractive. It meant the ride in his truck would be free of expectation at least.

She lifted her chin. "Maybe I know important information."

He grabbed her arm in the same place the policeman had, but with much more force. "You know important people. That's why you're out. Don't think Slash has any good feelings for you personally. If it wasn't for this job, he'd leave you to rot in there."

She stumbled as he dragged her down the stairs. Slash got arrested the same night she had, but he could run his business from a prison as well as downtown Oakview, sometimes better, since he couldn't get high while incarcerated. Champagne wished there was hope he'd give her a job that wouldn't be horrible, but there were no jobs with Slash outside the parameters of that word.

"I'm taking you back to your stupid little town." His smile was malicious. "And then I get to beat you up, good enough that even your old roommate will believe it when you say you want out."

The wound across the underside of her hair, along the back of her neck, throbbed with her fear. "What do you mean?"

"Slash is mad and wants revenge. He's got a great plan for your friend Candy, and all her little religious helpers."

Champagne's mouth went dry and her throat clogged. "Wha- what is he going to do?"

The man shoved her into the truck and slammed the door. Through the open window, a smirk preceded his words. "I'm not stupid enough to tell you." He rounded the vehicle and sat behind the wheel. "You're going to call her up and say you want to be rescued. When she picks you up, you'll act scared and helpless."

Like I am. Completely scared and totally helpless.

He sped through the parking lot toward the exit gate. "You'll stay with her and get to know her church people. You'll ask questions and act like a good little convert until Slash contacts you with further instruction."

"No."

The man slammed on his brakes and Champagne's forehead smashed into the dashboard. "You'll do exactly as you're told. Remember that baby sister of yours you used to protect?" He put the truck in gear and pressed on the gas. "She's grown into a sweet young teenager. Pretty too. You say no, or try to double-cross Slash, and he'll get her to replace you."

Champagne covered her face with her hands and fought complete despair. Would it ever end? No, it wouldn't. The prison she lived in had no bail, and no exit door. *God, if You're there, do something.*

She doubted God would bother listening to a prayer for her, not after all she'd done. But He might hear a prayer for Candy.

If not, they were all lost.

Sign up for the author newsletter at
www.kimberlyrae.com
to keep updated on the latest releases.

OTHER BOOKS BY KIMBERLY RAE

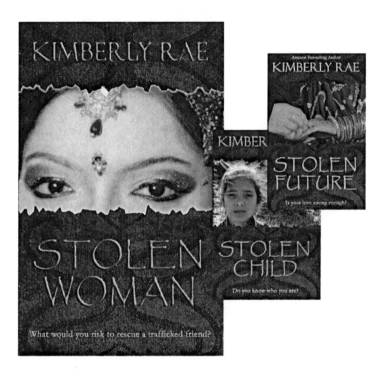

Human Trafficking...Asha knew nothing about it before meeting 16-year-old Rani, stolen from her home and forced into prostitution in Kolkata, India. Asha must help this girl escape, but Mark, a third-generation missionary, keeps warning her away from the red-light district and its workers. Will she ever discover why? And will they ever stop their intense arguments long enough to admit their even more intense feelings for one another? When Asha sneaks out one last time in a desperate attempt to rescue her friend, someone follows her through the night. Is freedom possible? Or will she, too, become one of the stolen?

Jasmina, a young girl in India, and her brother, Samir are sold by their father to a man promising them an education and good jobs.

They soon discover the man is providing an education, not in a school, but as a slave in his sweatshop garment factory. While Samir quickly submits to his new life of misery, Jasmina never stops planning an escape.

She comes to realize that escape doesn't always mean freedom.

FIND THESE AND OTHER BOOKS AT
www.kimberlyrae.com

ABOUT THE AUTHOR

Award-winning author of over 20 books, Kimberly Rae has been published over 200 times and has work in 5 languages.

Rae lived in Bangladesh, Uganda, Kosovo, and Indonesia. She rafted the Nile River, hiked the hills at the base of Mount Everest, and stood on the equator in two continents, but Addison's Disease now keeps her in the U.S. She currently writes from her home in Lenoir, North Carolina, where she lives with her husband and two young children.

Rae's Stolen Series, suspense and romance novels on fighting human trafficking, are all Amazon bestsellers.

Find out more or order autographed books at
www.kimberlyrae.com.

CPSIA information can be obtained at www.ICGtesting.com
Printed in the USA
LVOW10s1448270716

498006LV00019B/666/P